FOUNDATIONS OF BIOMOLECULES, CELL BIOLOGY AND BIOSTATISTICS

Dr. Rajesh Verma

Assistant Professor

PG Department of Zoology

Veer Kunwar Singh University, Ara –Bihar

Naveena Yadav

Assistant Professor

Department of Botany

Durgawati Mahavidyalaya, Bichhiya, Dumri

Kaimur (Bhabua), Bihar

ISBN 979-8-89984-156-9

Made with ♥ on the Notion Press Platform

www.notionpress.com

CONTENTS

CONTENTS

PREFACE

The study of life, in its myriad forms and processes, begins at the molecular level, where biomolecules orchestrate the functions essential for existence. Foundations of Biomolecules, Cell Biology and Biostatistics is a comprehensive academic resource designed to provide students and scholars of the life sciences with a clear, integrative understanding of the fundamental components of biological systems. This book seeks to build a bridge between the molecular framework of living organisms and the quantitative techniques necessary for modern biological analysis.

The genesis of this book lies in the growing need for an interdisciplinary approach to biological education—one that not only introduces the basic building blocks of life such as carbohydrates, proteins, lipids, nucleic acids, and enzymes, but also connects these molecules to the cellular structures and functions they support. In today's data-driven scientific environment, it is crucial that students gain familiarity with biostatistics—a discipline that equips them with the tools to critically analyze biological data, draw valid conclusions, and make informed decisions in research and applied settings.

Structured in a logical sequence, the book begins with an in-depth exploration of biomolecules, emphasizing their chemistry, structure, and roles in physiological processes. Following this, the text delves into cell biology, covering the ultrastructure of prokaryotic and eukaryotic cells, cellular organelles, membranes, and processes such as cell division, intracellular transport, and energy conversion. These chapters are enriched with diagrams, illustrations, and examples to enhance conceptual clarity.

The concluding section on biostatistics introduces readers to essential statistical methods commonly used in the biological sciences. Topics include data types, measures of central tendency and dispersion, probability distributions, hypothesis testing, correlation, regression, and analysis of variance (ANOVA). Real-world biological examples and exercises are incorporated to reinforce learning and highlight the relevance of statistical analysis in experimental biology.

This book is intended for undergraduate and postgraduate students in biology, zoology, botany, biotechnology, microbiology, and related fields. It also serves as a valuable reference for educators and researchers who wish to strengthen their foundational knowledge or seek a cohesive overview that integrates molecular biology with quantitative analysis.

We are deeply grateful to our academic institutions and colleagues whose support and feedback have been instrumental in the development of this manuscript. Our aim is to cultivate curiosity, critical thinking, and analytical skills among learners, thereby fostering a deeper appreciation for the complexity and beauty of life at the cellular and molecular level.

We hope that this book not only informs but also inspires readers to pursue further inquiry in the life sciences.

Dr. Rajesh Verma

Assistant Professor

PG Department of Zoology

Veer Kunwar Singh University, Ara -Bihar

ACKNOWLEDGMENT

The completion of this book, *Foundations of Biomolecules, Cell Biology and Biostatistics,* has been a journey of learning, collaboration, and unwavering support from numerous individuals and institutions. I express my deepest gratitude for their invaluable contributions, unwavering encouragement, and thoughtful guidance, all of which have played a pivotal role in the successful completion of this work. Their support has not only enriched the quality of this research but also inspired me to overcome challenges and remain committed throughout the journey.

First and foremost, I extend my heartfelt gratitude to my parents, **Shri R.P. Verma (Tarun)** and **Smt. Parvati Verma**, whose blessings, unwavering love, and encouragement have been the cornerstone of my academic and personal pursuits. Their values and teachings have always guided me toward the path of perseverance and excellence.

I am deeply indebted to **Prof. Shailendra Kumar Chaturvedi**, Honorable Vice Chancellor of Veer Kunwar Singh University, Ara, for his visionary leadership, scholarly guidance, and constant support throughout this endeavor. I also express my sincere gratitude to **Prof. (Dr.) Dhirendra Kumar Singh**, former Registrar of Veer Kunwar Singh University, Ara, for his encouragement and invaluable contributions to my academic journey.

A special note of appreciation goes to **Prof. (Dr.) Arvind Kumar**, my research guide, whose mentorship, critical insights, and encouragement have been pivotal in shaping this work. His tireless support and belief in my abilities have inspired me to delve deeper into the complexities of molecular biology and functional mechanisms.

I am immensely grateful to **Prof. (Dr.) Deenanath Pandit**, Postgraduate Department of Zoology, Veer Kunwar Singh University, Ara, for his scholarly advice and guidance. My thanks also go to **Ex-Prof. (Dr.) Anil Kumar Sinha** and **Ex-Prof. (Dr.) Ajit Kumar Sinha**, both of the Postgraduate Department of Zoology at Veer Kunwar Singh University, Ara, for their academic insights and encouragement. I also extend my thanks to **Prof. (Dr.) Anwar Imam**, Controller of Examinations, Veer Kunwar Singh University, Ara, for his steadfast support.

I wish to express my sincere appreciation to **Prof. (D.K. Dwivedi)** for his guidance and encouragement in the field of Education. His insights have added great value to this academic work. I am equally grateful to **Prof. (Dr.) Kamal Bauddh**, Raghunandan Teachers Training College, Patna, for his support and scholarly engagement that significantly contributed to the quality of this endeavor.

To my beloved wife, **Mrs. Aparna Kumari**, I owe a debt of gratitude for her patience, love, and unwavering encouragement. She has been my pillar of strength throughout this journey, providing me with the motivation and inspiration to see this project through. I also express my deepest gratitude to my sister, **Mrs. Ruma Verma**, for her constant support and belief in my abilities.

My heartfelt thanks go to my elder brother, **Mr. Sanjay Verma**, **Mr Rajeev Verma** and his wife, **Mrs. Rakhi Verma**, as well as my younger brother Mr. Rajnish Verma alias Swadarshan Prakash, Religious Saint of India and my brother-in-law, **Mr. Krishna Kumar Prasad Saini**, for their encouragement and faith in my endeavors. I am also profoundly grateful to my father-in-law, **Prof. (Dr.) Ravindra Bhakt**, whose wisdom and blessings have always been a source of guidance.

The contributions of my colleagues and peers cannot be overstated. My heartfelt thanks to **Dr. Kanhaiya Singh**, Assistant

Professor, A.J. College, Vikramganj, **Dr. Alok Prakash Diwakar, Dr. Ajay Kumar Upadhyay**, and **Ravi Shankar Kumar**, Assistant Teacher as resource persons with the Government of Bihar. Special thanks to **Dr. Anupma Singh**, Assistant Professor, S.B. College, Ara. I sincerely thank you for your moral support and encouragement to **Dr. Sushma Kumari Singh** Principal Incharge Durgawati Mahavidyalaya, Kaimur. I also express my gratitude to **Mr. Manish Kumar, Mr. Deep Narayan Pandit, Mr. Chandan Pandit** and **Miss. Shivangi Priya** are associated with the Education Department, Veer Kunwar Singh University, Ara, for their support.

A special note of gratitude is reserved for **Dr. Anil Kumar**, Principal Teacher (Bihar Govt.) and **Mr. Gaurav Kumar**, Research Scholar, GLA University, Mathura, whose unwavering support and significant contributions have been instrumental in shaping the depth and quality of this work. **Dr. Anil Kumar's** profound insights, meticulous approach, and dedication to research have enriched the academic rigor of this book. **Mr. Gaurav Kumar's** enthusiasm, analytical skills, and collaborative spirit have provided valuable perspectives that greatly enhanced the scope and execution of this Book. Their combined efforts and commitment to excellence have been a source of inspiration and an integral part of this journey, for which I am deeply thankful.

A heartfelt and special thanks to **Ms. Naveena Yadav**, daughter of **Mr. Trilochan Yadav** and **Mrs. Bharti Yadav**, for her invaluable support and encouragement throughout this journey. Her enthusiasm, keen interest, and unwavering belief in the vision of this work have been a source of great motivation. Her contributions, whether through insightful discussions or steadfast encouragement, have significantly enriched the process, and for this, I remain profoundly grateful.

Gaurav Kumar. To **Md. Mazharul Haque** Hod.- History, **Md. Nehal Akhter** HoD- Sociolgy, and **Md. Ziauddin**, HoD- Zoology at Al Hafeez, your expertise and input have been invaluable. Thanks also go to my students, **Jaydev**, **Yashaswi, Master Mrinal Mrityunjay**, **Kumar Mrityunjay Rakesh**, and **Mr. Anil Kumar**, for their enthusiasm and assistance.

To my cherished children, **Jaydev** and **Yashaswi**, thank you for your love and understanding, which have been a source of immense motivation and joy. To my nephews, **Mrinal Mrityunjay** whose enthusiasm has been inspiring.

Finally, I offer my heartfelt respect and gratitude to my Guru, **Priyatoshanand Avadhoot**, whose teachings have profoundly shaped my perspective on life and scholarship.

This work is a testament to the collective efforts of many individuals. To all those who supported me, whether mentioned here or not, I extend my deepest gratitude. It is your encouragement and belief in my abilities that have made this book possible.

Dr. Rajesh Verma

Assistant Professor

PG Department of Zoology

Veer Kunwar Singh University, Ara -Bihar

ABOUT THE AUTHORS

Dr. Rajesh Verma is an accomplished academician and researcher, currently serving as an Assistant Professor in the PG Department of Zoology at Veer Kunwar Singh University, Ara, Bihar. With dual Ph.D. degrees in Zoology and Education from Patna University, his academic journey reflects an unwavering commitment to interdisciplinary excellence. Dr. Verma has also attained multiple postgraduate qualifications in Psychology, Philosophy, and Educational Management from IGNOU, alongside various diplomas in leadership and technology integration. His teaching career spans over two decades, including roles at Nalanda Open University, D.K. College, and government schools. He has also held key administrative positions such as Nodal Officer for NAAC and RUSA and served as a resource person in teacher training programs under the Bihar Education Project. A prolific writer, Dr. Verma has authored over 65 research papers, 17 books, and holds 6 published and granted patents. His contributions have earned him several accolades, including the Best Teacher Award from the Didi Ji Foundation.

Naveena Yadav is an Assistant Professor in the Department of Botany at Durgawati Mahavidyalaya, Bichhiya, Dumri, Kaimur (Bhabua), Bihar. She has made significant academic contributions with the publication of 3 books and over 5 research papers in reputed international journals. Her work focuses on ecological and botanical sciences, reflecting her dedication to both teaching and research. Her scholarly achievements and commitment to environmental education underscore her role as a rising academic voice in the field.

CHAPTER 1

BIOMOLECULES – STRUCTURE AND FUNCTION

Biomolecules are the essential building blocks of life, playing a central role in the structure and function of cells. These organic compounds, including carbohydrates, proteins, lipids, nucleic acids, and enzymes, are involved in virtually every cellular process. They enable organisms to grow, reproduce, respond to their environment, and maintain homeostasis. Understanding the chemistry and biological roles of biomolecules is fundamental to the study of life sciences, as these molecules form the structural and functional framework of all living organisms.

THE CHEMISTRY OF BIOMOLECULES

Biomolecules are primarily composed of carbon, hydrogen, oxygen, nitrogen, phosphorus, and sulfur. These elements are abundant in nature and form stable covalent bonds, which provide the flexibility needed to form the complex structures observed in living organisms. The carbon atom is especially important due to its ability to form four strong covalent bonds, enabling the creation of diverse molecular structures. Biomolecules are also characterized by functional groups—specific groups of atoms that impart unique chemical properties to the molecule. For example, amino groups ($-NH_2$) are found in amino acids, while hydroxyl groups ($-OH$) are present in alcohols and sugars. These functional groups are critical

CARBOHYDRATES: ENERGY AND STRUCTURE

Carbohydrates are organic molecules composed of carbon, hydrogen, and oxygen, and they serve as the primary energy source for living organisms. The simplest form of carbohydrates, monosaccharides like glucose and fructose, provide immediate energy for cellular processes. These monosaccharides can be linked together through glycosidic bonds to form disaccharides (e.g., sucrose) and polysaccharides (e.g., starch, glycogen, and cellulose). Polysaccharides are important for both energy storage and structural support. For example, starch is a storage form of glucose in plants, while glycogen serves the same function in animals. Cellulose, a structural polysaccharide, is crucial for the integrity of plant cell walls. The structure of carbohydrates is intricately linked to their biological function, whether it be for energy storage or providing structural support in various organisms.

PROTEINS: CATALYSTS, STRUCTURES, AND TRANSPORTERS

Proteins are complex molecules composed of amino acids, and they are essential for a wide range of biological functions. They act as enzymes, catalysts that speed up biochemical reactions, and also serve as structural components, transporters, and signaling molecules. Proteins are made up of 20 different amino acids, each with a unique side chain (R group). The sequence of these amino acids determines the protein's three-dimensional structure and, consequently, its function. The structure of proteins is classified into four levels: primary structure (the linear sequence of amino acids), secondary structure (local folding into alpha-helices and beta-pleated sheets), tertiary structure (overall three-dimensional shape), and quaternary structure (the assembly of multiple polypeptide chains). Proteins are involved in virtually every cellular process, from catalyzing metabolic reactions to maintaining cell shape and mediating communication between cells. Hemoglobin, for example, is a protein that binds oxygen in the lungs and transports it to tissues throughout the body.

Lipids: Energy Storage and Membrane Structure

Lipids are hydrophobic molecules that include fats, oils, phospholipids, and steroids. They play critical roles in energy storage, insulation, and the formation of biological membranes. Triglycerides, which consist of three fatty acids linked to a glycerol molecule, are the primary form of energy storage in animals. Phospholipids, composed of two fatty acids, a glycerol backbone, and a phosphate group, form the structural basis of cell membranes. In aqueous environments, phospholipids arrange themselves into bilayers, with hydrophilic phosphate heads facing outward and hydrophobic fatty acid tails facing inward. This unique arrangement allows the formation of a semipermeable membrane that regulates the entry and exit of substances in and out of the cell. Lipids also include steroids such as cholesterol, which is crucial for maintaining membrane fluidity and serves as a precursor for the synthesis of hormones such as estrogen and testosterone.

Nucleic Acids: The Blueprint of Life

Nucleic acids, including DNA (deoxyribonucleic acid) and RNA (ribonucleic acid), are responsible for storing and transmitting genetic information. DNA is a double-stranded molecule that encodes the genetic instructions necessary for the development, functioning, and reproduction of all living organisms. The structure of DNA consists of two long chains of nucleotides, with each nucleotide composed of a sugar, a phosphate group, and one of four nitrogenous [illegible] (A), thymine (T), cytosine (C), or [illegible]

DNA are held together by complementary base pairing, with adenine pairing with thymine and cytosine pairing with guanine. RNA, a single-stranded molecule, plays several roles in protein synthesis and gene regulation. Messenger RNA (mRNA) carries genetic information from DNA to the ribosome, where proteins are synthesized. Transfer RNA (tRNA) and ribosomal RNA (rRNA) also contribute to protein synthesis by translating genetic information into functional proteins.

Enzymes: Catalysts of Biochemical Reactions

Enzymes are proteins that catalyze biochemical reactions, accelerating the rate of reactions without being consumed in the process. By lowering the activation energy required for a reaction to occur, enzymes allow reactions to proceed much faster than they would in their absence. Enzymes are highly specific, meaning that each enzyme catalyzes a particular reaction or group of reactions. This specificity is determined by the enzyme's active site, a region that binds to the substrate and facilitates the reaction. Enzyme activity can be regulated in various ways, such as through allosteric regulation, where the binding of a molecule at a site other than the active site alters enzyme activity, or through feedback inhibition, where the end product of a metabolic pathway inhibits the activity of an enzyme involved in an earlier step in the pathway. Enzymes are critical for maintaining the biochemical processes necessary for life, from digestion to cellular metabolism.

The Interconnectedness of Biomolecules

Although each class of biomolecule has its own specialized function, they are all interconnected within the cell. The various biomolecules work together in highly coordinated networks to maintain cellular homeostasis and facilitate complex biological processes. For example, enzymes often rely on substrates that are carbohydrates, proteins, or lipids. Proteins, in turn, are synthesized based on the genetic instructions encoded in nucleic acids. This interconnectedness allows for the regulation and coordination of cellular activities, ensuring that the cell functions efficiently and responds to changes in its environment.

1.1 Carbohydrates: Classification and Function

Carbohydrates are organic molecules composed of carbon (C), hydrogen (H), and oxygen (O), typically in the ratio of 1:2:1. These molecules play a crucial role in the biological processes of all living organisms, serving as the primary energy source for cellular functions. Carbohydrates also contribute significantly to structural components in cells and tissues, and are involved in various regulatory and signaling processes.

CLASSIFICATION OF CARBOHYDRATES

Carbohydrates can be broadly categorized into four main types based on the complexity of their structure: monosaccharides, disaccharides, oligosaccharides, and polysaccharides.

Carbohydrate Types

Type	Example	Source
Monosaccharide	Glucose	Basic energy source
Disaccharide	Sucrose	Table sugar
Oligosaccharide	Cell recognition	Cell surfaces
Polysaccharide	Starch	Plants
Polysaccharide	Glycogen	Animals

1. **Monosaccharides:**

   Monosaccharides are the simplest form of carbohydrates. These are single sugar units that are sweet, water-soluble, and the basic building blocks of more complex carbohydrates. The most common monosaccharides are:

   - **Glucose ($C_6H_{12}O_6$):** A vital energy source for the body, glucose is the most important monosaccharide. It is metabolized in cells through the process of glycolysis to produce ATP, the energy currency of the cell.
   - **Fructose:** Known for its sweet taste, fructose is found in fruits, honey, and some vegetables. It is metabolized in the liver and can be converted into glucose or other compounds used for energy.
   - **Galactose:** A less sweet monosaccharide, galactose is primarily found as part of the disaccharide lactose, the sugar found in milk. Galactose is converted into glucose in the body and used for energy production.

2. **Disaccharides:**

   Disaccharides are formed by the condensation of two monosaccharides through a glycosidic bond. These molecules are also sweet and water-soluble. Some common disaccharides include:

   - **Sucrose** (Glucose + Fructose): Commonly known as table sugar, sucrose is obtained from sugarcane and sugar beets and is widely used as a sweetener in food products.
   - **Lactose** (Glucose + Galactose): The sugar found in milk, lactose provides energy for infants and some adults. Some individuals have lactose intolerance due to a deficiency of the enzyme lactase.

- **Maltose** (Glucose + Glucose): Known as malt sugar, maltose is produced during the digestion of starch and is found in products like malted beverages.

3. **Oligosaccharides:**
Oligosaccharides are carbohydrates composed of 3 to 10 monosaccharide units linked together by glycosidic bonds. These are often found in plant foods such as legumes, and they have significant roles in cell recognition, signaling, and communication. They are frequently present as glycoproteins or glycolipids on the surface of cell membranes, contributing to immune system function and cell-to-cell communication.

4. **Polysaccharides:**
Polysaccharides are long chains of monosaccharide units and are typically classified into storage or structural types. They can be linear or branched, and they vary greatly in size and complexity.
   - **Starch:** The primary storage polysaccharide in plants, starch is composed of long chains of glucose molecules. It is found in foods like potatoes, rice, and wheat and can be broken down into glucose units for energy release.
   - **Glycogen:** This is the storage polysaccharide in animals, primarily stored in the liver and muscles. Glycogen is highly branched, allowing for rapid breakdown and release of glucose when the body requires energy.
   - **Cellulose:** A structural polysaccharide found in plant cell walls, cellulose provides rigidity and strength to the plant structure. Although humans cannot digest cellulose due to its β-1,4 linkage, it is an essential component of dietary fiber, aiding in digestion and bowel health.

FUNCTIONS OF CARBOHYDRATES

Carbohydrates perform several vital functions in living organisms, impacting everything from energy production to cellular communication.

1. **Energy Storage and Release**: Carbohydrates are the body's main source of energy. Glucose, derived from dietary carbohydrates, is metabolized through glycolysis, the citric acid cycle, and oxidative phosphorylation in mitochondria to produce ATP. This ATP is then used in various cellular processes, such as muscle contraction, protein synthesis, and active transport across cell membranes. When glucose is not immediately needed for energy, it is stored in the form of glycogen in muscles and the liver for later use.
2. **Structural Components**: Carbohydrates also serve as critical structural components. In plants, cellulose is the main structural polysaccharide, providing mechanical strength to plant cell walls. It ensures that plants maintain their shape and can resist mechanical stress. Similarly, chitin is a carbohydrate that forms the exoskeletons of arthropods like insects and crustaceans, offering protection and structural integrity.
3. **Cell Signaling**: Carbohydrates play an important role in cellular communication and recognition. On the surface of cells, carbohydrates are often attached to proteins (forming glycoproteins) or lipids (forming glycolipids). These carbohydrate chains act as markers, allowing cells to identify and interact with each other. For instance, glycoproteins and glycolipids are involved in the immune system's ability to distinguish between self and non-self cells, and they also play a role in hormone and neurotransmitter signaling.
4. **Sparing Protein and Fat Use**: Adequate carbohydrate intake helps preserve proteins and fats by preventing them from

being used as an energy source. This is especially important during prolonged periods of fasting or intense exercise. When carbohydrate reserves are low, the body begins to break down fat stores to release fatty acids for energy. If carbohydrate consumption is insufficient, proteins can also be catabolized for energy, which may lead to muscle loss and impaired cellular functions. A lack of carbohydrates can lead to ketosis, a condition where the body begins to use fat as a primary energy source, resulting in the accumulation of ketones in the blood.

Carbohydrates are essential biomolecules that contribute to various aspects of cellular function. Their classification into monosaccharides, disaccharides, oligosaccharides, and polysaccharides reflects their diverse structural forms and functional roles. As the primary energy source in most organisms, carbohydrates support critical metabolic processes, while also playing key roles in structure, signaling, and metabolic regulation. Understanding carbohydrates and their function is fundamental to the study of biochemistry and cellular biology, highlighting their importance in maintaining life processes.

1.2 Proteins and Amino Acids: Structure and Biological Role

Proteins are essential biomolecules that serve as the building blocks for nearly all cellular structures and functions. Composed of long chains of amino acids, proteins play an integral role in a multitude of biological processes, making them the most versatile class of molecules in terms of both structure and function. Proteins are involved in almost every biological reaction, from catalysis to structural support, and are crucial for maintaining cellular integrity and homeostasis.

Structure of Amino Acids

The fundamental building blocks of proteins are amino acids. These organic compounds are composed of a central carbon atom, also known as the α-carbon, to which four different groups are attached:

1. **Amino Group ($-NH_2$):** A basic group that can accept a proton (H^+) in solution.
2. **Carboxyl Group (–COOH):** An acidic group that can donate a proton.
3. **Hydrogen Atom (H):** A single hydrogen atom attached to the α-carbon.
4. **Variable R Group (Side Chain):** The distinctive part of the amino acid, often referred to as the "R group," which varies between different amino acids. The nature of the R group determines the specific properties of the amino acid (such as whether it is hydrophobic, hydrophilic, acidic, or basic).

There are 20 standard amino acids that make up proteins, each with a unique side chain. These amino acids can be classified into two categories:

- **Essential Amino Acids:** These must be obtained through the diet, as the human body cannot synthesize them. Examples include leucine, lysine, and tryptophan.
- **Non-Essential Amino Acids:** These can be synthesized by the body from other compounds. Examples include alanine, asparagine, and glutamic acid.

Levels of Protein Structure

Proteins are complex molecules with distinct levels of structure that are crucial for their function. The structure of a protein dictates its activity, interactions, and stability.

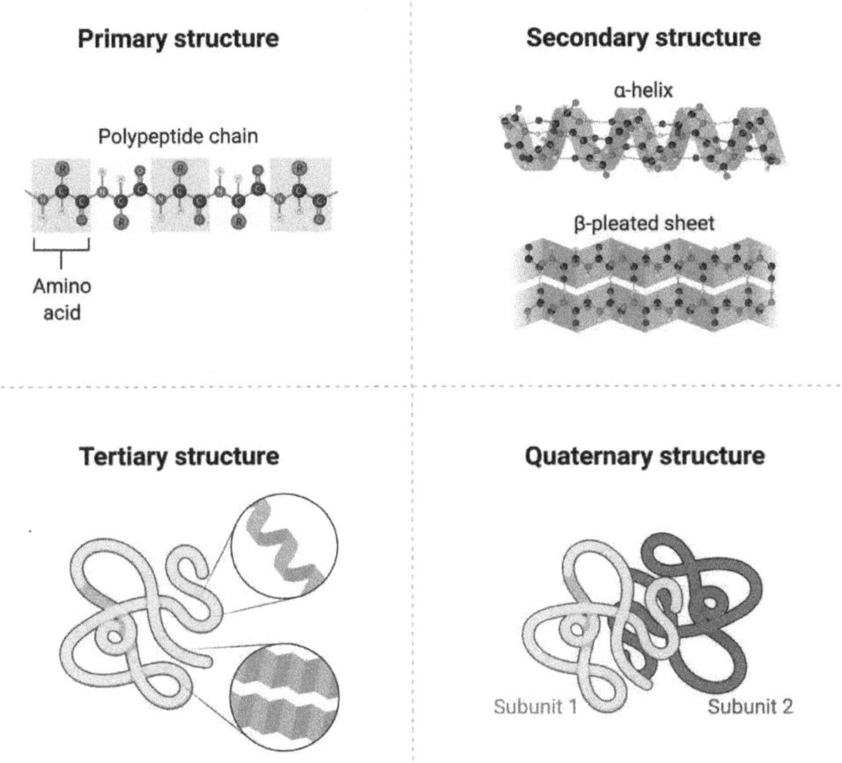

***Figure:** Levels of Protein Structure*

1. **Primary Structure**: The primary structure of a protein refers to the linear sequence of amino acids in a polypeptide chain, linked together by peptide bonds (a type of covalent bond between the carboxyl group of one amino acid and the amino group of another). The sequence of amino acids is determined by the genetic code, and even a small change in this sequence can drastically alter the function of the protein.
2. **Secondary Structure**: The secondary structure refers to localized folding patterns within the polypeptide chain, primarily stabilized by hydrogen bonds between the backbone atoms. The most common secondary structures are:

- **α-Helix**: A right-handed spiral or coil, where the carbonyl oxygen of one amino acid forms a hydrogen bond with the amide hydrogen of another amino acid located four residues away in the chain.
- **β-Sheets**: Sheets formed by linking two or more polypeptide chains through hydrogen bonds, creating a pleated structure. The strands may run parallel or antiparallel to each other.

3. **Tertiary Structure**: The tertiary structure refers to the three-dimensional shape of the protein, which is formed by further folding of the secondary structure. This folding is driven by interactions between the side chains (R groups) of the amino acids. These interactions include:

- **Hydrophobic Interactions**: Nonpolar side chains tend to cluster in the interior of the protein, away from the aqueous environment.
- **Hydrogen Bonds**: These bonds form between polar side chains and help stabilize the protein structure.
- **Ionic Bonds**: Oppositely charged side chains may form salt bridges.
- **Disulfide Bridges**: Covalent bonds between sulfur atoms of cysteine residues can form disulfide bridges, stabilizing the protein's structure.

4. **Quaternary Structure**: Some proteins consist of multiple polypeptide chains (subunits), and the quaternary structure refers to the arrangement of these subunits into a functional protein. Each subunit has its own primary, secondary, and tertiary structures, and the overall protein function depends on how these subunits interact. A well-known example of a protein with quaternary structure is **hemoglobin**, which consists of four polypeptide subunits that work together to transport oxygen in the blood.

FUNCTIONS OF PROTEINS

Proteins are incredibly versatile and serve a wide variety of functions in biological systems. Their functional diversity is directly linked to their complex and highly specific three-dimensional structures.

1. **Enzymatic Activity:** Enzymes are proteins that catalyze biochemical reactions, increasing the rate of reactions without being consumed in the process. They are highly specific to the substrates they bind and convert them into products. Examples of enzymes include **amylase**, which breaks down starches into sugars, and **DNA polymerase**, which is involved in DNA replication.
2. **Structural Support:** Proteins are a key component of the structural framework of cells and tissues. For example, **keratin** provides structural support to hair, nails, and skin, while **collagen** gives strength and flexibility to connective tissues, such as tendons, ligaments, and cartilage.
3. **Transport:** Proteins are involved in the transport of molecules across cell membranes and within the body. **Hemoglobin**, a protein found in red blood cells, binds to oxygen in the lungs and carries it to tissues throughout the body. The membrane proteins form channels and transporters that regulate the movement of ions and small molecules across the cell membrane.
4. **Defense:** The immune system relies heavily on proteins to protect the body from pathogens. **Antibodies** are proteins produced by immune cells that specifically recognize and neutralize foreign invaders, such as bacteria and viruses. These proteins are critical for the body's defense mechanisms.
5. **Hormonal Role:** Many hormones are proteins or peptides, and they regulate various physiological processes in the

lowers blood glucose by promoting cellular uptake of glucose, while glucagon raises blood glucose levels by stimulating the release of glucose from the liver.

6. **Movement**: Proteins are essential for movement in both cells and organisms. **Actin** and **myosin** are two proteins found in muscle fibers that interact to facilitate muscle contraction. These proteins also play a role in cell division, intracellular transport, and the movement of organelles within cells.
7. **Storage**: Some proteins function to store essential molecules within cells. **Ferritin** is a protein that stores iron in the liver and other tissues, releasing it when needed for processes like hemoglobin synthesis.

Proteins are integral to virtually all biological functions. Their versatility stems from the unique combination of amino acids that make up their structure and their ability to fold into complex three-dimensional shapes. These structures enable proteins to perform an array of tasks, from catalyzing reactions to providing structural integrity, transporting molecules, and defending the body. The diversity in protein functions is a testament to the complexity of life and highlights the importance of understanding protein structure and function in the study of biology.

1.3 Lipids: Types and Significance

Lipids are a diverse group of hydrophobic molecules composed primarily of carbon (C) and hydrogen (H), with smaller amounts of oxygen (O). Unlike carbohydrates and proteins, lipids are not polymers; instead, they are characterized by their inability to dissolve in water, making them essential for many biological functions. They play vital roles in energy storage, membrane structure, insulation, protection, and signaling. Their unique structural properties also allow them to interact with various cellular and molecular systems, making them indispensable to the proper functioning of living organisms.

TYPES OF LIPIDS

Lipids can be classified into three broad categories: simple lipids, compound lipids, and derived lipids. These classifications are based on their structural components and complexity.

1. **Simple Lipids:** Simple lipids are the basic, non-polar molecules consisting of fatty acids and alcohols. They are the most common type of lipid found in the body.
   - **Fats and Oils (Triglycerides):** Triglycerides are composed of one molecule of glycerol (a three-carbon alcohol) and three fatty acids. These fatty acids may be saturated (no double bonds between carbon atoms) or unsaturated (one or more double bonds between carbon atoms). Triglycerides are the primary form of energy storage in animals and plants. Fats are solid at room temperature, while oils are liquid, primarily due to the presence of unsaturated fatty acids.
   - **Waxes:** Waxes are esters of long-chain alcohols and fatty acids. They are hydrophobic and serve as protective coatings for plants and animals. For example, beeswax is used by bees to construct hives, while plant leaves are coated with a waxy layer that prevents water loss.
2. **Compound Lipids:** Compound lipids contain additional functional groups, such as phosphate or carbohydrate groups, that give them specific roles in the body.
   - **Phospholipids:** Phospholipids are composed of a glycerol backbone, two fatty acid chains, and a phosphate group. The fatty acid chains are

amphipathic (having both hydrophilic and hydrophobic regions). This property is critical for their role in forming the **phospholipid bilayers** that constitute the structural framework of cell membranes. The amphipathic nature of phospholipids allows them to form stable membranes in aqueous environments, with hydrophobic tails facing inward and hydrophilic heads facing outward.

- o **Glycolipids:** Glycolipids are lipids that contain a carbohydrate group in addition to fatty acids. These molecules are primarily found on the surface of cell membranes, where they play a significant role in cell recognition and communication. The carbohydrate portion of glycolipids interacts with the environment, helping cells identify each other and participate in signaling pathways.

3. **Derived Lipids:** Derived lipids are derived from simple and compound lipids through hydrolysis or other enzymatic processes. These lipids have diverse functions, including signaling and regulation.
   - o **Steroids:** Steroids are a group of lipids characterized by a structure of four fused carbon rings. Cholesterol is the most well-known steroid and serves as a precursor for the synthesis of other important steroids, including **testosterone** and **estrogen** (hormones that regulate sexual characteristics and reproduction) and **corticosteroids** (involved in stress response and immune function). Cholesterol is also essential for maintaining membrane fluidity and stability.
   - o **Fat-soluble Vitamins:** Certain vitamins, including **vitamin A, vitamin D, vitamin E**, and **vitamin K**, are fat-soluble, meaning they require lipids for absorption and transport. These vitamins play essential roles in vision, bone health, antioxidant protection, and blood clotting, respectively.

They are absorbed through the intestinal tract in the presence of dietary fats and are stored in body tissues, such as the liver and adipose tissue.

FUNCTIONS OF LIPIDS

Lipids are integral to many critical physiological processes, and their functions extend far beyond energy storage. Below are the primary functions of lipids in living organisms:

1. **Energy Storage**: Lipids are the most energy-dense macromolecules, providing approximately 9 kcal per gram, more than twice the energy provided by carbohydrates and proteins. Triglycerides stored in adipose tissue serve as an efficient long-term energy reserve. When energy is needed, triglycerides are broken down into fatty acids and glycerol, which can be metabolized to generate ATP through cellular respiration. Lipids are particularly important for energy storage in animals, as they provide a compact and efficient means of storing energy for periods of fasting or prolonged physical activity.
2. **Membrane Structure**: One of the most critical functions of lipids is their role in the formation of biological membranes. Phospholipids, the major components of cell membranes, form bilayers that create a semi-permeable barrier between the internal cell environment and the external surroundings. This membrane structure not only provides protection but also regulates the movement of molecules in and out of cells and organelles. The lipid bilayer's hydrophobic core acts as a barrier to water-soluble substances, while embedded proteins control the passage of specific molecules, such as ions, nutrients, and waste products.

3. **Insulation and Protection**: Lipids also play an essential role in providing insulation and protecting internal organs. **Adipose tissue**, which consists of lipid-storing cells, forms an insulating layer beneath the skin, helping to regulate body temperature by reducing heat loss. Additdipose tissue cushions vital organs, such as the heart and kidneys, providing mechanical protection from physical trauma.
4. **Signaling Molecules**: Many lipids function as signaling molecules, influencing cellular communication and the regulation of biological processes. **Steroid hormones**, such as estrogen, testosterone, and cortisol, regulate a wide range of physiological functions, including growth, metabolism, immune response, and reproductive processes. **Prostaglandins**, derived from fatty acids, act as local signaling molecules involved in inflammation, pain response, and blood clotting.
5. **Fat-soluble Vitamin Absorption**: Lipids are crucial for the absorption and transport of fat-soluble vitamins (A, D, E, and K). These vitamins are dissolved in the lipid-rich environment of the digestive system and are absorbed into the bloodstream along with dietary fats. Once absorbed, they are transported via lipoproteins to various tissues in the body. For example, vitamin D, which is involved in calcium metabolism and bone health, requires lipids for proper absorption and storage.

Lipids are fundamental to life, playing diverse roles in energy storage, cellular structure, insulation, signaling, and nutrient absorption. Their hydrophobic nature enables them to form essential components of cell membranes, while their energy-dense properties make them an efficient means of storing energy. The lipids serve as precursors to important hormones and vitamins that regulate various physiological processes. Understanding the different types and functions of lipids is critical to appreciating their vital role in maintaining the integrity and function of living organisms.

1.4 Nucleic Acids: DNA and RNA – Structure and Function

Nucleic acids are essential macromolecules responsible for storing, transmitting, and expressing genetic information. The two primary types of nucleic acids, **deoxyribonucleic acid (DNA)** and **ribonucleic acid (RNA)**, are integral to cellular function, and their structures are key to the storage and transmission of genetic instructions.

STRUCTURE OF NUCLEOTIDES

Both DNA and RNA are polymers made up of repeating units called nucleotides. Each nucleotide consists of three components:

1. **A nitrogenous base**: The nitrogenous bases are categorized into two groups:
   - **Purines:** Adenine (A) and Guanine (G).
   - **Pyrimidines:** Cytosine (C), Thymine (T) in DNA, and Uracil (U) in RNA.
2. **A pentose sugar**: The sugar molecule is a five-carbon ring structure.
   - In **DNA**, the sugar is **deoxyribose**, which lacks one oxygen atom on the 2' carbon (hence the name "deoxy").
   - In **RNA**, the sugar is **ribose**, which has a hydroxyl group (-OH) at the 2' position.
3. **A phosphate group**: The phosphate group, attached to the 5' carbon of the sugar, links adjacent nucleotides through phosphodiester bonds, forming the backbone of the nucleic acid chain.

DNA – DEOXYRIBONUCLEIC ACID

Structure of DNA: DNA is a double-stranded molecule that forms a chain of nucleotides, and the two strands run in opposite directions, known as **antiparallel orientation.** The two strands are held together by **hydrogen bonds** between complementary nitrogenous bases:

- **Adenine (A)** pairs with **Thymine (T).**
- **Guanine (G)** pairs with **Cytosine (C).**

This specific base pairing (A–T, G–C) ensures accurate replication and transmission of genetic information.

FUNCTION OF DNA:

- **Storage of Genetic Information**: DNA carries the genetic blueprint for all living organisms. The sequence of nitrogenous bases in DNA encodes the instructions necessary for building and maintaining an organism.
- **Template for RNA Synthesis**: During **transcription**, a segment of DNA is used as a template to synthesize messenger RNA (mRNA), which carries the genetic code from the DNA to the ribosome for protein synthesis.
- **Replication**: Before a cell divides, **DNA replication** ensures that each daughter cell receives an identical copy of the genetic material. This process allows for the inheritance of traits from one generation to the next, contributing to genetic continuity.

RNA – RIBONUCLEIC ACID

Structure of RNA: Unlike DNA, RNA is **single-stranded** and contains the sugar **ribose.** One significant difference between RNA and DNA is that RNA contains the base **Uracil (U)** instead of Thymine (T), making its base pairing slightly different:

- **Adenine (A)** pairs with **Uracil (U)** in RNA.

- **Guanine (G)** pairs with **Cytosine (C)**.

The single-stranded structure of RNA allows it to perform a variety of functions within the cell, including serving as a messenger between DNA and the protein synthesis machinery.

Types of RNA: There are several types of RNA, each with a specific role in gene expression and cellular function:

1. **Messenger RNA (mRNA)**: mRNA is synthesized during transcription and carries the genetic code from the DNA to the ribosome, where it serves as a template for protein synthesis during translation.
2. **Transfer RNA (tRNA)**: tRNA is involved in translation by carrying specific amino acids to the ribosome, where it matches the mRNA codons with the corresponding amino acids to build proteins.
3. **Ribosomal RNA (rRNA)**: rRNA is a structural component of ribosomes, which are the cellular machines that synthesize proteins. rRNA helps catalyze the formation of peptide bonds between amino acids during protein synthesis.
4. **Other Types of RNA**: There are also other specialized forms of RNA, such as small nuclear RNA (snRNA), which is involved in RNA splicing, and ribozymes, which are RNA molecules with enzymatic activity that catalyze specific biochemical reactions.

FUNCTIONS OF RNA:

- **Protein Synthesis**: The primary role of RNA is in **protein synthesis**. mRNA transcribes the genetic information from DNA and carries it to the ribosome, where tRNA translates the code into a specific sequence of amino acids to form proteins.

- **Gene Regulation:** RNA molecules, such as microRNAs (miRNA) and small interfering RNAs (siRNA), are involved in regulating gene expression by influencing the stability and translation of mRNA. These small RNAs play critical roles in controlling the levels of specific proteins in the cell.
- **Catalytic Activity:** Certain RNA molecules, such as ribozymes, can catalyze biochemical reactions, a function previously believed to be exclusive to proteins. This highlights the versatility of RNA in cellular processes, supporting the hypothesis that RNA may have played a central role in the origin of life.

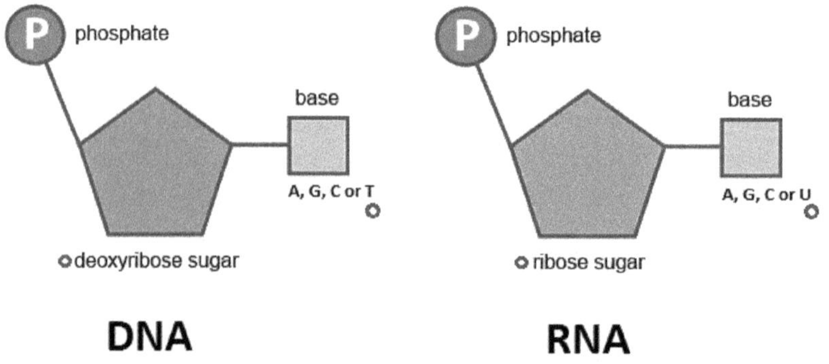

Figure: Structure of DNA and RNA

Nucleic acids, DNA and RNA, are the fundamental molecules responsible for the storage, transmission, and expression of genetic information. The structure of DNA, with its double-helix configuration and complementary base pairing, ensures the faithful replication and inheritance of genetic material. RNA, on the other hand, is central to the process of protein synthesis and gene regulation. Understanding the structure and function of nucleic acids is crucial for comprehending the molecular mechanisms that govern cellular activities, inheritance, and the synthesis of proteins, all of which are essential for life.

1.5 Enzymes: Classification, Mechanism, and Regulation

Enzymes are essential biological catalysts that accelerate the rate of chemical reactions without being consumed in the process. They are crucial for virtually every biochemical process in living organisms, from digestion to DNA replication, metabolism, and cellular signaling. Enzymes are highly specific, both in the reactions they catalyze and in the substrates they interact with. Understanding their classification, mechanism of action, factors affecting their activity, and regulation is fundamental to many areas of biology and medicine.

Classification of Enzymes

Enzymes are classified into six major categories based on the type of reaction they catalyze. This classification is based on the **International Union of Biochemistry and Molecular Biology (IUBMB)** system, and it includes:

1. **Oxidoreductases:** These enzymes catalyze oxidation-reduction (redox) reactions, where electrons are transferred between molecules. An example is **dehydrogenases**, which remove hydrogen atoms from substrates, often in metabolic pathways like glycolysis.
2. **Transferases:** These enzymes facilitate the transfer of functional groups (e.g., methyl, acetyl) from one molecule to another. **Kinases**, for instance, transfer phosphate groups from ATP to proteins or other substrates in signaling pathways.
3. **Hydrolases:** Hydrolases catalyze the hydrolysis of various bonds, breaking them down by the addition of water. **Proteases**, which break down proteins into smaller peptides or amino acids, are a well-known example.
4. **Lyases:** Lyases catalyze the breaking of chemical bonds by mechanisms other than hydrolysis or oxidation, often

forming a double bond or a ring structure. For example, **decarboxylases** remove a carboxyl group from amino acids.

5. **Isomerases**: These enzymes catalyze the rearrangement of atoms within a molecule, converting one isomer into another. An example is **phosphoglucoisomerase**, which converts glucose-6-phosphate into fructose-6-phosphate during glycolysis.
6. **Ligases**: Ligases are enzymes that join two molecules, usually by forming a new chemical bond between them. This process often requires ATP. **DNA ligase**, which joins DNA fragments during replication and repair, is a prime example.

Mechanism of Enzyme Action

Enzyme action involves several key steps, which work together to lower the activation energy required for a reaction to occur, thus increasing the reaction rate:

1. **Substrate Binding**: Enzymes possess a specific region called the **active site**, where the substrate binds. The **lock-and-key model** suggests that the active site has a specific shape that fits the substrate precisely. In contrast, the **induced-fit model** proposes that the enzyme's active site undergoes a conformational change upon substrate binding, improving the fit and enhancing catalysis.
2. **Catalysis**: Once the substrate binds to the enzyme's active site, the enzyme stabilizes the **transition state** of the reaction. By lowering the activation energy, the enzyme allows the reaction to proceed faster than it would in the absence of the enzyme.
3. **Product Release**: After the reaction, the enzyme releases the **product(s)**, and the enzyme itself returns to its original state, ready to catalyze another reaction cycle. The process of enzyme catalysis is typically very efficient, with enzymes

often facilitating thousands or even millions of reactions per second.

Factors Affecting Enzyme Activity

Several factors influence the activity of enzymes, determining how effectively they catalyze reactions. Key factors include:

1. **Temperature:** Enzymes have an **optimum temperature** range in which they function most efficiently. At temperatures below this range, enzyme activity slows, while temperatures above the optimum can cause denaturation, where the enzyme loses its functional shape.
2. **pH:** Similarly, enzymes have an **optimum pH** range. For example, digestive enzymes in the stomach work best at acidic pH, while others, like those in the small intestine, function best in neutral or slightly alkaline conditions. Extreme deviations in pH can affect the ionic bonds and the overall shape of the enzyme, reducing its activity.
3. **Substrate Concentration:** The reaction rate typically increases with an increase in substrate concentration, as more substrate molecules are available for the enzyme to act upon. This relationship only holds up to a certain point, known as **saturation**, where all active sites on the enzyme molecules are occupied, and increasing substrate concentration no longer increases the reaction rate.
4. **Inhibitors:**
   - **Competitive Inhibitors:** These molecules resemble the substrate and bind to the enzyme's active site, preventing the actual substrate from binding. The effect of competitive inhibition can be overcome by increasing substrate concentration.

- o **Non-competitive Inhibitors:** These inhibitors bind to a site other than the active site (called an allosteric site), causing a conformational change in the enzyme that reduces its activity. Non-competitive inhibition cannot be overcome by increasing substrate concentration.

5. **Cofactors and Coenzymes:** Many enzymes require non-protein molecules, known as cofactors (which may be metal ions like magnesium or zinc), or coenzymes (organic molecules, often derived from vitamins, such as NAD^+ or FAD) for their activity. These molecules assist in the enzyme's catalytic function, often by participating directly in the reaction mechanism.

ENZYME REGULATION

Enzymes are not only influenced by environmental factors but are also regulated by a variety of mechanisms to ensure proper cellular function. This regulation helps control metabolic pathways and maintains homeostasis within the organism. Key regulatory mechanisms include:

1. **Allosteric Regulation:** Allosteric enzymes have regulatory sites (allosteric sites) that are distinct from the active site. When an effector molecule binds to an allosteric site, it induces a conformational change in the enzyme, altering its activity. Allosteric activators increase enzyme activity, while allosteric inhibitors decrease it. This type of regulation is essential in controlling pathways like glycolysis.
2. **Feedback Inhibition:** In many biochemical pathways, the end product of a pathway inhibits the activity of an enzyme that acts earlier in the pathway. This regulation ensures that the cell does not overproduce certain molecules. For example, in the biosynthesis of amino acids, the accumulation of the

final product can inhibit the first enzyme in the pathway, preventing unnecessary synthesis.

3. **Covalent Modification**: Enzymes can be regulated by the addition or removal of chemical groups, such as phosphate groups (phosphorylation) or methyl groups (methylation). These modifications can activate or deactivate the enzyme by inducing conformational changes, altering its activity. Protein kinases add phosphate groups, while phosphatases remove them.
4. **Gene-Level Regulation**: The expression of enzymes is also regulated at the genetic level. The synthesis of enzymes can be upregulated or downregulated based on the cell's needs, allowing for more efficient responses to changes in the environment. For example, certain enzymes may be synthesized in response to the presence of a substrate or in response to hormonal signals.

Enzymes are essential catalysts in all living organisms, enabling chemical reactions to occur at rates sufficient for life. Their classification into six broad categories reflects the wide variety of reactions they catalyze, from redox reactions to the formation of new bonds. Enzymes work by binding substrates at their active sites and lowering the activation energy required for reactions. The activity of enzymes is finely tuned by factors such as temperature, pH, and the presence of inhibitors. The enzymatic function is regulated through allosteric interactions, feedback inhibition, covalent modification, and gene expression, ensuring that metabolic processes are tightly controlled and responsive to cellular needs. Understanding enzyme structure, function, and regulation is crucial for fields ranging from biochemistry to medicine.

CONCLUSION

Biomolecules are the fundamental building blocks of life and play a crucial role in the structure, function, and regulation of living organisms. Carbohydrates, as one of the primary sources of energy, are essential for cellular metabolism, providing fuel for processes like respiration and energy storage in the form of glycogen and starch. Proteins, with their diverse structures and functions, serve as the molecular machines of the cell, performing tasks ranging from catalyzing biochemical reactions as enzymes to providing structural support in cells and tissues through proteins like collagen and keratin. Lipids, though hydrophobic, are vital for energy storage, forming the backbone of cell membranes in the form of phospholipids and providing insulation and protection to organs. Nucleic acids, specifically DNA and RNA, store and transmit genetic information, ensuring that genetic instructions are passed down from generation to generation, facilitating cellular functions, and enabling evolution. Enzymes, as specialized proteins, are essential for catalyzing biochemical reactions at a rate that is necessary for sustaining life. They lower the activation energy required for chemical reactions, enabling vital processes such as digestion, DNA replication, and energy production. The interaction and balance of these biomolecules underpin all biological processes, and together they create the intricate web of life. Understanding the chemical structure and function of these biomolecules is foundational for exploring areas such as physiology, molecular biology, genetics, and biotechnology. Their study not only provides insights into how life functions at a molecular level but also enables advancements in medical, agricultural, and environmental sciences, where biomolecular knowledge is applied to create solutions for pressing challenges, from disease treatment to food security.

QUESTIONS

- What are the different types of carbohydrates, and how do they function in the body?
- Describe the structure and function of amino acids and proteins.
- What is the difference between simple and compound lipids? Provide examples.
- Explain the structure and function of nucleic acids, particularly DNA and RNA.
- How do enzymes function as biological catalysts, and what factors affect their activity?
- What are the roles of lipids in the body? Mention at least two types of lipids.
- Discuss the classification of enzymes and their mechanisms of action.
- How do proteins contribute to cell structure and function? Give examples.

CHAPTER 2

CELL BIOLOGY AND ULTRASTRUCTURE

Cell biology is the branch of biology that focuses on the study of cells, which are the fundamental units of life. Every living organism, regardless of its complexity, is made up of cells. From unicellular organisms such as bacteria and protozoa to multicellular organisms like plants, animals, and humans, cells serve as the basic building blocks of life. Understanding cell biology is essential for a comprehensive understanding of how organisms grow, develop, reproduce, and maintain their functions. The study of cells includes an examination of their structures, processes, and interactions with other cells and the environment. Cellular components, such as the nucleus, cytoplasm, organelles, and cell membrane, work in concert to perform the various tasks that sustain life. These cellular activities are governed by molecular machinery made up of biomolecules, such as proteins, lipids, nucleic acids, and carbohydrates, which all play specialized roles in maintaining cellular homeostasis.

The internal structure of a cell is highly organized, and each component has a specific function that contributes to the overall operation of the cell. One of the most vital aspects of cell biology is understanding how cellular structures support the cell's function. The cell membrane, for instance, serves as a selective barrier that controls the entry and exit of materials, maintaining the cell's internal environment. The cytoplasm contains a network of proteins and organelles that allow the cell to carry out its metabolic processes. The nucleus, often considered the control center of the cell, stores genetic information in the form of DNA and coordinates processes like gene expression and DNA replication. Organelles like the mitochondria are responsible for energy production, while ribosomes play an essential role in protein synthesis. The endoplasmic reticulum (ER) is involved in the synthesis of lipids and proteins, with the rough ER housing ribosomes for protein synthesis and the smooth ER involved in lipid metabolism and detoxification. The Golgi apparatus further processes proteins and lipids and packages them for transport to their final destinations. The lysosomes contain enzymes that break down waste materials and cellular debris, while the cytoskeleton provides structural support and enables cellular movement and division.

The complexity of cellular structure is mirrored by the sophistication of cellular processes. Each cellular activity, from energy production to waste disposal, is carefully coordinated to ensure that the cell functions efficiently. This coordination is facilitated by signaling pathways, which are intricate networks of molecules that transmit information within and between cells. For example, growth factors, hormones, and neurotransmitters act as signals that regulate cell division, differentiation, and response to external stimuli. The ability of a cell to respond to signals from its environment is crucial for the organism's survival. For instance, immune cells must recognize and respond to pathogens, while nerve cells transmit electrical signals that control movement and sensory perception. The study of these processes is central to understanding cellular function, and it provides insights into diseases such as cancer, neurodegenerative disorders, and immune system dysfunctions, which arise from errors in cellular regulation and signaling.

At the ultrastructural level, cell biology delves deeper into the organization of cellular components using advanced techniques such as electron microscopy, which allows the visualization of structures too small to be seen with light microscopy. Electron microscopy has endoplasmic reticulum, and Golgi apparatus, providing a deeper understanding of their roles within the cell. This level of detail has also contributed to our understanding of the dynamic nature of the cell. For instance, the study of cellular membranes has shown that they are not static but rather fluid structures that are constantly undergoing changes. Lipids and proteins within the membrane are able to move and interact, allowing the cell to adapt to changing conditions and communicate with its environment. The study of cellular components at the ultrastructural level has helped uncover the molecular machinery that drives cellular processes, such as protein folding, intracellular transport, and DNA replication.

Cell biology also emphasizes the importance of cellular diversity. Despite all cells sharing fundamental similarities, different cell types within multicellular organisms are specialized for specific functions. For example, muscle cells are specialized for contraction, while nerve cells are designed for transmitting electrical signals. Understanding the specialization of cells and how they work together to form tissues, organs, and systems is crucial to understanding how complex organisms function. This concept is explored in developmental biology, where the differentiation of stem cells into specialized cell types is studied. The ability of cells to differentiate and specialize is a key aspect of development, regeneration, and repair in multicellular organisms. The study of cellular communication and coordination helps to explain how cells cooperate to maintain homeostasis in the body, as seen in processes like immune responses, wound healing, and tissue growth.

At the molecular level, the study of cell biology also focuses on the molecules that regulate cellular functions. DNA, RNA, and proteins interact in highly coordinated ways to control cell behavior. For instance, transcription factors bind to specific sequences of DNA to regulate gene expression, which in turn determines the production of proteins. These proteins, in turn, control cellular processes like the cell cycle, metabolism, and apoptosis (programmed cell death). The regulation of these processes is crucial for maintaining the integrity of the organism. Disruptions in these molecular interactions can lead to diseases, such as cancer, where mutations in genes that control the cell cycle result in uncontrolled cell division. Understanding the molecular basis of cell function is essential for the development of new therapies and treatments for a wide range of diseases.

The cell biology is the study of the structural and functional units of life—cells. The understanding of cellular components, their organization, and their interactions is fundamental to biology, as it provides insights into the basic mechanisms of life. From energy production to genetic regulation, cells are the sites of all biochemical processes that sustain life. Advanced techniques, such as electron microscopy and molecular biology, have enabled scientists to examine cellular structures and processes in unprecedented detail. This has led to groundbreaking discoveries in medicine, genetics, and biotechnology, contributing to our understanding of both health and disease. Cell biology not only provides the foundation for understanding individual cellular functions but also sheds light on the complexities of multicellular organisms and how cells coordinate to maintain life at the organismal level.

2.1 Cell Theory and Origin of Eukaryotic Cells (Endosymbiotic Theory)

Cell Theory: Historical Perspective and Principles

The concept of the cell as the fundamental unit of life has profound implications for biology, and its development was a milestone in our understanding of living organisms. The foundation of cell theory emerged in the 19th century, with key contributions from German scientists Matthias Schleiden and Theodor Schwann, as well as from Rudolf Virchow. The primary principles of cell theory are as follows:

1. **All living organisms are composed of one or more cells.** This principle asserts that whether an organism is unicellular (e.g., bacteria, protozoa) or multicellular (e.g., plants, animals), the cell is the basic unit of life, responsible for maintaining the characteristics of living systems.
2. **The cell is the basic unit of structure and function in all organisms.** This principle highlights the idea that the cell is not just a structural entity but also a functional one. Each cell carries out various processes, such as energy production, metabolism, and reproduction, which are necessary for the survival of the organism.
3. **All cells arise from pre-existing cells (Omnis cellula e cellula).** This principle, coined by Rudolf Virchow in 1855, challenged the idea of spontaneous generation and established that cells come from other cells through processes such as division, ensuring the continuity of life.

As scientific knowledge advanced, additional components were integrated into cell theory. These include the understanding that:

- **Cells contain hereditary information (DNA)**, which is passed down from parent to offspring during cell division. This is central to the transmission of genetic material, ensuring the continuity of traits across generations.
- **All energy flow (metabolism) occurs within cells.** Cellular metabolism, which encompasses all chemical reactions that occur within the cell, is essential for energy production and sustaining cellular activities. These processes, such as cellular respiration and photosynthesis, are fundamental to life.

Cell theory serves as the cornerstone of modern biology and provides a framework for understanding the biological processes that occur at the cellular level. The application of this theory spans a broad range of fields, from genetics and microbiology to medicine and biotechnology. It emphasizes the idea that the cell is not only the smallest living unit but also the most important one in ensuring the organization, maintenance, and function of living organisms.

The Origin of Eukaryotic Cells: The Endosymbiotic Theory

While the principles of cell theory established a unified view of cells, the origin of eukaryotic cells—the more complex cells that make up multicellular organisms—was a mystery for a long time. The evolutionary transition from prokaryotic cells (which are simpler, smaller, and lack membrane-bound organelles) to eukaryotic cells (which are larger, have a defined nucleus, and contain membrane-bound organelles) marked a major leap in biological complexity. How did these more complex cells arise? The answer lies in the endosymbiotic theory, which was proposed by American biologist Lynn Margulis in the 1960s.

Margulis' endosymbiotic theory suggests that the mitochondria and chloroplasts found in eukaryotic cells are the evolutionary descendants of free-living prokaryotes (bacteria) that were engulfed by a primitive host cell. According to the theory, these prokaryotes established a symbiotic relationship with their host cell, providing some form of benefit to the host (such as enhanced energy production) in exchange for a protected environment and access to nutrients. Over time, these engulfed prokaryotes evolved into permanent, integrated organelles within the host cell, eventually becoming mitochondria (in animal and fungal cells) and chloroplasts (in plant cells).

This theory explains how eukaryotic cells, which are significantly engulfment of prokaryotic organisms by a host cell marks a crucial point in cellular evolution, allowing for the development of multicellular life. Through this symbiotic relationship, eukaryotic cells gained specialized structures that significantly enhanced their efficiency in energy production, among other functions, leading to the emergence of more complex forms of life.

Supporting Evidence for the Endosymbiotic Theory

The endosymbiotic theory is supported by a range of compelling evidence, which suggests that mitochondria and chloroplasts are more closely related to certain prokaryotic groups than to the eukaryotic host cells they reside in. Some of the most significant pieces of evidence include:

1. **Presence of Circular DNA:** Mitochondria and chloroplasts each contain their own circular DNA, which is similar to the DNA found in bacteria. This is in contrast to the linear chromosomes found in the nucleus of eukaryotic cells. The presence of circular DNA suggests that these organelles may have originated from bacteria that had a similar method of storing genetic information.
2. **Independent Replication:** Both mitochondria and chloroplasts replicate independently of the host cell through a process similar to binary fission, the method of cell division used by prokaryotic cells. This further supports the idea that these organelles were once independent prokaryotes that divided and reproduced on their own, even within the host cell.
3. **Ribosomal Similarity:** The ribosomes within mitochondria and chloroplasts are similar in size and structure to those found in prokaryotes (specifically, the 70S ribosomes found

in bacteria), rather than the larger 80S ribosomes found in eukaryotic cells. This similarity in ribosome structure suggests a close evolutionary relationship between these organelles and prokaryotic cells.

4. **Genetic Similarity to Specific Prokaryotes:** Phylogenetic analyses, which examine the genetic relationships between different organisms, have shown that the DNA sequences of mitochondria are closely related to the DNA of certain proteobacteria (especially alpha-proteobacteria), while the DNA of chloroplasts is closely related to cyanobacteria. This further strengthens the idea that mitochondria and chloroplasts are derived from these specific groups of prokaryotes.
5. **Dual Genetic Origins:** The endosymbiotic theory also explains the fact that mitochondria and chloroplasts have their own genomes but still depend on the host cell for many functions. Over time, many of the original genes of the engulfed prokaryotes were transferred to the host cell's nuclear genome, leaving only a small portion of the genetic material within the organelle. This gene transfer is consistent with the endosymbiotic model, as the host cell gradually took on more of the regulatory functions.

Implications of the Endosymbiotic Theory

The endosymbiotic theory has profound implications for our understanding of evolutionary biology. It suggests that the origin of eukaryotic cells was a highly complex event that involved cooperation between two different organisms, rather than a straightforward progression from simple to complex. The symbiotic relationship between a prokaryotic cell and its host would have provided advantages for both parties, making it an evolutionary strategy that likely took place around 1.5 to 2 billion years ago, marking the point at which eukaryotes first appeared.

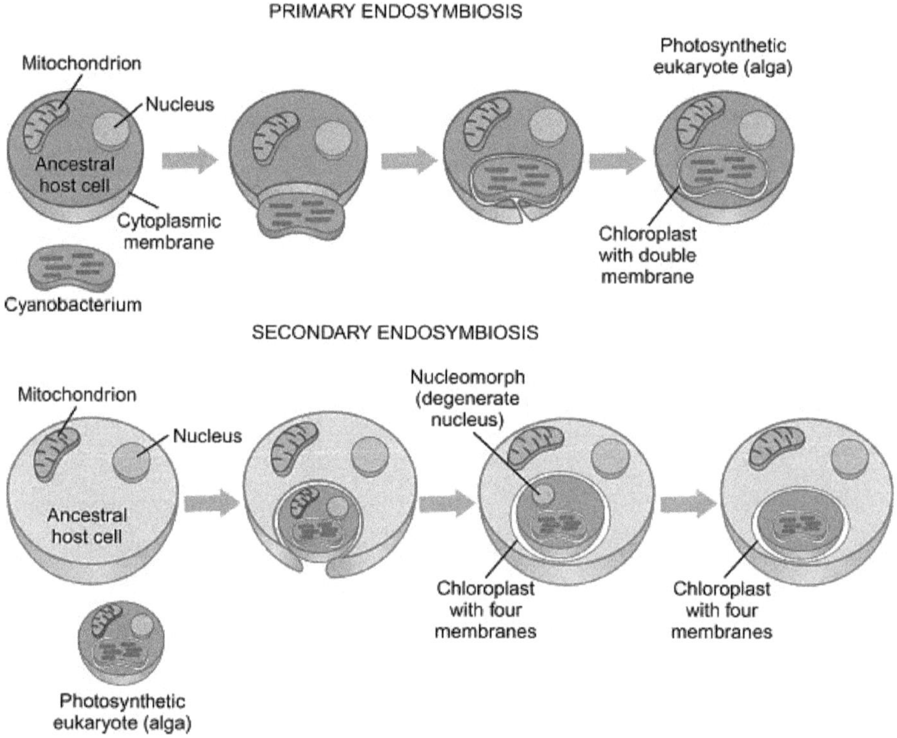

Figure: *Endosymbiotic Theory*

The transition from prokaryotic to eukaryotic life was crucial for the evolution of multicellular organisms, as eukaryotic cells could specialize and interact in ways that prokaryotes could not. The specialization of organelles, such as mitochondria for energy production and chloroplasts for photosynthesis, allowed eukaryotic cells to harness energy in more efficient ways, paving the way for more complex forms of life. This event also set the stage for the evolution of multicellularity, where individual cells could specialize in different functions and cooperate to form tissues and organs.

The endosymbiotic theory underscores the importance of symbiosis in the evolution of life. While symbiotic relationships are often viewed as mechanisms for cooperation and mutual benefit, the endosymbiotic theory illustrates how such interactions can also lead to evolutionary innovations that give rise to entirely new forms of life. In this case, the merging of two different life forms—prokaryotes and eukaryotes—led to the development of an entirely new cellular structure, one that was capable of more complex and diverse biological processes.

The cell theory and the endosymbiotic theory represent critical concepts in our understanding of cellular life. Cell theory provides the foundational principles for the study of all living organisms, emphasizing the importance of the cell as the basic unit of life. The endosymbiotic theory offers a compelling explanation for the origin of eukaryotic cells, proposing that mitochondria and chloroplasts evolved from free-living bacteria that were engulfed by a host cell, forming a symbiotic relationship that eventually led to the development of permanent organelles within the eukaryotic cell. The evidence supporting this theory has revolutionized our understanding of eukaryotic evolution, providing a glimpse into the profound changes that allowed for the emergence of complex, multicellular life forms. Together, these theories form the cornerstone of modern biology, offering insights into the structure, function, and evolution of cells and organisms.

2.2 Prokaryotic vs. Eukaryotic Cells

Cells are the fundamental units of life and can be broadly classified into two categories based on their structure and complexity: prokaryotic cells and eukaryotic cells. While both types of cells share certain common features, such as a plasma membrane and the presence of genetic material, they differ significantly in their internal the distinction between organisms like bacteria and archaea (prokaryotes) and those like plants, animals, fungi, and protists (eukaryotes). Understanding the key differences between these two types of cells provides a foundation for studying biology, evolution, and cellular function.

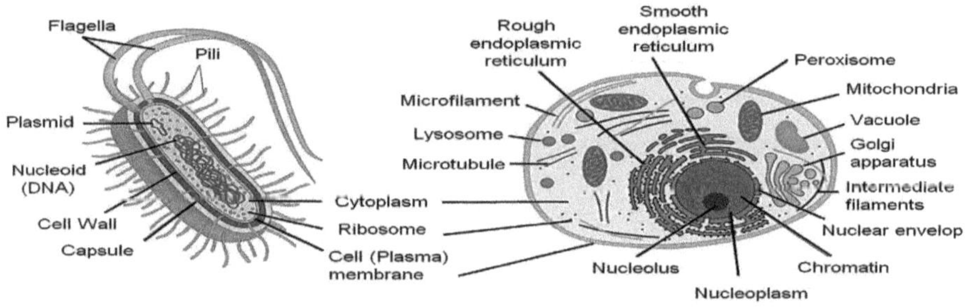

***Figure:** Prokaryotic vs. Eukaryotic Cell Structure*

KEY FEATURES OF PROKARYOTIC CELLS

Prokaryotic cells are generally simpler and smaller than eukaryotic cells, typically ranging from 0.1 to 5 micrometers in diameter, which allows for rapid nutrient exchange and faster growth and reproduction. Unlike eukaryotes, prokaryotes lack membrane-bound organelles such as the mitochondria, endoplasmic reticulum, and Golgi apparatus, making their cellular processes more dependent on the cytoplasm. They do not have a true nucleus; instead, their genetic material is located in the nucleoid, a region that is not enclosed by a membrane. The DNA is usually a single, circular chromosome, not associated with histones, and prokaryotes may also contain plasmids, which carry additional genes like those for antibiotic resistance. Prokaryotic ribosomes are smaller (70S) than those of eukaryotes (80S), but both types are involved in protein synthesis. Prokaryotes divide through binary fission, a simple and rapid form of asexual reproduction. Most prokaryotic cells also have a cell wall made of peptidoglycan that provides structural support and protection against environmental stress, with variations among different prokaryotic groups. This structural simplicity allows prokaryotic cells to adapt and thrive in a wide range of environments.

Key Features of Eukaryotic Cells

Eukaryotic cells are more complex and larger than prokaryotic cells, with a variety of features that support their higher degree of specialization and organization, which is evident in organisms like plants, animals, fungi, and protists. A key characteristic of eukaryotic cells is the presence of a true, membrane-bound nucleus, which contains the cell's genetic material in the form of linear chromosomes, tightly coiled around histones to form chromatin. Eukaryotic cells also contain several membrane-bound organelles, such as mitochondria (energy production), endoplasmic reticulum (synthesis of proteins and lipids), Golgi apparatus (protein sorting and packaging), and in plant cells, chloroplasts (photosynthesis). These organelles compartmentalize cellular functions, allowing for more efficient and complex processes than in prokaryotic cells. Eukaryotic cells are generally larger, ranging from 10 to 100 micrometers, and their increased size accommodates the intricate internal structures needed for cellular specialization. The DNA in eukaryotes is organized into multiple linear chromosomes within the nucleus, unlike the single circular chromosome in prokaryotes. Eukaryotic cells also contain larger 80S ribosomes, although those found in mitochondria and chloroplasts are more similar to the 70S ribosomes of prokaryotes, which supports the endosymbiotic theory of their origin. Eukaryotic cell division occurs through mitosis for growth and tissue repair, and meiosis for the production of genetically diverse gametes. The composition of the cell wall varies among eukaryotes: plant cells have a cellulose wall, fungal cells contain chitin, and animal cells lack a cell wall, instead relying on a flexible plasma membrane for mobility and flexibility. Here's a table summarizing the key differences between

***Table:** Differences between prokaryotic and eukaryotic cells*

Feature	**Prokaryotic Cells**	**Eukaryotic Cells**
Nucleus	Absent (nucleoid region)	Present (membrane-bound nucleus)
Membrane-bound Organelles	Absent	Present (e.g., mitochondria, ER, Golgi)
Size	Small (0.1–5 µm)	Larger (10–100 µm)
DNA Structure	Circular DNA	Linear chromosomes with histones
Ribosomes	70S	80S (except 70S in mitochondria/ chloroplasts)
Cell Division	Binary fission	Mitosis and meiosis
Cell Wall	Peptidoglycan (bacteria)	Cellulose (plants), chitin (fungi), or absent (animals)
Example	*Escherichia coli* (bacteria)	*Homo sapiens*, *Arabidopsis*, *Saccharomyces* (plants, animals, fungi)
Metabolic Diversity	High; can be autotrophic or heterotrophic	Generally autotrophic or heterotrophic
Genetic Material Exchange	Horizontal gene transfer (e.g., plasmids)	Typically vertical gene transmission

Diversity in Prokaryotic Cells

Despite their relatively simple structure, prokaryotic cells exhibit remarkable metabolic and ecological diversity. Prokaryotes can be found in nearly every environment on Earth, from the depths of the oceans to extreme environments such as hot springs and acidic lakes. They can be autotrophic (able to produce their own food through processes like photosynthesis or chemosynthesis) or heterotrophic (requiring external sources of organic compounds for energy). Prokaryotes are essential to many biochemical cycles, such as nitrogen fixation and the decomposition of organic matter, contributing significantly to the global cycling of nutrients.

In addition to their metabolic diversity, prokaryotes also exhibit genetic diversity. Through processes such as horizontal gene transfer, prokaryotes can exchange genetic material between individuals, facilitating the spread of traits such as antibiotic resistance and metabolic capabilities. This ability to rapidly acquire and share genetic material contributes to the adaptability of prokaryotic populations, allowing them to thrive in a wide range of habitats.

The fundamental differences between prokaryotic and eukaryotic cells highlight the varying degrees of complexity in cellular structure and function. While prokaryotic cells are smaller, simpler, and lack membrane-bound organelles, eukaryotic cells are larger and more specialized, with compartmentalized structures that support more complex functions. These differences have profound implications for the organization of life, from unicellular prokaryotes to multicellular eukaryotes. Despite their simplicity, prokaryotes are remarkably diverse and play critical roles in ecological and biochemical processes, while eukaryotes exhibit the structural and functional complexity required for the development of multicellular life forms. Understanding these differences is key to understanding the evolution of life on Earth and the

2.3 Cell Wall and Cell Membrane Structure

CELL WALL

The cell wall is a rigid outer layer that surrounds the cell membrane in various types of cells, providing structural support and protection. It plays a key role in maintaining cell shape, preventing excessive water uptake, and protecting cells from mechanical and osmotic kingdoms, tailored to the specific needs and environments of the organism.

- **Bacteria**: In bacterial cells, the cell wall is primarily composed of peptidoglycan, a polymer of sugars and amino acids. This structure provides strength and rigidity, allowing bacteria to maintain their shape and resist osmotic pressure. The composition of peptidoglycan varies between different bacterial groups, with Gram-positive bacteria having a thick peptidoglycan layer, and Gram-negative bacteria possessing a thinner peptidoglycan layer along with an outer membrane.
- **Fungi**: In fungi, the cell wall is made of chitin, a tough, nitrogen-containing polysaccharide. Chitin gives fungal cells their rigidity and protection against environmental stresses, while also allowing for flexibility to enable growth. This composition distinguishes fungal cells from both plant and bacterial cells.
- **Plants**: The plant cell wall is made primarily of cellulose, a polymer of glucose, along with hemicellulose and pectin. Cellulose forms a rigid framework that provides structural support for plant cells, enabling them to stand upright and resist external pressures. The primary cell wall, found in young plant cells, is flexible, allowing for cell growth and expansion. Over time, plant cells can deposit a secondary cell wall, which adds additional strength and rigidity, especially in cells that require added structural support, such as those in wood and bark.

The core function of the cell wall is to provide protection and structural support, its specific composition varies across different kingdoms, highlighting the diversity in cellular architecture across life forms.

Cell Membrane (Plasma Membrane)

The cell membrane, or plasma membrane, is a dynamic structure that surrounds all cells and controls the movement of substances into and out of the cell. It is a selectively permeable barrier, allowing essential nutrients to enter, waste products to exit, and helping to maintain cellular homeostasis. The plasma membrane is made up primarily of a phospholipid bilayer, in which phospholipids arrange themselves in a way that exposes their hydrophilic (water-attracting) heads to the aqueous environment while burying their hydrophobic (water-repelling) tails within the membrane. This bilayer structure forms the foundation of the membrane and allows it to maintain its integrity while facilitating selective permeability.

The Fluid Mosaic Model, proposed by S.J. Singer and G.L. Nicolson in 1972, describes the structure of the cell membrane as a fluid, dynamic arrangement of lipids and proteins. The model highlights the membrane's flexibility, with proteins embedded within the lipid bilayer that can move laterally, allowing the membrane to adapt to various conditions. This model also emphasizes the heterogeneity of the membrane, where different proteins and lipids are distributed unevenly, forming a mosaic of components that carry out distinct functions.

- **Phospholipids**: The amphipathic nature of phospholipids, with their hydrophilic heads and hydrophobic tails, forms the basis of the membrane's structure. This arrangement allows the membrane to be selectively permeable to certain molecules, such as small non-polar molecules (e.g., oxygen and carbon dioxide), while limiting the passage of others. The bilayer also serves as a barrier to water-soluble substances.
- **Proteins**: Integral proteins, which span the entire bilayer, are responsible for transporting molecules across the membrane, acting as channels, carriers, or pum

facilitate both passive transport (e.g., through diffusion) and active transport (e.g., through energy-dependent processes like ion pumping). Peripheral proteins, which are attached to the outer or inner surface of the membrane, are involved in cell signaling, maintaining the cell's shape, and providing anchorage for the cytoskeleton.

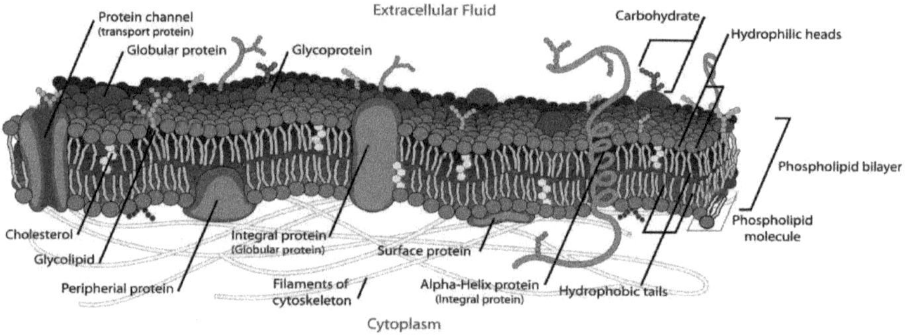

***Figure:** Fluid Mosaic Model of the Plasma Membrane*

- **Cholesterol:** Cholesterol molecules are interspersed within the phospholipid bilayer, particularly in animal cell membranes. Cholesterol helps maintain membrane fluidity by preventing the phospholipids from packing too closely together, which could otherwise make the membrane too rigid. It also helps to stabilize the membrane at varying temperatures, ensuring that it remains flexible under both high and low temperature conditions.
- **Glycoproteins and Glycolipids:** The outer surface of the plasma membrane is decorated with glycoproteins and glycolipids, which are proteins and lipids with carbohydrate chains attached to them. These molecules play a critical role in cell recognition and signaling. Glycoproteins, for example, can act as receptors for signaling molecules like hormones, and they are crucial for immune recognition. Glycolipids also

contribute to the recognition of self and non-self cells, a vital process for immune function.

Functions of the Cell Membrane

The cell membrane performs several essential functions that are critical to the survival and function of the cell. These functions include:

- **Regulation of Transport**: The cell membrane controls the movement of ions, nutrients, and waste products into and out of the cell. It does so via mechanisms such as passive diffusion, facilitated diffusion, active transport, and vesicular transport. This regulation is essential for maintaining the internal environment of the cell, which is necessary for biochemical reactions to occur efficiently.
- **Facilitation of Cell Signaling**: The membrane contains receptors (often glycoproteins) that bind to signaling molecules, such as hormones and neurotransmitters. This process triggers intracellular signaling pathways that regulate various cellular processes, such as growth, division, and apoptosis. Membrane proteins, such as G-protein-coupled receptors (GPCRs), play critical roles in this form of communication.
- **Enzymatic Activity**: The cell membrane provides a site for various enzymatic activities. Membrane-bound enzymes participate in essential metabolic processes, such as ATP synthesis in mitochondria, and the breakdown of macromolecules during digestion. The membrane also houses enzymes involved in the synthesis of lipids and proteins.
- **Anchorage of Cytoskeleton and Extracellular Matrix**: The

cell. This connection is crucial for maintaining the shape and stability of the cell. The membrane proteins anchor the cell to the extracellular matrix (ECM), which provides mechanical support and helps maintain tissue structure.

The cell wall and plasma membrane are both essential to maintaining the structural integrity and functional capabilities of cells. The cell wall provides support, protection, and shape to cells in plants, fungi, and bacteria, while the plasma membrane regulates the internal environment of the cell, facilitates communication, and supports essential biochemical processes. Together, these two structures form the foundation for cellular function, ensuring that cells can thrive and interact with their surroundings in a dynamic and controlled manner.

2.4 Cell Organelles: Nucleus, Mitochondria, Ribosomes, ER, Golgi, Lysosomes, Chloroplasts, Vacuoles

1. Nucleus

The nucleus is the control center of the cell, responsible for managing cellular activities, including growth, metabolism, protein synthesis, and reproduction. It is enclosed by a double membrane, called the nuclear envelope, which has pores that allow the selective exchange of materials between the nucleus and the cytoplasm. Inside the nucleus, chromatin (a complex of DNA and histone proteins) stores the cell's genetic information. During cell division, chromatin condenses to form distinct chromosomes. The nucleolus, located within the nucleus, is responsible for the synthesis of ribosomal RNA (rRNA) and the assembly of ribosome subunits, which are then exported to the cytoplasm for protein synthesis. The nucleus also plays a crucial role in regulating gene expression and controlling DNA replication, ensuring that the genetic instructions needed for cellular function are correctly transcribed and translated into proteins.

2. Mitochondria

Mitochondria are membrane-bound organelles often referred to as the "powerhouses" of the cell due to their role in generating energy. These organelles have a double membrane structure, with the inner membrane folding into structures known as cristae, which increase the surface area for enzymatic reactions involved in energy production. Mitochondria are the site of aerobic respiration, where glucose and oxygen are used to produce ATP (adenosine triphosphate), the primary energy carrier in cells. The outer membrane is permeable to ions and small molecules, while the inner membrane is more selective. Mitochondria contain their own circular DNA and 70S ribosomes, supporting the endosymbiotic theory, which suggests that mitochondria originated from free-living prokaryotes engulfed by ancestral eukaryotic cells. Mitochondria also play a role in regulating cellular metabolism, calcium signaling, and apoptosis (programmed cell death).

3. Ribosomes

Ribosomes are non-membranous organelles composed of ribosomal RNA (rRNA) and proteins. They are the sites of protein synthesis in cells, where mRNA is translated into polypeptides, which then fold into functional proteins. Ribosomes can be found either floating freely in the cytoplasm or attached to the rough endoplasmic reticulum (ER). Free ribosomes primarily synthesize proteins that function within the cytoplasm, whereas bound ribosomes synthesize proteins that are either secreted from the cell, incorporated into the cell membrane, or destined for specific organelles such as the lysosomes or the endoplasmic reticulum. Ribosomes are essential for cellular function, as proteins are vital for nearly all cellular processes, from metabolism to signaling.

4. Endoplasmic Reticulum (ER)

The endoplasmic reticulum (ER) is an extensive network of membrane-bound tubules and sacs that play a key role in the synthesis of proteins and lipids. The rough ER (RER) is studded with ribosomes on its cytoplasmic surface, which give it its "rough" appearance. This structure is primarily involved in the synthesis and modification of proteins that are secreted, incorporated into cell membranes, or sent to the lysosomes. The smooth ER (SER), which lacks ribosomes, is involved in lipid synthesis, detoxification of harmful substances, and storage of calcium ions. The smooth ER is particularly important in liver cells, where it helps to detoxify various metabolites, drugs, and other chemicals. The ER also plays a role in the folding and modification of newly synthesized proteins, ensuring that they are correctly formed before being transported to their final destinations.

5. Golgi Apparatus

The Golgi apparatus is a stack of flattened membrane-bound sacs known as cisternae, functioning as a central hub for modifying, packaging, and distributing proteins and lipids that have been synthesized in the ER. Proteins and lipids from the ER are transported in vesicles to the Golgi, where they are further modified by processes such as glycosylation, phosphorylation, and proteolysis. These modifications are crucial for the proper functioning of the proteins and lipids in their final destinations. Once processing is complete, the Golgi apparatus packages the molecules into vesicles, which are then sent to the appropriate locations, including the plasma membrane, lysosomes, or secretory vesicles. The Golgi apparatus plays a pivotal role in the sorting and trafficking of cellular molecules, ensuring that they reach their designated cellular compartments or are secreted outside the cell.

6. Lysosomes

Lysosomes are membrane-bound organelles containing hydrolytic enzymes that are responsible for breaking down and recycling cellular waste materials, old organelles, and foreign substances that enter the cell. These enzymes are acidic, and their function is optimized in the acidic environment inside the lysosome. Lysosomes are formed by the Golgi apparatus and are involved in processes such as autophagy, where damaged organelles or protein aggregates are engulfed by the cell and degraded. They also play a role in apoptosis, or programmed cell death, by releasing their enzymes to break down cellular components in a controlled manner. Lysosomes help maintain cellular homeostasis by eliminating waste products and recycling cellular components for reuse.

7. Chloroplasts (in Plants and Algae)

Chloroplasts are specialized organelles found in plant and algal cells, responsible for photosynthesis — the process by which light energy is converted into chemical energy stored in glucose molecules. Chloroplasts have a double-membrane structure, with the inner membrane forming a system of interconnected sacs called thylakoids, which are stacked into structures known as grana. The thylakoids contain chlorophyll, the pigment that captures light energy, and other proteins involved in the light-dependent reactions of photosynthesis. The stroma, the space surrounding the thylakoids, contains enzymes necessary for the Calvin cycle, where carbon dioxide is converted into glucose. Like mitochondria, chloroplasts contain their own DNA and 70S ribosomes, suggesting their evolutionary origin from free-living prokaryotes, as proposed by the endosymbiotic theory.

8. VACUOLES

Vacuoles are membrane-bound organelles that serve various functions in different types of cells. In plant cells, the central vacuole is large and occupies a significant portion of the cell's volume. It is primarily responsible for maintaining turgor pressure, which helps the cell maintain its shape and prevents it from wilting. The vacuole also stores a variety of substances, such as water, nutrients, pigments, and waste products. The vacuoles play a role in the breakdown of macromolecules, similar to lysosomes. In animal cells, vacuoles tend to be smaller and are involved in processes like endocytosis, where they engulf extracellular material, and storage, such as storing nutrients and ions.

The cell organelles are highly specialized structures that contribute to the cell's function and survival. From the energy-producing mitochondria to the protein-synthesizing ribosomes, each organelle plays an integral role in maintaining the integrity of the cell, facilitating complex metabolic processes, and supporting growth, division, and communication. The highly organized architecture of these organelles is essential for the overall functioning of the cell, and their coordination ensures that the cell operates efficiently and effectively.

2.5 Chromosome Structure and Nucleosome Concept

CHROMOSOMES

Chromosomes are highly organized structures composed of DNA and proteins, primarily histones. These structures are vital for packaging the genetic material in a compact and manageable form that can be accurately replicated and distributed during cell division. In eukaryotic cells, chromosomes are located in the nucleus, and they are composed of linear DNA molecules. The DNA in chromosomes is tightly coiled and condensed to fit within the cell's nucleus, but it can also be dynamically unpacked during cellular processes such as transcription and replication. There are two main types of chromatin within chromosomes:

- **Euchromatin**: This is the loosely packed form of chromatin that is actively transcribed. Euchromatin contains genes that are frequently expressed and can be accessed by the transcription machinery. Its loose configuration allows the DNA to be exposed and available for the processes of transcription and replication.
- **Heterochromatin**: In contrast, heterochromatin is densely packed and typically transcriptionally inactive. It often contains repetitive sequences and is associated with regions of the genome that are less likely to be expressed. Heterochromatin plays roles in maintaining the structural integrity of the chromosome and regulating gene expression.

The structure of chromosomes includes several critical components:

- **Centromere**: This is the constriction site on the chromosome that holds the two chromatids together. During cell division, the centromere is the attachment site for the spindle fibers that separate the chromatids into two daughter cells.
- **Telomeres**: These are the repetitive DNA sequences located at the ends of chromosomes. Telomeres serve to protect the integrity of the chromosome, preventing loss of genetic information during DNA replication and protecting the chromosome from degradation or fusion with other chromosomes.
- **Chromatid**: A chromatid refers to one half of a duplicated chromosome. After DNA replication, each chromosome consists of two chromatids joined at the centromere. During

cell division, these chromatids are separated to ensure that each daughter cell receives a complete set of chromosomes.

Nucleosome Concept

The concept of the nucleosome was proposed by Roger Kornberg in 1974 and represents the fundamental unit of chromatin structure. Nucleosomes are responsible for the first level of DNA compaction, playing a critical role in packaging the vast length of DNA into the small space of the cell's nucleus. A nucleosome consists of approximately 147 base pairs of DNA wrapped around a histone octamer. This octamer is made up of eight histone proteins, arranged in pairs: two copies each of histones H2A, H2B, H3, and H4. The DNA is wound around the histone core in a left-handed superhelix, forming a structure often described as "beads-on-a-string," where the nucleosomes appear as "beads" on a continuous "string" of DNA.

The histone octamer, the linker histone H1 binds to the DNA between nucleosomes, helping to stabilize the structure and regulate the spacing between nucleosomes. This results in a more compact and organized structure, which is essential for controlling access to genetic information and regulating gene expression. The nucleosome is crucial for gene regulation because the packaging of DNA into nucleosomes influences the accessibility of the DNA to the transcription machinery. Regions of the genome that are tightly packed in nucleosomes are less accessible for transcription, while regions that are more loosely packed are more readily transcribed.

Higher-order Chromatin Organization

Beyond the nucleosome, chromatin undergoes additional levels of compaction to organize the DNA into structures suitable for the functions it must perform. The nucleosome "beads-on-a-string" structure is further coiled into a more compact form, known as the **solenoid** or 30 nm fiber. This higher-order structure involves the nucleosomes winding into helical fibers, which significantly condense the DNA.

As the cell prepares for cell division, chromatin undergoes even further compaction. The 30 nm fibers fold and loop into larger structures, forming **looped domains**, which are critical for ensuring that each chromosome can be properly segregated during cell division. During mitosis and meiosis, these looped domains condense even further, forming the characteristic **metaphase chromosomes** that can be observed under a microscope. The highly condensed nature of these chromosomes ensures that the genetic material is accurately distributed between the daughter cells during cell division, reducing the risk of genetic errors.

The organization of DNA into chromosomes is a complex process involving several levels of compaction. The nucleosome represents the most basic level of DNA packaging, which, through further folding and looping, results in the highly condensed chromosomes necessary for cell division. The regulation of chromatin structure is also a key factor in controlling gene expression and maintaining the stability of the genome.

Cell biology bridges the gap between molecular biology and anatomy, serving as a foundational discipline that connects the microscopic mechanisms of life with the structural organization of organisms. By examining the ultrastructure of cells and their various components, scientists can unravel how life functions at both the molecular and cellular levels. This field provides insight into how organelles work together to maintain homeostasis, how signals are transmitted within and between cells, and how cells grow, divide, differentiate, and respond to their environment. Understanding these processes is crucial for advancements in medicine, genetics, developmental biology, and biotechnology. One of the key areas of cells. Unlike simpler prokaryotic cells, eukaryotic cells exhibit compartmentalization through membrane-bound organelles such as the nucleus, mitochondria, endoplasmic reticulum, and Golgi apparatus, allowing them to carry out highly specialized functions. The development of these organelles, particularly mitochondria and chloroplasts, is believed to have arisen through endosymbiosis—an evolutionary process that highlights the dynamic and interconnected nature of life.

The packaging of genetic material into chromosomes within the nucleus exemplifies the sophistication of cellular organization. DNA, tightly coiled around histone proteins to form chromatin, ensures the efficient storage and regulation of genetic information, enabling precise control over gene expression. This structural organization plays a critical role in cell division processes like mitosis and meiosis, which are essential for growth, repair, and reproduction in multicellular organisms. Advances in cell imaging and molecular techniques have further enabled scientists to explore cellular dynamics in real time, revealing the complex interplay between cellular structures and biochemical pathways. As such, the study of cells not only enhances our understanding of life's smallest units but also informs treatments for diseases like cancer, neurodegeneration, and genetic disorders. Ultimately, the cell remains the focal point of all biological phenomena, acting as both the building block and the blueprint of life itself.

QUESTIONS

- What are the three key principles of cell theory?
- Explain the endosymbiotic theory and its significance in the origin of eukaryotic cells.
- What are the major differences between prokaryotic and eukaryotic cells?

- Describe the structure and function of the cell membrane.
- What are the main functions of the organelles in a eukaryotic cell, such as the nucleus, mitochondria, and ribosomes?
- How does the structure of chromosomes relate to gene expression and cell division?
- What is the role of nucleosomes in DNA packaging and gene regulation?
- Compare the structure of the plant and animal vacuoles in terms of their functions.

CHAPTER 3

CELL CYCLE AND DIVISION

The cell cycle is a highly ordered and regulated series of stages through which a cell passes to grow, replicate its DNA, and ultimately divide into two daughter cells. This process is fundamental to life, enabling growth, tissue repair, development, and reproduction. The cycle is broadly divided into two main phases: interphase and the mitotic phase (M phase). Interphase, which comprises the majority of the cell cycle, is further subdivided into the $G1_1$ (Gap 1), S (Synthesis), and G_2 (Gap 2) phases. During G_1, the cell increases in size and synthesizes proteins and organelles essential for DNA replication. In the S phase, DNA replication occurs, resulting in the duplication of chromosomes. G_2 involves further cell growth and preparation for division, including the synthesis of microtubules and other components necessary for mitosis. The M phase includes both mitosis and cytokinesis, where the nucleus and then the cytoplasm divide, respectively. In addition to these stages, certain cells may exit the cycle into a quiescent state known as G_0, where they remain metabolically active but no longer divide—this is typical for nerve and muscle cells.

Cell division occurs through two primary mechanisms: mitosis and meiosis. **Mitosis** is the process by which somatic cells divide, ensuring genetic consistency by producing two genetically identical daughter cells, each with the same number of chromosomes as the parent cell. Mitosis is critical for growth, maintenance, and asexual reproduction in multicellular organisms. It consists of several sequential phases: prophase, metaphase, anaphase, and telophase, followed by cytokinesis. In prophase, chromatin condenses into visible chromosomes, and the mitotic spindle begins to form. During metaphase, chromosomes align at the cell's equatorial plane. In anaphase, sister chromatids are pulled apart to opposite poles, and in telophase, the nuclear envelope re-forms around each set of chromosomes. Cytokinesis, the division of the cytoplasm, follows, completing the formation of two daughter cells.

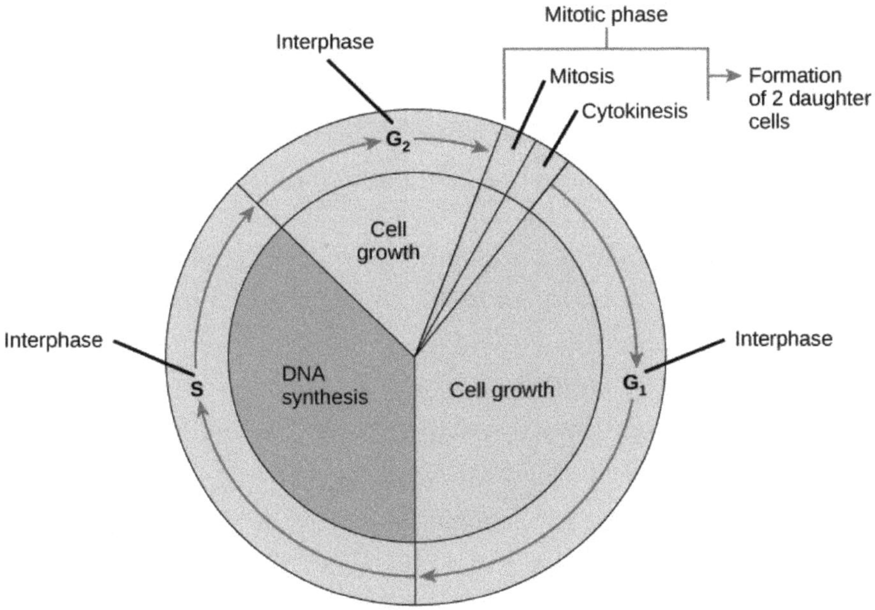

Figure: *Overview of the Cell Cycle*

The meiosis is a specialized form of cell division that occurs in germ cells to produce gametes—sperm and eggs—in sexually reproducing organisms. It reduces the chromosome number by half, ensuring that the zygote formed during fertilization has the correct diploid number. Meiosis involves two successive divisions: meiosis I and meiosis II. Meiosis I is a reductional division, where homologous chromosomes pair up, exchange genetic material through crossing over (during prophase I), and then segregate into two daughter resulting in four non-identical haploid gametes. This genetic variation introduced by crossing over and independent assortment of chromosomes is vital for evolution and the survival of species.

Regulation of the cell cycle is mediated by checkpoints and regulatory proteins such as cyclins and cyclin-dependent kinases (CDKs), which ensure that each phase is completed accurately before the next begins. For instance, the G_1 checkpoint verifies cell size and DNA integrity, the G_2 checkpoint ensures successful DNA replication, and the spindle checkpoint during metaphase checks for proper chromosome alignment and attachment to spindle fibers. Any malfunction in these regulatory mechanisms can lead to uncontrolled cell division and potentially cancer. Thus, a proper understanding of the cell cycle and its regulation is central not only to developmental biology but also to medical science, particularly in areas such as cancer research, regenerative medicine, and reproductive biology.

3.1 Phases of the Cell Cycle

The cell cycle is the series of events that a cell undergoes from the time it is formed until it divides to produce two daughter cells. This cycle is central to all aspects of biological development, growth, tissue repair, and reproduction. It is a highly regulated process that ensures the accurate replication and distribution of genetic material. The cell cycle is broadly divided into two main phases: interphase and the mitotic (M) phase. Some cells exit the active cycle and enter a resting, non-dividing phase known as G_0.

INTERPHASE

Interphase is the longest phase of the cell cycle, typically occupying about 90% of a cell's life. It is the period during which the cell prepares for division by growing, replicating its DNA, and synthesizing the necessary proteins and organelles. Interphase is further subdivided into three sequential stages: G_1 (first gap), S (synthesis), and G_2 (second gap).

G_1 Phase (First Gap): In this initial phase, the cell undergoes significant growth. It increases in size, produces RNA, and synthesizes proteins necessary for DNA replication and general cellular function. The G_1 phase is a period of intense biosynthetic activity. The cell also duplicates its organelles to ensure that each daughter cell will have the proper cellular machinery. A crucial checkpoint, the G_1 checkpoint (also called the restriction point), occurs here. At this checkpoint, the cell assesses whether conditions are favorable for DNA synthesis. Factors such as nutrient availability, cell size, and DNA integrity are evaluated. If any of these criteria are not met, the cell may enter the quiescent G_0 phase instead of progressing to the S phase.

S Phase (Synthesis): During the S phase, the cell synthesizes a complete copy of the DNA in its nucleus. Each chromosome is duplicated, resulting in two identical sister chromatids joined at a centromere. This ensures that each daughter cell will receive an exact copy of the genetic material. Along with DNA replication, the centrosome — the microtubule-organizing center — is also duplicated, a process that is vital for the later stages of mitosis when the spindle apparatus forms.

G_2 Phase (Second Gap): Following DNA replication, the cell enters the G_2 phase, where it continues to grow and produce proteins, particularly those necessary for mitosis. At this stage, the cell undergoes final preparations for division, including the synthesis of microtubules required for chromosome separation. The G_2 checkpoint ensures that DNA replication has been successfully completed without damage or errors. If any issues are detected, the cell cycle is arrested, and repair mechanisms are activated. Only after passing this checkpoint does the cell proceed to the mitotic phase.

MITOTIC (M) PHASE

The M phase encompasses both mitosis (karyokinesis) and cytokinesis, the processes by which a parent cell divides into two genetically identical daughter cells. This phase ensures that each daughter cell receives an equal and accurate distribution of chromosomes and sufficient cytoplasmic material to survive and function. Mitosis is divided into five distinct stages:

1. **Prophase:** Chromatin condenses into visible chromosomes, and each consists of two sister chromatids. The nuclear envelope begins to disintegrate, and the centrosomes move to opposite poles of the cell, forming the mitotic spindle.
2. **Prometaphase:** The nuclear envelope completely breaks down. Spindle fibers attach to the kinetochores, protein complexes on the centromeres of each chromosome.
3. **Metaphase:** Chromosomes align at the cell's equatorial plane, known as the metaphase plate. This alignment ensures that each daughter cell will receive one copy of each chromosome.
4. **Anaphase:** Sister chromatids are separated and pulled toward opposite poles of the cell by shortening spindle fibers. This separation ensures genetic consistency between daughter cells.
5. **Telophase:** Chromosomes reach the poles and begin to decondense back into chromatin. The nuclear envelope re-forms around each set of chromosomes, resulting in two distinct nuclei.

Cytokinesis is the final step, where the cytoplasm divides. In animal cells, a contractile ring composed of actin filaments pinches the cell into two. In plant cells, a cell plate forms along the center line of the cell, eventually developing into a new cell wall.

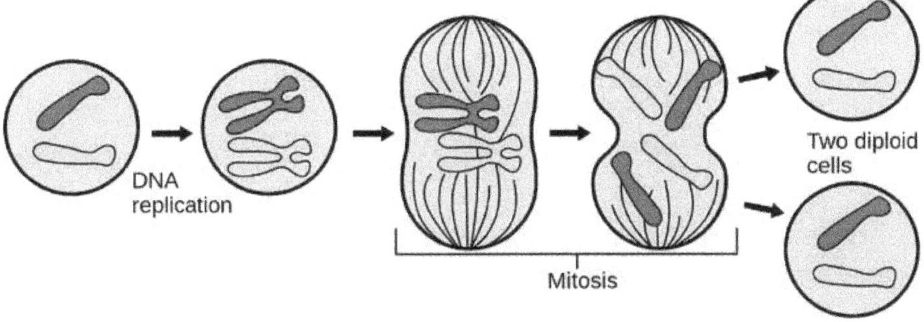

***Figure:** Mitosis Phases*

G_0 PHASE (QUIESCENT STAGE)

Not all cells continuously cycle. Many enter a dormant phase known as the G_0 phase, where they are metabolically active but not actively dividing. This phase can be temporary or permanent, depending on the cell type and its environmental context.

- **Permanently in G_0:** Neurons and cardiac muscle cells typically do not re-enter the cell cycle once they have matured. They remain in a stable, non-dividing state throughout the organism's life.
- **Reversible G_0:** Liver cells and some immune cells can re-enter the cell cycle in response to injury or specific stimuli, contributing to tissue repair and regeneration.

G_0 is crucial for maintaining tissue homeostasis and preventing uncontrolled cell proliferation. Dysregulation of this phase can lead to excessive cell division or loss of necessary cell types.

REGULATION OF THE CELL CYCLE

The cell cycle is controlled by a complex network of regulatory proteins and checkpoints

Among the most important regulators are cyclins and cyclin-dependent kinases (CDKs).

Cyclins and CDKs: Cyclins are proteins whose concentrations vary cyclically during the cell cycle. They activate CDKs, a group of enzymes that phosphorylate target proteins to drive cell cycle progression. Different cyclin-CDK complexes regulate specific transitions, such as G_1/S and G_2/M.

- **Cyclin D/CDK4/6:** Controls progression through G_1.
- **Cyclin E/CDK2:** Initiates DNA replication at the G_1/S transition.
- **Cyclin A/CDK2:** Regulates S phase.
- **Cyclin B/CDK1:** Triggers entry into mitosis.

Checkpoints:

Three main checkpoints ensure proper cell cycle progression:

1. **G_1 Checkpoint:** Verifies cell size, nutrients, and DNA integrity.
2. **G_2 Checkpoint:** Ensures DNA replication is complete and error-free.
3. **M Checkpoint (Spindle Checkpoint):** Confirms that all chromosomes are properly attached to the spindle before anaphase begins.

If errors are detected, the cell can delay progression to allow repair. If damage is irreparable, the cell may undergo programmed cell death (apoptosis) to prevent the propagation of defective cells.

Tumor Suppressors and Cell Cycle Arrest: Key tumor suppressor genes, such as **p53**, play a central role in monitoring DNA damage. Upon detecting damage, p53 can arrest the cell cycle at the G_1 checkpoint to allow repair or initiate apoptosis if the damage is too severe. Mutations in p53 are found in over 50% of human cancers, underscoring its importance in preventing tumor development.

Implications in Health and Disease

The precise regulation of the cell cycle is critical for normal growth and development. Aberrations in cycle control can lead to uncontrolled cell division, a hallmark of cancer. Many anticancer therapies target cell cycle regulators, aiming to halt the proliferation of tumor cells. For example, CDK inhibitors are being developed as potential treatments for various cancers. Understanding cell cycle dynamics also informs regenerative medicine, aging research, and the development of targeted therapies.

3.2 Mitosis: Process and Significance

Mitosis is a highly regulated process of nuclear division in eukaryotic cells that ensures the equal distribution of replicated genetic material into two daughter cells. It is essential for various biological functions, including organismal growth, tissue maintenance, repair, and asexual reproduction. Unlike meiosis, which produces gametes with half the chromosome number, mitosis maintains the chromosome number, making the resulting daughter cells genetically identical to the parent cell. Mitosis typically occurs in somatic (non-reproductive) cells and consists of a series of distinct but continuous phases: **prophase, metaphase, anaphase, and telophase**, followed by **cytokinesis**, the division of the cytoplasm. The entire process ensures that each daughter cell inherits a complete and accurate copy of the genome.

Phases of Mitosis

1. Prophase

Prophase marks the beginning of mitosis and is characterized by significant cellular rearrangements. The chromatin fibers — which are loosely packed DNA-protein complexes during interphase —

chromosome now appears as two sister chromatids joined at a central region called the **centromere**.

The mitotic spindle begins to form. This structure is composed of microtubules that originate from the centrosomes, which migrate to opposite poles of the cell. The **nucleolus** disappears, and the **nuclear envelope** starts to disintegrate, allowing the spindle microtubules access to the chromosomes.

2. Metaphase

During metaphase, the spindle fibers fully attach to the chromosomes at specialized protein structures called **kinetochores**, which are located on the centromeres. The chromosomes align along the equatorial plane of the cell, known as the **metaphase plate**. This alignment is critical to ensure that, during separation, each daughter cell will receive an identical set of chromosomes.

The **metaphase checkpoint**, or spindle assembly checkpoint, occurs here. It is a control mechanism that ensures every chromosome is correctly attached to the spindle apparatus. This prevents the unequal distribution of genetic material, which could lead to aneuploidy (abnormal chromosome numbers), often associated with cancer and genetic disorders.

3. Anaphase

Anaphase is a pivotal stage where sister chromatids — the identical copies of each chromosome — are pulled apart. The centromeres split, and spindle fibers shorten, drawing the chromatids toward opposite poles of the cell. This ensures that each pole receives a complete and identical set of chromosomes.

The separation is driven by motor proteins and the depolymerization of microtubules. Anaphase is often the shortest phase of mitosis but is crucial for maintaining genetic consistency.

4. Telophase

In telophase, the events of prophase and metaphase are essentially reversed. The separated chromosomes arrive at the opposite poles and begin to **de-condense** back into the less visible chromatin state. The **nuclear envelope re-forms** around each set of chromosomes, creating two distinct nuclei within a single cell. The **nucleolus reappears**, and the spindle fibers disassemble. This marks the end of nuclear division, but the process of cell division concludes only after the cytoplasm is partitioned — a process known as **cytokinesis.**

CYTOKINESIS

Cytokinesis is the final step in the cell cycle, following mitosis, and it physically separates the two daughter cells. The mechanism of cytokinesis differs between animal and plant cells due to structural differences:

- **In animal cells**, a contractile ring composed of **actin and myosin filaments** forms beneath the plasma membrane. This ring contracts, forming a **cleavage furrow** that pinches the cell into two genetically identical daughter cells.
- **In plant cells**, due to the presence of a rigid cell wall, a different mechanism occurs. Vesicles from the Golgi apparatus coalesce at the center of the cell to form the **cell plate**. This plate eventually develops into the **middle lamella**, which becomes the new cell wall that separates the two daughter cells.

SIGNIFICANCE OF MITOSIS

Mitosis plays a foundational role in multicellular organisms and has broad biological significance:

- **Genetic Stability:** Mitosis ensures that each daughter cell receives an exact copy of the parent cell's DNA. This is crucial for maintaining genetic integrity across generations of cells.
- **Growth and Development:** From a fertilized egg to a fully grown adult, mitosis enables organisms to grow by increasing the number of cells. It is responsible for the development of tissues, organs, and the overall body structure.
- **Tissue Repair and Regeneration:** Mitosis allows for the replacement of damaged or dead cells. For example, skin cells, intestinal lining cells, and blood cells are continuously renewed through mitotic division.
- **Asexual Reproduction:** In unicellular organisms such as **Amoeba** and **Paramecium**, mitosis serves as the mode of reproduction. The organism divides into two identical offspring, each genetically identical to the parent.
- **Maintenance of Chromosome Number:** Unlike meiosis, which reduces the chromosome number by half for sexual reproduction, mitosis maintains the diploid chromosome number in somatic cells, ensuring cellular function and organismal stability.

The mitosis is not merely a process of cell division; it is the basis of life continuity, structural integrity, and organismal function. Its accuracy and regulation are vital, as errors in mitosis can lead to mutations, developmental defects, or cancer. Understanding mitosis not only provides insights into fundamental biological processes but also informs biomedical research, regenerative medicine, and cancer therapies.

3.3 Meiosis: Stages and Genetic Importance

Meiosis is a specialized type of cell division that occurs in sexually reproducing organisms. Unlike mitosis, which produces two identical diploid daughter cells, meiosis reduces the chromosome number by half, resulting in the formation of haploid cells — the **gametes** (sperm and egg in animals, or spores in plants). This process is crucial for maintaining a constant chromosome number across generations and introducing genetic variability, which fuels evolution and adaptation.

Overview of Meiosis

Meiosis comprises two sequential nuclear divisions — Meiosis I and Meiosis II — but only a single round of DNA replication.

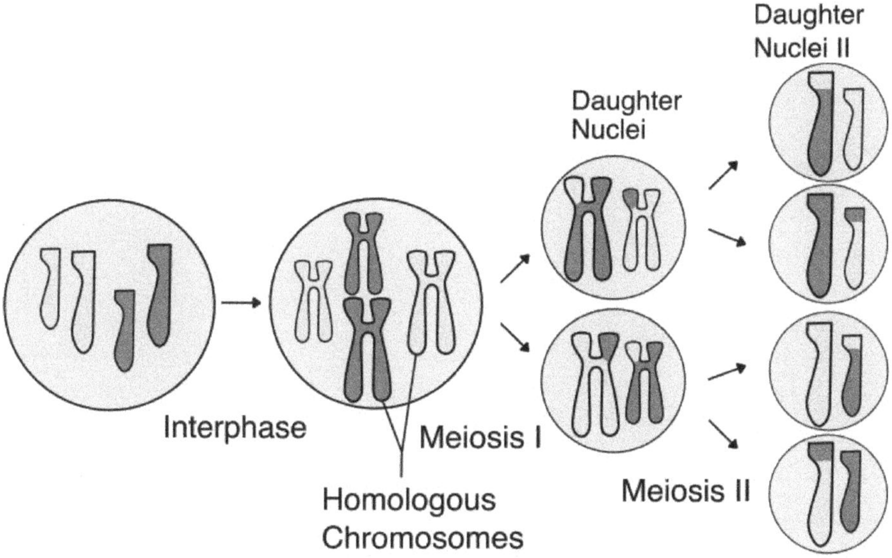

***Figure:** Meiosis I and II with Genetic Variation*

This unique arrangement leads to the production of four haploid cells from one diploid parent cell. Each of these divisions plays a distinct role:

- **Meiosis I (Reductional Division):** Homologous chromosomes (one from each parent) are separated, reducing the chromosome number by half.

- **Meiosis II (Equational Division):** Similar to mitosis, sister chromatids of each chromosome are separated, but no further reduction in chromosome number occurs.

MEIOSIS I: REDUCTIONAL DIVISION

Meiosis I is the more complex of the two meiotic divisions and involves several critical events, especially during Prophase I, which set the stage for genetic recombination.

Prophase I

Prophase I is the longest and most complex phase of meiosis and is subdivided into five distinct stages, each defined by key chromosomal events:

1. **Leptotene:**
   Chromosomes start to condense and become visible under a microscope. Each chromosome consists of two sister chromatids, although they are not yet distinctly separated.
2. **Zygotene:**
   Homologous chromosomes (chromosomes of the same type, one from each parent) begin to pair up in a process called synapsis. This results in the formation of bivalents or tetrads, each consisting of four chromatids.
3. **Pachytene:**
   Synapsis is complete, and homologous chromosomes are closely aligned. At this stage, crossing-over occurs — a crucial event in which non-sister chromatids exchange genetic material at specific points known as chiasmata. This process generates new combinations of alleles, contributing to genetic variation.
4. **Diplotene:**
   Synapsed chromosomes begin to repel each other but remain connected at chiasmata where crossing-over occurred. In

oocytes, this stage can last for months or even years (e.g., in humans).

5. **Diakinesis:**

   Chromosomes condense further, the chiasmata move toward the ends of the chromosomes (terminalization), and the nuclear envelope breaks down in preparation for metaphase.

Metaphase I

Homologous chromosome pairs (bivalents) align randomly along the metaphase plate. Spindle fibers attach to the centromeres of each homolog. This random alignment contributes to independent assortment, another mechanism for genetic variation.

Anaphase I

The homologous chromosomes are pulled to opposite poles of the cell by spindle fibers. Importantly, sister chromatids remain attached at their centromeres, unlike in mitosis.

Telophase I and Cytokinesis

Chromosomes de-condense slightly, and a nuclear membrane may briefly re-form in some species. Cytokinesis follows, resulting in two haploid cells, each with half the original chromosome number (but each chromosome still consists of two chromatids).

Meiosis II: Equational Division

Meiosis II resembles a typical mitotic division but starts with haploid cells. It serves to separate the sister chromatids of each chromosome.

Prophase II

If the chromosomes had de-condensed in telophase I, they now re-condense, and a new spindle apparatus forms. The nuclear envelope breaks down again, if it had reformed.

Chromosomes align individually along the equatorial plate of each haploid cell. Each chromosome's centromere is attached to spindle fibers from opposite poles.

Anaphase II

Sister chromatids finally separate and move toward opposite poles. This event is analogous to anaphase in mitosis.

Telophase II and Cytokinesis

Chromosomes arrive at the poles, de-condense, and nuclear membranes re-form. Cytokinesis divides the cytoplasm, resulting in four genetically distinct haploid cells.

In males, this typically produces four sperm cells. In females, usually only one large egg and three smaller polar bodies are produced due to unequal cytokinesis.

Genetic Importance of Meiosis

Meiosis is not only a mechanism of gamete formation but also a source of genetic innovation. Its importance can be summarized through three key contributions:

1. Reduction of Chromosome Number

By halving the chromosome number, meiosis ensures that when gametes fuse during fertilization, the resulting zygote has the correct diploid number. Without this reduction, chromosome numbers would double with each generation.

2. Genetic Recombination

- **Crossing-over:** During **pachytene of prophase I**, homologous chromosomes exchange segments, creating new allele combinations and increasing genetic diversity.
- **Independent Assortment:** The **random orientation of homologs** during metaphase I means each gamete receives

a random mix of maternal and paternal chromosomes. The number of possible combinations is 2^n, where n is the haploid number of chromosomes (e.g., 2^{23} in humans = over 8 million combinations).

3. Basis of Evolution and Natural Selection

Genetic variation resulting from meiosis provides raw material for **evolutionary change**. Organisms with favorable traits are more likely to survive and reproduce, leading to **adaptive evolution** over generations.

Table: *Comparison: Mitosis vs. Meiosis*

Feature	Mitosis	Meiosis
Number of Divisions	One	Two
Number of Daughter Cells	Two	Four
Chromosome Number	Diploid (2n)	Haploid (n)
Genetic Identity	Identical to parent	Genetically unique
Crossing Over	Absent	Present in Prophase I
Function	Growth, repair, asexual reproduction	Gamete formation for sexual reproduction

Disorders Related to Cell Division

Errors during meiosis or mitosis can lead to **chromosomal abnormalities**, some of which have significant clinical consequences:

1. Non-Disjunction

Failure of homologous chromosomes or sister chromatids to separate properly during anaphase can lead to **aneuploidy** — an abnormal number of chromosomes.

- **Down syndrome (Trisomy 21):** An extra copy of chromosome 21 due to non-disjunction.
- **Turner syndrome (XO):** A female with only one X chromosome.
- **Klinefelter syndrome (XXY):** A male with an extra X chromosome.

2. Cancer

In contrast to meiotic errors, mitotic failures can lead to **uncontrolled cell proliferation**, a hallmark of cancer. Faulty checkpoints, such as those involving tumor suppressors like **p53**, allow cells with damaged DNA to divide uncontrollably.

Meiosis is an elegant and essential biological process that not only facilitates sexual reproduction but also promotes genetic variation — the cornerstone of biodiversity and evolutionary success. Its precise regulation and timing are crucial for healthy development, and its failure can result in profound genetic disorders or developmental abnormalities. Understanding meiosis provides critical insights into heredity, genetic disorders, and the molecular basis of life itself.

The cell cycle and its two major division processes—mitosis and meiosis—are fundamental to the continuity and diversity of life. The cell cycle is a carefully regulated series of events that prepare a cell for division, ensuring the accurate replication and distribution of genetic material. Mitosis, the process by which somatic cells divide, plays a critical role in growth, tissue repair, and cellular renewal. During mitosis, a parent cell divides to produce two genetically identical daughter cells, each retaining the full complement of chromosomes. This process ensures the maintenance of genetic stability across generations of cells, a vital function in multicellular organisms. In contrast, meiosis occurs in germ cells and is central to sexual reproduction. It reduces the chromosome number by half, resulting in four genetically distinct haploid gametes. Through mechanisms such as crossing over and independent assortment, meiosis introduces genetic variation—an essential driver of evolution and species adaptation.

A deeper understanding of these processes not only sheds light on basic biological principles like development, heredity, and gene expression, but also provides crucial insights into human health and disease. Errors in cell cycle regulation or division can lead to severe consequences, such as uncontrolled cell proliferation seen in cancer or chromosomal abnormalities like Down syndrome. In medical research, targeting cell cycle checkpoints and division machinery has led to the development of cancer therapies that selectively inhibit rapidly dividing cells. Advances in assisted reproductive technologies, stem cell research, and regenerative medicine are grounded in a thorough understanding of mitotic and meiotic mechanisms. In biotechnology, harnessing the principles of cell division enables innovations such as cloning, genetic engineering, and the production of genetically modified organisms (GMOs). Thus, studying the cell cycle, mitosis, and meiosis is not only vital for understanding life's continuity but also for driving progress in science, medicine, and technology.

QUESTIONS:

- Explain the phases of the cell cycle, highlighting the key events of each phase.
- What is the significance of the G_0 phase in the cell cycle? Discuss its role in cellular function.
- Describe the process of mitosis and its phases. How does mitosis contribute to growth and tissue repair?
- Compare and contrast mitosis and meiosis in terms of their

- Discuss the stages of meiosis I, with emphasis on the process of crossing over and its genetic significance.
- What are the major differences between mitosis and meiosis, particularly in terms of chromosome number and genetic variation?
- Explain the regulation of the cell cycle. How do cyclins and tumor suppressor genes, like p53, control cell division?
- Identify and explain the consequences of errors in cell division, including conditions like Down syndrome and cancer.

CHAPTER 4

MORPHOLOGY AND REPRODUCTIVE STRUCTURES IN PLANTS

The study of plant morphology — particularly the form and structure of reproductive organs — is pivotal in understanding how plants propagate, adapt to their environments, and evolve over time. Reproductive morphology provides critical insights into plant taxonomy, as structural features like flower parts, seed types, and fruiting bodies often serve as key diagnostic characters for plant identification and classification. In flowering plants (angiosperms), reproduction is primarily sexual and is centered around the flower, a complex reproductive organ composed of sepals, petals, stamens, and carpels. The male reproductive structures, known as stamens, bear pollen-laden anthers, while the female structures, or carpels, contain the ovary, style, and stigma. The intricate design of these parts facilitates pollination, which may be mediated by wind, insects, water, or animals. In contrast, non-flowering plants such as gymnosperms, pteridophytes, bryophytes, and algae exhibit a range of reproductive strategies, including spores, cones, and alternation of generations. The morphological diversity seen in reproductive structures is an evolutionary response to habitat, pollinator availability, and survival strategies, helping plants to colonize a vast array of ecological niches.

The sexual reproduction, many plants also exhibit asexual reproduction through mechanisms such as vegetative propagation (e.g., runners, rhizomes, tubers, bulbs) and apomixis, where seeds are produced without fertilization. These methods allow for rapid reproduction remains the primary source of genetic variation, which is essential for evolution and adaptation. The process of fertilization in flowering plants begins with pollination and culminates in the fusion of male and female gametes to form a zygote, which develops into a seed. The ovary matures into a fruit, serving both to protect the seed and aid in its dispersal. Morphological adaptations such as fleshy fruits, winged seeds, and specialized flower shapes are directly linked to reproductive success by enhancing seed dispersal and pollinator attraction. The structural complexity of reproductive organs and their interactions with biotic (e.g., pollinators) and abiotic (e.g., wind) agents illustrate the deep interconnection between plant form and ecological function. Studying these features not only enriches our understanding of plant life cycles but also has practical applications in agriculture, horticulture, plant breeding, and conservation biology.

4.1 Inflorescence Types and Functions

Inflorescence refers to the mode of arrangement of flowers on the floral axis of a plant. It represents a crucial morphological feature in angiosperms and plays a significant role in taxonomy, pollination strategies, plant reproductive biology, and even ornamental value. The study of inflorescence types provides insight into the evolutionary strategies employed by plants to maximize reproductive success. Flowers are not typically borne singly in nature; instead, they are organized in specific patterns to increase visibility to pollinators and to optimize fertilization. Inflorescences help plants synchronize blooming, ensure efficient use of resources, and often adapt to specific environmental conditions or pollination vectors, such as insects, wind, or birds.

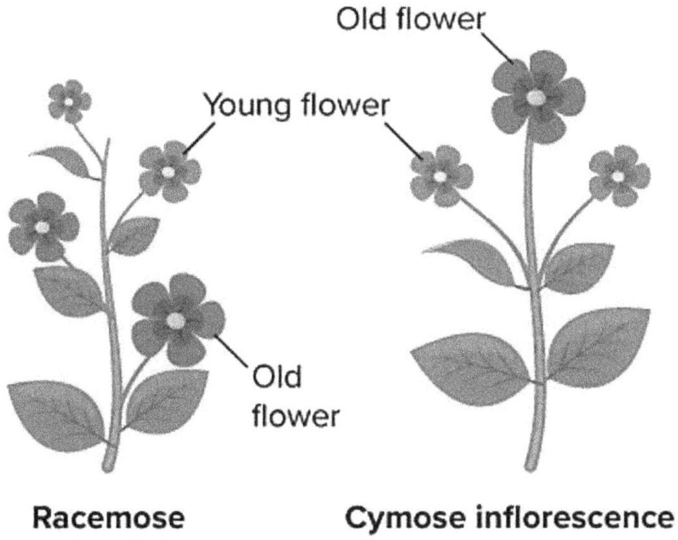

Figure: *Types of Inflorescence*

Inflorescences can be classified broadly into three major categories based on the growth pattern of the main axis and the sequence of flower development: **racemose (indeterminate), cymose (determinate), and special types.** This classification is based on the activity of the apical meristem. In **racemose inflorescence**, the main axis continues to grow indefinitely, and the flowers are produced in a successive manner, with the youngest flowers located towards the apex. In contrast, **cymose inflorescence** is characterized by the termination of the main axis into a flower, hence limiting further growth. In this type, flowers develop in a basipetal order, with the oldest flower at the top and younger ones towards the base. **Special inflorescences** represent unique or modified types of arrangements that do not conform strictly to either racemose or cymose patterns and are often seen in highly evolved angiosperm families.

A. Racemose (Indeterminate) Inflorescence

Racemose inflorescences are defined by continuous growth of the main floral axis without terminating in a flower. The lateral flowers develop acropetally (from base to apex), ensuring that the oldest flowers are at the base while younger buds are found at the top. Racemose inflorescence types are highly diverse and are adapted for various reproductive strategies.

- **Raceme**: This is a simple and unbranched inflorescence with stalked (pedicellate) flowers arranged along the main axis. The flowers bloom in acropetal succession. *Example: Brassica (mustard).*
- **Spike**: Similar to raceme, but the flowers are sessile (without stalks). This arrangement allows for compactness and is common in wind-pollinated species. *Example: Achyranthes.*
- **Catkin**: A drooping spike-like inflorescence bearing unisexual flowers. It is generally found in wind-pollinated trees where the dangling structure facilitates dispersal of pollen. *Example: Mulberry, Willow.*
- **Spadix**: A thick, fleshy spike often enclosed within a large bract called a spathe. The enclosing spathe may be brightly colored to attract pollinators. This type is commonly seen in monocots. *Example: Arum, Banana.*
- **Corymb**: In this form, flowers have pedicels of unequal length such that all flowers appear at the same level, forming a flat or slightly convex top. *Example: Candytuft (Iberis).*
- **Umbel**: Short flower stalks arise from a common point on the top of the peduncle, resembling an umbrella structure. This inflorescence is typical in the family Apiaceae. *Example: Onion, Coriander.*

- **Capitulum (Head)**. A compact inflorescence with sessile flowers (florets) on a flattened receptacle. It may have ray florets (for attraction) and disc florets (for reproduction). This is characteristic of the family Asteraceae. *Example: Sunflower, Marigold.*

B. Cymose (Determinate) Inflorescence

In cymose inflorescence, the main axis terminates into a flower, stopping further elongation. The growth is determined and flowers are produced in a basipetal sequence — the terminal flower blooms first followed by the development of lateral flowers. This pattern results in a more compact and often symmetric floral arrangement.

- **Uniparous (Monochasial) Cyme**: The main axis ends in a flower, and only one lateral branch arises at a time, which also ends in a flower. This continues in a zigzag manner. It may further be classified as:
  - o *Helicoid cyme*: The successive lateral branches develop on the same side. *Example: Heliotropium.*
  - o *Scorpioid cyme*: The branches develop on alternate sides. *Example: Cotton.*
- **Biparous (Dichasial) Cyme**: Two lateral branches arise below the terminal flower and continue to develop in the same pattern. This type often results in a more symmetrical appearance. *Example: Bougainvillea, Dianthus.*
- **Multiparous (Polychasial) Cyme**: More than two lateral flowers branch out below the terminal flower. This type is typically dense and appears in clusters. *Example: Calotropis, Nerium.*

Cymose inflorescences are often associated with precise, small energy and resources, particularly in plants adapted to short growing seasons or limited environments.

C. Special Inflorescences

Special inflorescences deviate from the typical racemose and cymose patterns. These are highly evolved structures often seen in specific plant families and are adaptations to unique pollination strategies.

- **Cyathium**: A cup-shaped structure surrounded by involucral bracts containing a single female flower in the center, surrounded by multiple male flowers, each reduced to a single stamen. This is typical of *Euphorbia* and is considered a highly condensed inflorescence.
- **Verticillaster**: Appears as a whorl of flowers at a node but is actually a pair of opposite cymes. Common in the family Lamiaceae. *Example: Ocimum (Tulsi).*
- **Hypanthodium**: A hollow, pear-shaped receptacle with an apical opening (ostiole). Flowers are borne on the inner surface – male flowers near the opening, female and sterile flowers towards the base. It is typical of figs. *Example: Ficus.*

These specialized inflorescences often develop in response to unique ecological pressures or specific pollination syndromes. For instance, hypanthodium in figs is tightly associated with fig-wasp mutualism, an example of co-evolution between plant and insect.

Functions and Biological Significance of Inflorescence

Inflorescences offer numerous biological and ecological advantages to plants. The arrangement and structure of flowers in an inflorescence greatly influence pollination efficiency and reproductive success.

- **Facilitation of Pollination:** The clustered arrangement increases floral display, attracting more pollinators. In wind-pollinated species, structures like catkins or spikes enhance the dispersal range of pollen grains.
- **Protection of Floral Buds:** Floral clusters protect the developing flowers from environmental stress and herbivores. The spatial arrangement often minimizes damage to reproductive organs.
- **Synchronized Blooming:** Inflorescences promote mass blooming, which is advantageous in attracting pollinators and ensuring cross-pollination. This is critical in plant species with short reproductive windows.
- **Resource Optimization:** Sharing vascular and structural support across multiple flowers within the same inflorescence reduces energy expenditure compared to solitary flowering.
- **Seed Dispersal Strategy:** Some inflorescence types assist not only in reproduction but also in dispersal. For instance, in dandelions (composite flowers), the inflorescence matures into a dispersal unit aided by wind.

The diversity in inflorescence types reflects the wide array of evolutionary strategies plants have adopted to adapt to various ecological niches. Whether promoting wind pollination through catkins, attracting insects with showy umbels, or forming tightly packed capitula for efficient reproduction, inflorescences are critical components of the plant's reproductive arsenal. Understanding these structures is essential in fields ranging from systematics and ecology to horticulture and agriculture.

4.2 Flower Structure and Variations

The flower is the most specialized and often th

reproductive unit. It is an evolutionary marvel that has contributed immensely to the success and diversification of angiosperms on Earth. Typically borne on a stalk called the pedicel, the flower is a modified shoot in which the internodes are compressed and the appendages are specialized into floral organs. The primary function of a flower is sexual reproduction, facilitating gamete formation, pollination, fertilization, and ultimately leading to the formation of fruit and seeds.

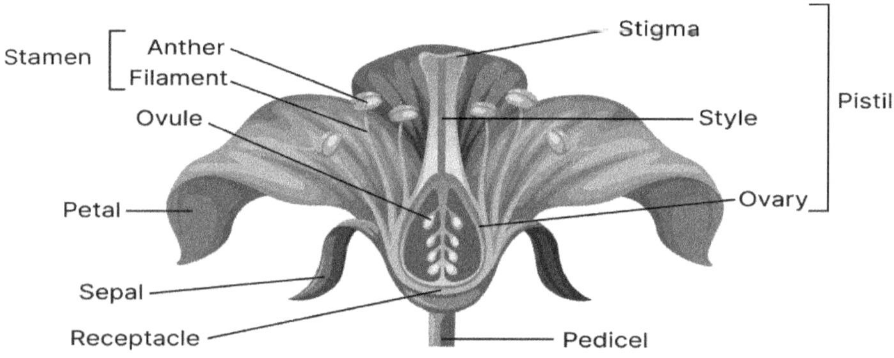

Figure: Structure of a Typical Flower

Structurally, a typical flower is composed of four distinct concentric whorls of appendages arranged on the floral receptacle: **calyx**, **corolla**, **androecium**, and **gynoecium**. These whorls are specialized to perform protective, attractive, and reproductive roles. The variations in these floral parts are key to plant classification and have ecological relevance in pollination mechanisms.

Parts of a Typical Flower

1. **Calyx (Sepals)**: The calyx forms the outermost whorl and consists of units called sepals. Typically green and leaf-like, sepals serve a protective function, especially in the bud stage, shielding the inner whorls from mechanical injury, desiccation, and pathogens. Sepals may be:

- o **Polysepalous:** Free sepals.
- o **Gamosepalous:** Sepals are united, forming a tubular structure.

  In some flowers, sepals may become petaloid (colored) to enhance the visual appeal for pollinators. This is especially common in flowers lacking distinct petals.

2. **Corolla (Petals):** The second whorl consists of petals, which are often brightly colored, fragrant, and of varied shapes and sizes. Their primary function is to attract pollinators through visual cues and scent. Petals may be:
   - o **Polypetalous:** Free petals.
   - o **Gamopetalous:** United petals forming a corolla tube. Shapes of corolla include:
   - o **Rotate** (wheel-shaped, e.g., Solanum),
   - o **Tubular** (tube-shaped, e.g., disc florets of sunflower),
   - o **Campanulate** (bell-shaped, e.g., bellflower),
   - o **Papilionaceous** (butterfly-shaped, e.g., pea).

The petal arrangement also contributes to floral symmetry and pollination efficiency.

3. **Androecium (Stamens):** This is the male reproductive whorl composed of stamens, each consisting of a **filament** (stalk) and an **anther** (pollen-producing structure). The anther typically contains two lobes, each with two pollen sacs. Variations in androecium include:
   - o **Free stamens:** Not attached to each other or other floral parts.
   - o **United stamens:**
     - o **Monadelphous:** Stamens united by their filaments into

- o **Diadelphous**: Two bundles of stamens (e.g., pea).
- o **Polyadelphous**: More than two bundles (e.g., citrus). Positional variations:

- o **Epipetalous**: Stamens attached to petals (e.g., brinjal).
- o **Epiphyllous**: Stamens attached to perianth (e.g., lily). The androecium plays a vital role in pollen presentation and dispersal, often co-evolving with specific pollinators.

4. **Gynoecium (Carpels or Pistils)**: The innermost whorl and female reproductive part of the flower is the gynoecium. It may consist of a single carpel (monocarpellary), multiple free carpels (apocarpous), or multiple fused carpels (syncarpous). Each carpel has three parts:
   - o **Stigma**: The receptive surface for pollen.
   - o **Style**: The stalk connecting stigma to ovary.
   - o **Ovary**: The basal, swollen part containing one or more ovules. Based on ovary position relative to other floral whorls, flowers are categorized as:
   - o **Hypogynous**: Ovary is superior (e.g., mustard, brinjal).
   - o **Epigynous**: Ovary is inferior (e.g., guava, cucumber).
   - o **Perigynous**: Ovary is half-inferior, enclosed by a floral cup (e.g., rose).

Floral Variations and Special Morphological Features

Flowers show immense diversity in form and structure to suit their reproductive strategies and environmental conditions. These variations are often used in plant identification and classification.

1. **Symmetry**:
   - o **Actinomorphic (Radial Symmetry)**: Flower can be divided into equal halves along any vertical plane. These are typically accessible to a variety of pollinators. *Example: Datura, mustard.*
   - o **Zygomorphic (Bilateral Symmetry)**: Flower can be divided into equal halves in only one plane. This often indicates specialization for a particular type of pollinator. *Example: Pea, bean.*
   - o **Asymmetric (Irregular)**: No symmetry present. Rare in occurrence. *Example: Canna.*
2. **Sexuality**:
   - o **Unisexual Flowers**: Contain either androecium or gynoecium, but not both. They are either staminate (male) or pistillate (female). *Example: maize, cucumber.*
   - o **Bisexual Flowers (Hermaphroditic)**: Contain both androecium and gynoecium. *Example: hibiscus, mustard.* Based on the distribution of unisexual flowers, plants may be:
   - o **Monoecious**: Both male and female flowers present on the same plant (e.g., maize).
   - o **Dioecious**: Male and female flowers occur on separate plants (e.g., papaya).
3. **Insertion of Floral Whorls (Based on Ovary Position)**:
   - o **Hypogynous Flowers**: The other whorls are below the ovary, which is said to be superior. This is considered the most primitive condition.
   - o **Epigynous Flowers**: The other floral whorls arise above the ovary, which is inferior.

- **Perigynous Flowers:** The ovary is situated in the center, and the other floral parts are attached to the rim of the floral cup (thalamus). The ovary is half-inferior.

4. **Aestivation:**
   Aestivation refers to the mode of arrangement of sepals or petals in floral buds. It is a key feature in classification.
   - **Valvate:** Sepals or petals touch each other at the margin without overlapping (e.g., Calotropis).
   - **Twisted:** One margin of each petal overlaps the next one in the same direction (e.g., China rose).
   - **Imbricate:** Petals overlap irregularly without a fixed pattern (e.g., Cassia).
   - **Quincuncial:** Among five petals, two are internal, two external, and one is partly internal and external (e.g., guava).

Function and Biological Significance of Flowers

The flower serves as the primary site for all reproductive processes in angiosperms. Each part of the flower contributes uniquely to reproduction:

- **Gamete Formation:** Stamens and carpels produce male and female gametes, respectively. The anthers generate pollen grains containing sperm cells, while ovules contain the egg cell.

- **Pollination:** Flowers are often adapted for self or cross-pollination. Features such as color, scent, nectar, and floral shape are tailored to attract specific pollinators like bees, butterflies, birds, or even wind and water.

- **Fertilization**: The pollen tube from a germinating pollen grain facilitates the delivery of male gametes to the ovule, leading to fertilization.
- **Seed and Fruit Formation**: After fertilization, the ovule matures into a seed, and the ovary develops into a fruit, aiding in seed dispersal.
- **Genetic Variation**: Through processes like cross-pollination and genetic recombination during gamete formation, flowers help generate variation within species — the raw material for evolution.

Flowers also have ecological and economic importance. They provide nectar and pollen to pollinators and are used extensively in agriculture, horticulture, perfume industries, and traditional medicines. Their structural variations serve as key diagnostic features in taxonomy, helping botanists in plant identification and phylogenetic classification.

4.3 Fruit Types and Development

Fruits represent the final stage in the reproductive process of flowering plants. Botanically, a fruit is defined as the **mature and ripened ovary** of a flower, usually containing one or more seeds. Fruits are critical in protecting developing seeds, facilitating their dispersal, and often serving as a nutritional resource for various animals and humans. The development and structural diversity of fruits reflect complex interactions between floral morphology, fertilization, and ecological adaptations.

DEVELOPMENT OF FRUIT

Fruit development begins after successful **fertilization** of the ovule by developing into a fruit, while the **ovules** transform into seeds. This process is influenced by hormones such as auxins, gibberellins, and cytokinins, which regulate cell division, enlargement, and differentiation.

Key stages in fruit development include:

- **Fertilization**: Triggers hormonal changes initiating fruit formation.
- **Ovary enlargement**: As the ovary wall expands, tissues differentiate into various fruit layers (pericarp).
- **Seed development**: Ovules mature into viable seeds.
- **Fruit maturation**: Involves biochemical changes such as sugar accumulation, color development, and texture modification.

In some plants, fruits may develop **without fertilization**, a phenomenon known as **parthenocarpy**. Parthenocarpic fruits are **seedless** and are commercially significant. Examples include **banana**, **pineapple**, and certain varieties of **grapes**. These can arise naturally or be induced through the application of plant growth regulators.

Classification of Fruits

Fruits are broadly classified based on their **origin** and **structure**. The main categories include **simple**, **aggregate**, and **multiple (composite)** fruits.

1. Simple Fruits

These fruits develop from the **mature ovary of a single pistil** (whether monocarpellary or syncarpous). Depending on the texture of the pericarp, simple fruits can be either **fleshy** or **dry**.

A. Fleshy Simple Fruits

In these, the pericarp remains soft and succulent at maturity.

- **Drupe**. Also called a stone fruit, it has a thin epicarp, fleshy mesocarp, and a hard, stony endocarp enclosing a single seed. *Example: Mango, Coconut, Peach.*
- **Berry**: The entire pericarp is fleshy and often contains multiple seeds. *Example: Tomato, Grapes, Guava.*
- **Pome**: The edible part is primarily the fleshy thalamus; the ovary becomes embedded within. *Example: Apple, Pear.*

B. Dry Simple Fruits

These are characterized by a dry, often hard pericarp at maturity. They can be further classified based on dehiscence:

i. Dehiscent Dry Fruits: These split open at maturity to release seeds.

- **Legume**: Develops from a single carpel and splits along two sutures. *Example: Pea, Bean.*
- **Capsule**: Formed from a syncarpous ovary, splits in various ways. *Example: Cotton, Datura.*
- **Silique**: A long fruit with two valves and a partition in the middle. *Example: Mustard.*

ii. Indehiscent Dry Fruits: These do not open at maturity; seeds remain enclosed.

- **Nut**: One-seeded fruit with a hard, woody pericarp. *Example: Cashew, Oak.*
- **Caryopsis**: Characteristic of grasses; seed coat is fused with the pericarp. *Example: Wheat, Maize.*
- **Achene**: Single-seeded fruit with free pericarp. *Example: Sunflower.*
- **Samara**: Winged achene aiding in wind dispersal. *Example: Maple.*

Aggregate fruits arise from a **single flower with multiple free carpels (apocarpous gynoecium)**. Each carpel develops into a separate fruitlet, and the cluster is collectively called an aggregate fruit.

- **Strawberry**: The fruitlets (achenes) are embedded on a fleshy receptacle.
- **Custard Apple**: Individual fruitlets coalesce on a common receptacle.

These fruits often have diverse pollination strategies and exhibit various dispersal adaptations. Aggregate fruits demonstrate how evolutionary modifications in floral structure can lead to varied fruit morphologies.

3. Multiple (Composite) Fruits

Multiple fruits develop from an entire **inflorescence**, meaning they arise from the combined ovaries of multiple flowers that are tightly packed together.

- **Pineapple (Ananas)**: The individual fruits of the spike inflorescence fuse together with floral parts and bracts forming a single, compact unit.
- **Fig (Ficus)**: Arises from a hypanthodium inflorescence. The flowers are enclosed within a fleshy receptacle.

Jackfruit: Each flower of the catkin inflorescence contributes to the formation of the large composite fruit.

These fruits often serve as important food sources and exhibit complex structural integration, emphasizing the significance of inflorescence type in fruit morphology.

Fruit Wall (Pericarp)

In most fleshy fruits, the ovary wall transforms into the **pericarp**, which may differentiate into three distinct layers:

1. **Epicarp (Exocarp)**: The outermost layer, forming the skin or peel. Its texture can vary from smooth (e.g., grape) to leathery or tough (e.g., citrus). The epicarp provides protection and contributes to fruit coloration due to the presence of pigments like anthocyanins or carotenoids.
2. **Mesocarp**: The middle layer, often the fleshy, edible portion of the fruit. In drupes like mango, it is thick and juicy, whereas in coconut, it becomes fibrous.
3. **Endocarp**: The innermost layer that directly surrounds the seed(s). Its nature varies—hard and stony in mango (forming the seed pit), membranous in tomato, or papery in apples.

In dry fruits, these layers are not as distinct, and the pericarp is typically thin, rigid, and protective.

Functions of Fruits

Fruits serve several critical biological and ecological functions:

1. **Protection of Seeds**: Fruits encase and safeguard developing seeds from physical damage, predation, and environmental stress.
2. **Seed Dispersal**: Fruits often aid in dispersal through various agents:
   - **Wind**: Lightweight or winged fruits (e.g., samaras).
   - **Water**: Buoyant fruits with fibrous husks (e.g., coconut).
   - **Animals**: Fleshy, attractive fruits encourage ingestion and dispersal through defecation (endozoochory), while dry fruits with hooks or barbs cling to fur (epizoochory).
3. **Nutritional Resource**: Fruits are a major source of food for humans and animals, rich in vitamins (especially Vitamin C), minerals, fiber, and antioxidants.

4. **Embryo Protection from Desiccation**: The pericarp helps maintain internal moisture levels, preventing desiccation of the embryo, especially in seeds with delayed germination.
5. **Reproductive Success**: The adaptive features of fruits enhance seed viability, dispersal, and germination potential, thereby contributing to plant survival and evolution.

The study of fruit types and development highlights the evolutionary innovation of angiosperms in safeguarding and dispersing their progeny. The vast diversity of fruit forms is a reflection of ecological interactions, especially those involving pollinators, seed dispersers, and environmental conditions. Understanding fruit morphology and classification is not only essential for botanists and horticulturists but also underpins agricultural productivity and food security.

4.4 Seed Structure and Germination

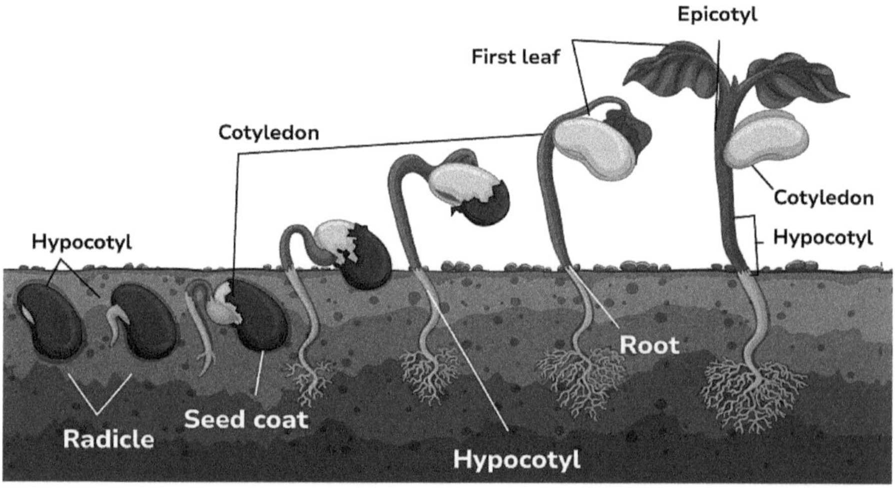

Figure: Seed Structure and Germination Types

Seeds are a crucial component of plant reproduction, serving as the vehicle for propagating species across generations. A seed is the mature ovule of a flowering plant and contains all the essential structures for the growth of a new plant under favorable conditions. The complexity of seed structure allows plants to survive in various environmental conditions and ensures successful colonization. This section discusses the structure of seeds, the process of seed germination, and the factors influencing this process.

STRUCTURE OF A SEED

The structure of a seed varies between different groups of plants, particularly between **dicots** and **monocots.** While they share some common features, the differences between them reflect evolutionary adaptations.

A. Dicot Seed (e.g., Bean, Pea)

Dicot seeds typically have two cotyledons, which are the primary storage organs for nutrients. The major components of a dicot seed are as follows:

- **Seed Coat:** The seed coat consists of two layers, the **testa** (outer layer) and **tegmen** (inner layer), which provide protection to the seed. The testa is often tough and impermeable, which helps prevent premature water absorption and protects against mechanical damage and pathogens.
- **Cotyledons:** These are the seed's first leaves, often modified to store food, providing the necessary nutrients for the developing embryo. In dicots, there are two cotyledons. They may be fleshy or membranous, and they serve as the primary food reserve for the embryo during early stages of growth.
- **Embryo:** The embryo consists of the **radicle** (embryonic root), **plumule** (embryonic shoot), and the **embryonic axis,** which connects the root and shoot. The radicle eventually develops into the root system, while the plumule grows into

- **Hilum**: The hilum is a scar that marks the attachment site of the seed to the ovary wall. It is often visible as a small mark or dent on the seed surface and is crucial in identifying the seed's orientation and development.
- **Micropyle**: Located near the hilum, the micropyle is a small pore in the seed coat that allows water absorption at the time of germination. It is the point where the pollen tube enters during fertilization and serves as the main route for water uptake during germination.

B. Monocot Seed (e.g., Maize, Rice)

Monocot seeds, unlike dicots, have a single cotyledon, which has adapted to function differently. Key features of monocot seeds include:

- **Single Cotyledon (Scutellum)**: The scutellum in monocot seeds serves as the food storage area. It is typically thin and is positioned adjacent to the endosperm, where most of the food reserves are stored. This cotyledon absorbs nutrients from the surrounding endosperm during early seedling development.
- **Endosperm**: Unlike dicots, monocots have a prominent **endosperm**, which acts as the primary food reserve. The endosperm is rich in starch and serves to nourish the developing embryo. It remains intact throughout germination and provides nutrients until the plant can produce its own food.
- **Aleurone Layer**: The aleurone is a layer of cells surrounding the endosperm. It is rich in enzymes that are activated during germination, breaking down starches in the endosperm into sugars for the growing embryo.

- **Embryo**: The embryo in monocots also consists of the **radicle** (protected by a specialized covering called the **coleorhiza**) and the **plumule** (protected by the **coleoptile**). The coleorhiza and coleoptile serve as protective sheaths, ensuring that the radicle and plumule are safeguarded during the initial stages of growth.

GERMINATION

Germination is the process by which a seed develops into a new plant. It is initiated when a seed absorbs water, triggering enzymatic activity and metabolic changes that lead to the growth of the embryo. The primary goal of germination is to establish the seedling as an independent organism capable of photosynthesis and nutrient uptake. There are several stages in the germination process, including imbibition (water absorption), activation of metabolic processes, and growth of the embryo's root and shoot.

Types of Germination

Germination can occur in different forms depending on the type of seed and its environmental conditions. The two primary types of germination are **epigeal** and **hypogeal**, with a third rare type known as **vivipary**.

1. **Epigeal Germination**: In epigeal germination, the **cotyledons** rise above the soil surface. This occurs when the hypocotyl (stem below the cotyledons) elongates rapidly, lifting the cotyledons out of the soil. The cotyledons then begin to function as the first photosynthetic structures. *Example: Bean, Pea.*
2. **Hypogeal Germination**: In hypogeal germination, the cotyledons remain below the soil surface, and the **epicotyl**

shoot upward. The cotyledons remain buried and do not play a direct role in photosynthesis. *Example: Maize, Rice.*

3. **Vivipary**: In viviparous germination, seeds begin to germinate while still attached to the parent plant or within the fruit. This type of germination is typical of plants growing in wet or coastal areas, like **mangroves**, where seeds can begin to sprout before detaching from the parent. *Example: Mangrove, Red Mangrove.*

Factors Influencing Germination

Several environmental factors affect the rate and success of seed germination. These include:

- **Water**: Water is essential for seed germination as it activates enzymes and softens the seed coat. It also helps in the transport of nutrients and serves as a medium for metabolic processes. Without adequate water, the seed cannot absorb the necessary energy for growth.
- **Oxygen**: Oxygen is required for cellular respiration, the process by which the seed converts stored food into energy. Insufficient oxygen can inhibit seedling growth and delay or prevent germination.
- **Temperature**: Each species has an optimal temperature range for germination. Some seeds require cold temperatures (cold stratification) to break dormancy, while others thrive at warmer temperatures. Temperature influences enzyme activity and metabolic processes essential for seedling growth.
- **Light**: Light requirements vary among species. Some seeds need light to germinate (positive photoblastic seeds), while others germinate better in darkness (negative photoblastic seeds). In some cases, light can trigger the synthesis of hormones necessary for seedling growth.

Dormancy

Dormancy is a natural phenomenon that prevents seeds from germinating under unfavorable conditions. It serves as a protective mechanism, ensuring that seeds only germinate when environmental conditions are conducive to survival. Seed dormancy can be caused by various factors, such as:

- **Hard Seed Coat**: A tough, impermeable seed coat can prevent water and oxygen from entering the seed, thus delaying germination. This type of dormancy is often broken by physical processes like **scarification**, which weakens or damages the seed coat.
- **Immature Embryo**: Some seeds have an underdeveloped embryo that requires a period of time to mature before it can begin germination. This type of dormancy is commonly broken through **stratification**, a process in which seeds are exposed to cold, moist conditions for an extended period.
- **Chemical Inhibitors**: The seed may contain chemicals that inhibit germination until the environmental conditions change. These inhibitors are often broken down by light, temperature fluctuations, or other environmental cues.

Breaking Dormancy

There are several techniques to break seed dormancy in agricultural and horticultural practices:

- **Scarification**: Physical damage to the seed coat, often through mechanical means or chemical treatment, allows water and oxygen to penetrate the seed and initiate germination.
- **Stratification**: A period of cold, moist treatment that mimics

- **Hormonal Treatments**: Treatments with plant hormones like **gibberellins** can promote germination in certain seeds by overcoming chemical inhibitors or stimulating embryo growth.

Functions of Seeds

Seeds are vital to the reproductive strategy of plants, offering several functions:

- **Ensuring Species Continuity**: Seeds allow plants to reproduce sexually and propagate their genetic material to the next generation.
- **Dispersal**: Seeds are dispersed by various mechanisms such as wind, water, and animals, which helps in colonizing new environments and maintaining genetic diversity.
- **Food Source**: Seeds provide a nutritional source for humans and animals. They are rich in carbohydrates, proteins, and lipids, making them an essential part of many diets.
- **Genetic Diversity**: By enabling sexual reproduction, seeds promote genetic variability, which enhances a plant's ability to adapt to changing environments.

The study of seed structure and germination reveals the intricate biological processes that ensure plant survival and reproduction. Seeds are marvels of evolutionary design, optimizing the chances of successful growth under diverse conditions. Through an understanding of these mechanisms, we gain valuable insights into plant biology, agriculture, and ecology.

This chapter highlights the remarkable structural and functional diversity of plant reproductive parts, ranging from inflorescences to seeds. The intricate design of these reproductive structures plays a pivotal role in plant classification, as it allows for the differentiation of species and the understanding of their evolutionary relationships.

Inflorescences, the arrangements of flowers on a stem, vary significantly across plant groups, with each pattern adapted to maximize reproductive success by facilitating pollination through various mechanisms such as wind, insects, or animals. The flowers themselves, as the reproductive organs of plants, exhibit a wide variety of forms and structures tailored to specific modes of pollination, fertilization, and seed dispersal. Following fertilization, seeds develop to ensure the continuation of species, often featuring specialized structures that enhance their survival and dispersal in diverse environments.

Understanding the morphology of these reproductive parts is crucial for applications in agriculture, horticulture, and environmental science. In agriculture, knowledge of plant reproductive structures aids in crop classification, breeding, and genetic improvement, allowing for the development of varieties with desirable traits such as higher yield, pest resistance, or climate adaptability. Horticulturists can also apply this knowledge to enhance the cultivation and management of ornamental plants and ensure the successful propagation of plant species. Additionally, in the field of environmental science, reproductive morphology plays a vital role in ecosystem restoration efforts. By studying how plants reproduce and adapt to changing environments, researchers can identify species that are resilient to stressors like climate change or habitat destruction, aiding in the restoration of degraded ecosystems.

Reproductive morphology is not only essential for the survival of individual species but also for the broader functioning of ecosystems. It influences plant-pollinator interactions, the establishment of plant communities, and the provision of ecosystem services such as food, oxygen, and habitat. Thus, a comprehensive understanding of plant reproductive structures enriches our ability to manage and conserve plant biodiversity, ensuring the [illegible]

QUESTIONS

- What are the main types of inflorescences in plants? Provide examples.
- Explain the difference between racemose and cymose inflorescences.
- Describe the structure and function of the flower's calyx and corolla.
- What is the difference between actinomorphic and zygomorphic flowers?
- Define simple fruits and provide examples of fleshy and dry fruits.
- What are the three types of fruit development based on origin?
- Compare dicot and monocot seed structure.
- What factors influence seed germination and dormancy in plants?

CHAPTER 5

ANATOMY OF PLANT TISSUES

The anatomy of plant tissues is fundamental to the plant's ability to grow, adapt, and thrive in various environmental conditions. Plant tissues are specialized structures formed from a group of cells that work together to carry out specific functions. These tissues are classified into two major types: meristematic tissues and permanent tissues. The distinction between these two types of tissues lies primarily in their capacity for cell division, differentiation, and specialization. Each tissue type contributes in unique ways to the overall structure, growth, and function of the plant, making them essential for the plant's development and survival.

Meristematic tissues are composed of actively dividing cells, which are responsible for the growth and formation of new tissues. They are found in specific regions of the plant known as meristems. These regions include the apical meristems at the tips of roots and shoots, responsible for primary growth (lengthening), and the lateral meristems, such as the vascular cambium and cork cambium, responsible for secondary growth (thickening). Meristematic tissues play a crucial role in the plant's ability to adapt to its environment, as they allow for continuous growth throughout the plant's life. The undifferentiated nature of cells in meristematic tissues allows them to differentiate into various specialized cells and tissues as needed, contributing to the plant's ability to form new structures like leaves, flowers, and roots in response to environmental stimuli.

Permanent tissues are composed of differentiated and specialized for various vital functions such as support, transport, and storage. Permanent tissues can be further classified into simple and complex tissues. Simple permanent tissues consist of cells that are structurally similar and perform a single function. Examples include parenchyma, collenchyma, and sclerenchyma, each contributing to functions such as photosynthesis, support, and strength, respectively. Complex permanent tissues, on the other hand, are made up of different types of cells working together to perform specific functions. The two main types of complex tissues in plants are xylem and phloem, which are crucial for the transport of water, nutrients, and food throughout the plant. The structure of xylem cells, such as tracheids and vessel elements, enables the movement of water, while phloem cells, including sieve tube elements and companion cells, facilitate the transport of nutrients and sugars produced during photosynthesis. These permanent tissues work together to ensure the plant's survival, growth, and reproduction in a variety of environmental conditions, highlighting their importance in maintaining homeostasis and promoting efficient functioning across the plant's body.

The differentiation of plant tissues into meristematic and permanent categories is not just a structural distinction, but one that governs the plant's physiological processes. For instance, meristematic tissues enable plants to continually adapt to environmental changes, whether by growing taller in search of light or by developing thicker stems for better support. Permanent tissues, meanwhile, provide the stability necessary for these changes to occur, ensuring that the plant maintains its structure and is able to transport essential nutrients and water throughout its various parts. The specialization within these tissues allows the plant to thrive in diverse ecological niches, whether in arid deserts where water transport is critical or in temperate forests where rapid growth and support are necessary. The cooperation between meristematic and permanent tissues thus enables plants to survive, adapt, and grow under a wide range of conditions, making them highly efficient in resource acquisition and management.

The anatomy and organization of plant tissues form a dynamic system that supports plant life from the cellular level to the entire organism, ensuring their survival, adaptation, and success in the natural world. Understanding how these tissues function and interconnect provides essential insights into plant biology, growth regulation, and ecological adaptation.

5.1 Meristematic Tissues: Root and Shoot Meristems

Meristematic tissues form the foundation of plant growth and development, enabling plants to continually elongate and diversify into complex structures. These tissues consist of **actively dividing cells** that retain the potential to differentiate into various specialized cells and tissues. Meristematic cells are typically small, with thin cell walls, abundant cytoplasm, and prominent nuclei. They lack large vacuoles and are characterized by their rapid cell division, making them crucial for both primary and secondary growth in plants. The concept of **meristems** lies at the heart of understanding plant development, as they provide the cells necessary for a plant to grow, adapt to environmental changes, and reproduce. The **root apical meristem (RAM)** and **shoot apical meristem (SAM)** are key players in this process, with specialized functions and regions that contribute to overall plant structure and function. These cells enable the plant to expand in size, form specialized tissues, and adapt to different ecological niches.

CLASSIFICATION OF MERISTEMS

Meristems are classified based on their location and function in the plant body. The classification includes **apical meristems, intercalary**

meristems, and **lateral meristems**. Each of these meristems plays a unique role in the growth and development of the plant.

A. APICAL MERISTEMS

Apical meristems are located at the tips of the plant's roots and shoots. These meristems are responsible for **primary growth**, which leads to an increase in the length of the plant. The two primary types of apical meristems are the **shoot apical meristem (SAM)** and the **root apical meristem (RAM)**.

1. **Shoot Apical Meristem (SAM)**: The shoot apical meristem is located at the apex of the plant shoot and is responsible for producing the stem, leaves, and floral organs. It consists of two main regions:

- **Tunica**: The outer layer of cells in the SAM, which divides in a plane parallel to the surface, contributing to the growth in the lateral direction.
- **Corpus**: The inner mass of cells in the SAM, which divides in various planes, contributing to the growth in the vertical direction. The cells of the corpus give rise to the various tissues that make up the plant body, including the vascular system, ground tissue, and dermal tissue.

The shoot apical meristem plays a central role in controlling the development of plant architecture, producing leaves, lateral shoots, and flowers in an organized pattern. It regulates the development of **axillary buds** (the buds found in the leaf axils), which may develop into branches or flowers, depending on the plant's growth and environmental conditions. This ability of the SAM to form and maintain the structure of the shoot is vital for **branching** and **reproductive success** in plants.

2. **Root Apical Meristem (RAM)**: The root apical meristem is found at the tip of the plant's root, behind the protective

root cap. The RAM is responsible for producing the tissues of the root, including the epidermis, cortex, endodermis, pericycle, and vascular tissues. The RAM also plays a key role in the root's ability to elongate and penetrate the soil, seeking out water and nutrients. As the root tip grows, cells in the RAM divide and differentiate into specialized tissue layers that form the **root cap** and the internal tissues. The root cap protects the growing tip and helps in soil penetration, while the tissues derived from the RAM allow for **water and nutrient absorption** and the development of **lateral roots.**

The **RAM** is functionally important for the overall plant's survival, as the growth of roots determines the plant's ability to anchor itself in the soil, access nutrients, and establish a symbiotic relationship with microorganisms like mycorrhizal fungi. The RAM also controls the formation of **lateral roots**, which allow the plant to expand its root system and explore a larger volume of soil for nutrients and water.

B. Intercalary Meristems

Intercalary meristems are found at the internodes (regions between leaves) or the bases of leaves in some plants, especially in **monocots** like grasses. These meristems are vital for the **regeneration** of plant parts and the **recovery** of damaged tissues. When a plant is grazed, cut, or damaged, intercalary meristems allow the plant to **regrow** by promoting the growth of new tissues. This regenerative ability is particularly important for plants that face frequent disturbances or environmental stresses. Intercalary meristems contribute to the growth of new **leaf blades** and **stem tissues** in the region where the plant has been damaged, allowing the plant to continue its growth and development despite adverse conditions.

Monocots, such as grasses, have a distinct advantage due to the rapidly and maintain **photosynthetic productivity**. This type of growth is essential for these plants, particularly in grasslands and other ecosystems where herbivory and environmental disturbances are frequent.

C. Lateral Meristems

Lateral meristems contribute to the **secondary growth** of plants, which leads to an increase in the **girth** or thickness of the plant. This growth is essential for woody plants, which require thickened stems to support their structure, transport water, and withstand mechanical stresses. The two major types of lateral meristems are the **vascular cambium** and the **cork cambium** (also known as **phellogen**).

1. **Vascular Cambium**: The vascular cambium is a **cylindrical layer** of meristematic cells found between the xylem and phloem tissues in the vascular bundle. The vascular cambium is responsible for the production of **secondary xylem** (wood) towards the inside and **secondary phloem** towards the outside. This process increases the thickness of the plant's stems and roots and contributes to the formation of wood, which is vital for support and transport in large plants and trees. The vascular cambium enables the plant to grow in girth, providing structural support to **trees** and **woody shrubs** that need to carry out long-distance transport of water and nutrients.
2. **Cork Cambium (Phellogen)**: The cork cambium is responsible for producing the **periderm**, a protective outer layer that replaces the epidermis in plants undergoing secondary growth. The cork cambium produces **cork cells** to the outside and **phelloderm** cells to the inside. The cork acts as a barrier to prevent water loss, pathogen invasion, and physical damage, while the phelloderm provides some

additional structural support. The formation of the periderm is especially important in woody plants, which need protection from external factors as they age and expand.

FEATURES OF MERISTEMATIC CELLS

Meristematic cells exhibit distinct features that set them apart from differentiated plant cells. These include:

- **Isodiametric shape:** Meristematic cells are often spherical or cuboidal, which allows for maximum flexibility and division.
- **Dense cytoplasm:** The cytoplasm is rich in cellular organelles, including **ribosomes**, **mitochondria**, and **endoplasmic reticulum**, reflecting the cell's high metabolic activity and capacity for protein synthesis.
- **Prominent nucleus:** The nucleus is large and centrally located, reflecting the cell's role in rapid division and regulation of the cell cycle.
- **Thin primary cell walls:** The primary cell walls of meristematic cells are thin and flexible, which allows for cell division and expansion.
- **Absence of vacuoles:** Meristematic cells lack large vacuoles, which differentiates them from mature cells that typically contain large central vacuoles for storage.
- **No intercellular spaces:** These cells are tightly packed together, forming a continuous sheet of undifferentiated cells that can quickly divide and differentiate.

FUNCTION OF MERISTEMS

Meristems are the key regions responsible for the continuous growth

1. **Drive Organogenesis**: Meristematic cells produce the new cells that will differentiate into roots, stems, leaves, and flowers, thus driving the overall growth and development of plant organs.
2. **Regulate Tissue Patterning**: The division and differentiation of meristematic cells are crucial for the formation of well-organized tissues within the plant, allowing for proper vascular, ground, and dermal tissue formation.
3. **Control Growth Direction and Rate**: Meristems control the direction of growth (vertical or horizontal) and regulate the overall rate of growth depending on environmental cues and internal signals.
4. **Initiate Vascular Development**: In the apical meristem, the formation of vascular tissues is initiated, which enables the transport of water, nutrients, and sugars throughout the plant body. This is crucial for the plant's nutrient transport system and for its survival.

Meristematic tissues are therefore the foundation of plant growth, development, and adaptation, allowing plants to respond to both internal and external signals, ensuring survival and reproduction in a variety of environments.

5.2 Permanent Tissues: Simple and Complex

Once meristematic cells undergo differentiation, they form permanent tissues that are specialized to perform specific functions in the plant body. Unlike meristematic cells, permanent tissues generally do not retain the ability to divide, although they can undergo changes to suit the functional needs of the plant. Permanent tissues are categorized into simple permanent tissues and complex permanent tissues, based on their structure, composition, and functions. While simple tissues are composed of only one type of cell, complex tissues consist of multiple types of cells working together in a coordinated manner to carry out their functions. These tissues are fundamental to the growth, support, transport, and metabolic processes of the plant.

A. Simple Permanent Tissues

Simple permanent tissues consist of a single type of cell, each performing distinct roles based on its structural characteristics. These tissues play essential roles in processes such as storage, support, and protection.

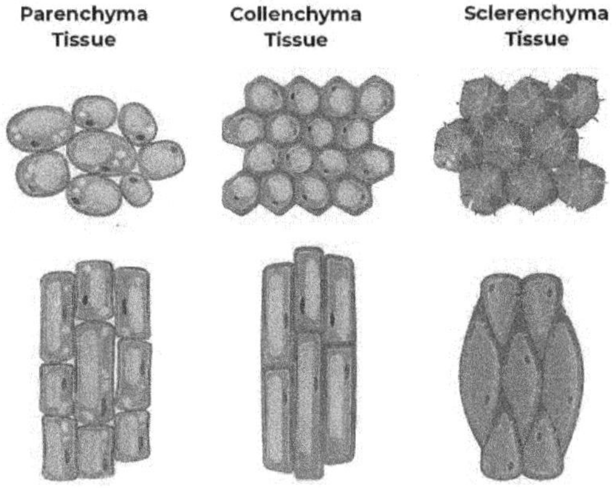

Figure: Simple Permanent Tissues

1. Parenchyma

Parenchyma is the most common type of simple permanent tissue and is composed of living cells that have thin primary cell walls and intercellular spaces. These cells are typically isodiametric, meaning they have a similar length, width, and height, although they can vary depending on their specific function. Parenchyma is found in many plant organs, including the cortex, pith, mesophyll, and in the vascular tissues (xylem and phloem).

- **Functions:**

- **Storage**: Parenchyma cells are primarily responsible for storing starch, sugars, and water. In some cases, they also store proteins and lipids.
- **Photosynthesis**: In some regions, such as the mesophyll of leaves, parenchyma cells contain chloroplasts and are known as chlorenchyma. These cells play a critical role in photosynthesis by converting carbon dioxide and water into glucose using light energy.
- **Buoyancy**: Certain parenchyma cells, especially those found in aquatic plants, are modified to form aerenchyma. These cells have large intercellular spaces, which provide buoyancy and allow the plant to float on water.

2. Collenchyma

Collenchyma cells are living cells that have unevenly thickened walls primarily made of cellulose and pectin. These cells are often found in the petioles, leaf midribs, and young stems of plants. Unlike parenchyma cells, collenchyma cells provide flexible support to the plant while still allowing for growth and elongation.

1. **Functions**:

- **Support**: Collenchyma provides mechanical support to growing parts of the plant. It is particularly important in regions where flexibility is needed, such as in the young stems and leaf veins.
- **Elasticity**: Due to its unevenly thickened walls, collenchyma allows for flexibility without compromising strength, enabling parts of the plant to bend and stretch without breaking.

3. Sclerenchyma

Sclerenchyma cells are dead cells that have thick, lignified cell walls, making them rigid and supportive. There are two main types of sclerenchyma cells: fibres and sclereids.

- **Fibres**: These are long, narrow, and tapered cells, often found in vascular bundles and fibrous plants like hemp and flax. They provide structural support to the plant.
- **Sclereids**: These are shorter, irregularly shaped cells found in seed coats, nutshells, and **stone cells** (like those in pears). Sclereids contribute to the **mechanical protection** of seeds and fruits.
- **Functions**:
- **Rigidity and Strength**: Sclerenchyma tissues are essential for providing **structural support to the plant. Their thick lignified walls make them particularly effective in strengthening plant tissues that need to resist external forces, such as in woody plants and fibrous tissues.**
- **Protection**: Sclerenchyma cells, particularly sclereids, also contribute to the **protection** of seeds and fruits by providing a hard, protective layer.

B. Complex Permanent Tissues

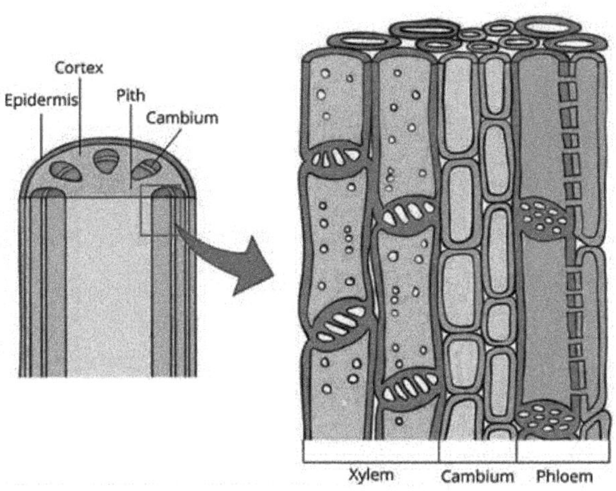

Figure: Complex Permanent Tissues

Complex permanent tissues are made up of more than one type of cell working together to perform specific functions, primarily related to transport. These tissues include xylem and phloem, which are responsible for the transport of water, minerals, and nutrients throughout the plant.

1. Xylem (Water-Conducting Tissue)

Xylem is a complex tissue responsible for the transportation of water and minerals from the roots to the aerial parts of the plant, such as the stem, leaves, and flowers. Xylem also provides structural support to the plant. It consists of several types of cells, each with a specific function:

- **Tracheids**: These are long, tapering cells that are lignified and help in the conduction of water. Tracheids are present in all vascular plants and serve as the primary water-conducting elements in gymnosperms and ferns.
- **Vessels**: These are cylindrical tubes formed by the end-to-end fusion of vessel elements. Vessels are more efficient at water transport than tracheids and are found primarily in angiosperms.
- **Xylem Parenchyma**: These are living cells that store water, nutrients, and other substances, such as starch. They also assist in the lateral movement of water and solutes.
- **Xylem Fibres**: These are long, lignified cells that provide structural support to the plant.
- **Functions**:
    - **Water and Mineral Transport**: The xylem is responsible for the upward movement of water and dissolved minerals from the roots to the shoot system. This transport is crucial for plant hydration and nutrient supply.

- o **Mechanical Support:** The lignified cell walls of xylem cells provide rigidity and strength, enabling the plant to maintain its upright structure.

1. Phloem (Food-Conducting Tissue)

Phloem is another complex tissue responsible for the transportation of food, particularly sugars produced during photosynthesis in the leaves, to the rest of the plant. It also helps in the movement of other organic molecules, such as amino acids and hormones. Phloem consists of several specialized cell types:

- **Sieve Tubes:** These are elongated, living cells that form continuous tubes through which sugars and other nutrients are transported. Sieve tubes have sieve plates at their ends that allow for the flow of materials between cells.
- **Companion Cells:** These are specialized parenchyma cells that are closely associated with sieve tube elements. Companion cells help in the metabolic functions of the sieve tubes, including loading and unloading sugars.
- **Phloem Parenchyma:** These cells store organic nutrients and assist in the lateral movement of sugars and other substances.
- **Phloem Fibres:** These are long, thick-walled cells that provide structural support to the phloem tissue.
- **Functions:**
- **Food Transport:** Phloem is responsible for the translocation of sugars and other organic compounds from the source (typically the leaves) to the sink (such as growing roots, fruits, and flowers).
- **Transport of Signaling Molecules:** Phloem also plays a role in the movement of plant hormones and other signaling molecules, which regulate growth and

3. Cambium

Cambium is a type of lateral meristematic tissue in plants that is responsible for secondary growth, meaning the increase in thickness or girth of stems and roots. It is located between the xylem and phloem in dicot plants and is made up of thin-walled, actively dividing cells. The cambium produces secondary xylem (wood) towards the inside and secondary phloem towards the outside, thereby forming part of the complex permanent tissues. This activity helps in the development of vascular tissues over time, making the plant stronger and enabling better transport of water, minerals, and food. Cambium plays a vital role in the formation of growth rings seen in woody plants.

Both xylem and phloem are essential for the plant's ability to synthesize and distribute nutrients, maintain hydration, and support growth. Together, they form the vascular system, ensuring the survival and proper functioning of the plant. The coordinated activities of simple and complex tissues contribute to the structural integrity, metabolism, and adaptability of plants in diverse environmental conditions.

5.3 Mechanical Tissues: Structure, Distribution, and Functions

Mechanical tissues are a specialized group of plant tissues that play a vital role in providing structural strength, protection, and flexibility to the plant body. These tissues are designed to withstand mechanical stress and support the plant as it grows and interacts with its environment. They help maintain the structural integrity of the plant, allowing it to resist forces such as wind, rain, and physical damage, which are essential for its survival and growth. The presence of mechanical tissues ensures that the plant can stand upright, transport water and nutrients efficiently, and protect its internal structures from damage.

Mechanical tissues can be classified into different types based on their structure, location, and function. These tissues are mainly collenchyma, sclerenchyma, xylem fibres, and phloem fibres. While all of these tissues serve the common purpose of providing mechanical support, their unique features and locations within the plant enable them to carry out specific functions suited to particular plant organs or conditions.

TYPES OF MECHANICAL TISSUES

A. Collenchyma

Collenchyma cells are living, elongated cells that are typically found beneath the epidermis in young stems and petioles of dicot plants. These cells are characterized by their unevenly thickened cell walls, primarily composed of cellulose and pectin. The thickening is concentrated at the corners of the cells, making the walls flexible and able to withstand tensile forces without breaking. Collenchyma is found in areas that are still growing and in regions of the plant that require both support and the ability to stretch or bend as the plant develops.

- **Structure**: Collenchyma cells have unevenly thickened walls, particularly at the corners. This allows them to flex under pressure while providing sufficient strength to support the plant.
- **Function**: The main function of collenchyma tissue is to provide flexibility and tensile strength to young plant parts such as petioles, leaf veins, and young stems. This tissue allows for the bending and growth of these plant parts while maintaining support, ensuring that they can withstand mechanical stress without breaking or collapsing.

B. Sclerenchyma

Sclerenchyma is a dead, lignified tissue found in various parts of the plant, including vascular bundles, seed coats, and hard stems. This tissue is primarily involved in providing rigidity and strength to mature plant parts. Sclerenchyma cells have thick, lignified cell walls, which makes them strong, stiff, and highly resistant to mechanical damage. The two main types of sclerenchyma cells are fibres and sclereids.

- **Fibres:** Fibres are long, narrow cells that are often found in the vascular bundles and in the bark of trees. These cells are heavily lignified, which makes them stiff and resistant to tensile forces. Fibres are often commercially valuable and are used in industries such as textiles (e.g., flax, jute, and hemp).
- **Sclereids:** Sclereids are shorter, irregularly shaped cells with thick lignified walls. These cells are commonly found in the seed coats of plants and in hard fruits such as pears, where they contribute to the gritty texture. They serve a protective function by providing structural strength and protection to the plant's reproductive structures.
- **Function:** The primary function of sclerenchyma is to provide structural support and rigidity to plant parts. It allows the plant to maintain its upright posture, withstand physical stress, and resist damage from external forces like wind or herbivory. Sclerenchyma is particularly important in mature, non-growing parts of the plant, such as woody stems and seed coats, where strength and durability are required.

C. Xylem Fibres

Xylem fibres are a type of sclerenchyma that are specifically associated with the xylem tissue, which is responsible for the transport of water and minerals from the roots to the rest of the plant. These fibres are dead cells with thick lignified walls that provide structural support to the xylem. Xylem fibres contribute to the tensile strength and stiffness of the plant, helping it maintain its structure while performing vital functions like water transport.

- **Structure**: Xylem fibres are elongated, lignified cells that are found alongside the vessel elements and tracheids in the xylem tissue.
- **Function**: Xylem fibres provide additional support to the xylem tissue, ensuring that the plant's vascular system remains intact and functional, especially under conditions of physical stress or wind load. These fibres also help in the mechanical stability of the plant by reinforcing the xylem vessels.

D. Phloem Fibres

Phloem fibres, also known as bast fibres, are long, narrow cells found in the phloem tissue, which is responsible for transporting food (sugars) from the leaves to other parts of the plant. Phloem fibres are typically associated with the phloem in dicot plants and are used commercially in jute, flax, and ramie industries. These fibres add strength and support to the phloem tissue, ensuring the structural integrity of the plant while it performs its food transport function.

- **Structure**: Phloem fibres are elongated, lignified cells that run parallel to the sieve tubes and companion cells in the phloem. They are composed of cellulose and lignin, making them strong and durable
- **Function**: The main function of phloem fibres is to provide structural support to the phloem and to the overall plant body. They help the plant maintain rigidity and resilience while also providing strength to the phloem tissue during food transport.

Distribution and Function of Mechanical Tissues

Mechanical tissues are distributed throughout various plant organs, including the leaves, stems, and roots, and are especially concentrated in areas that are subject to physical stress or require additional support. These tissues help plants to resist forces from the environment, such as wind, rain, and herbivory, and to maintain their erect posture and structural integrity.

1. **Support of Leaves, Stems, and Roots:** Mechanical tissues provide support to these critical plant structures, allowing them to stay upright and function effectively in the plant's photosynthetic and nutrient transport processes. For example, collenchyma supports the petioles and leaf veins, while sclerenchyma provides rigidity to the woody stems of trees.
2. **Erect Posture Against Environmental Forces:** Mechanical tissues help the plant withstand external stresses like wind and rain, preventing damage and collapse under such conditions. Xylem fibres and sclerenchyma in woody plants contribute to maintaining a plant's upright position under these conditions.
3. **Minimization of Mechanical Damage:** By providing flexibility and strength, mechanical tissues protect the plant from damage caused by environmental factors, such as tension and pressure. They also help prevent the collapse of plant tissues under their own weight.
4. **Protection of Vascular Tissues:** Mechanical tissues like sclerenchyma and xylem fibres offer protection to the plant's vascular system, which is critical for transporting water, nutrients, and food. They help ensure that the vascular tissues remain intact and functional, preventing damage from external forces.

The mechanical tissues are essential for providing strength, flexibility, and protection to plants. They allow plants to maintain their structure while resisting physical stresses and environmental challenges, ensuring the survival and growth of the plant throughout its life cycle.

5.4 Periderm: Origin, Structure, and Function

The periderm is a specialized tissue that forms a protective covering over the plant as it undergoes secondary growth, particularly in woody plants. As the plant grows in diameter, the epidermis, which originally protects the plant, becomes inadequate to provide continued protection. In response to this need, the plant develops the periderm, which functions as a secondary protective barrier. This tissue plays a key role in protecting internal plant tissues from environmental stressors such as desiccation, pathogens, and mechanical injury. It also reduces the loss of water through transpiration and facilitates gas exchange via specialized structures called lenticels.

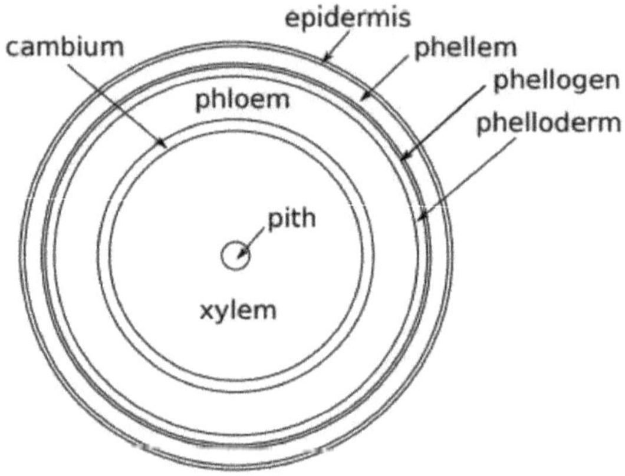

Figure: Periderm Structure with Lenticels

ORIGIN OF PERIDERM

The development of periderm begins with the formation of the cork cambium (also known as phellogen), a meristematic tissue that arises from the cortical cells of the plant during secondary growth. As the plant continues to grow in girth, the outermost layers of the stem, which are part of the epidermis, become unable to accommodate the expanding plant body. The epidermis eventually ruptures and peels off, and the cork cambium takes over the task of producing new tissues to replace the damaged epidermis.

- Cork cambium (phellogen) is responsible for the production of the cork (phellem) outwardly and the secondary cortex (phelloderm) inwardly. This process occurs through periclinal division, where the cork cambium cells divide parallel to the surface, resulting in the continuous formation of the periderm.
- As the secondary growth proceeds, the cork cambium continues to produce new layers of cork, which leads to the thickening of the periderm and the eventual shedding of

older, outer layers. This process allows the plant to maintain protection as it increases in size.

Components of Periderm

The periderm is composed of three primary components: cork cambium, cork, and secondary cortex. Each of these components plays a specific role in the structure and function of the periderm.

1. Phellogen (Cork Cambium)

- The **phellogen** is a **meristematic tissue**, meaning it consists of actively dividing cells that produce new tissue throughout the life of the plant. It arises from the **cortical cells** in the outer layers of the plant body.
- The cork cambium divides **periclinally** to produce two distinct tissues:
    - **Phellem (Cork)**: The outer layer of the periderm, consisting of dead, suberized cells that form a protective barrier.
    - **Phelloderm (Secondary Cortex)**: The inner layer, consisting of living parenchymatous cells that may be involved in functions such as storage or photosynthesis in some species.

The cork cambium remains active as long as secondary growth occurs, continuously producing layers of cork and secondary cortex, which thickens over time.

2. Phellem (Cork)

- The phellem is the outermost layer of the periderm, made up of dead, lignified cells that have undergone suberization, meaning they are impregnated with suberin, a waxy substance. This suberization renders the cork cell water and gases, providing an effective barrier against water loss and pathogen invasion.

- The phellem forms the protective outer layer that shields the plant from physical damage, desiccation, and pathogens. It serves as a robust defense system, ensuring the plant can survive harsh environmental conditions.
- Over time, as secondary growth continues, older layers of cork become compacted and die, while newer layers of cork are continually produced by the cork cambium.

3. Phelloderm

- The phelloderm is the inner layer of the periderm and consists of living parenchyma cells that are thin-walled and capable of performing various functions, such as storage and, in some species, photosynthesis.
- While it is not as prominent as the phellem, the phelloderm plays an important role in maintaining the overall health and function of the plant. In some plants, the cells of the phelloderm store nutrients or act as a reservoir for water, helping the plant maintain internal balance.

LENTICELS

One important feature of the periderm is the presence of lenticels, which are small, raised structures found in the outer surface of the bark. These specialized areas are composed of loosely arranged cells that allow gas exchange between the plant's internal tissues and the environment. Lenticels play an essential role in the process of respiration, allowing oxygen to enter the plant and carbon dioxide to exit, especially in woody plants where the cork layer may otherwise create a nearly impermeable barrier.

- **Structure:** Lenticels appear as raised spots or pores on the surface of the plant's bark. They are formed by loosely arranged cells in the periderm that create small openings through which gases can pass.
- **Function:** The primary function of lenticels is to facilitate the exchange of gases such as oxygen and carbon dioxide, which are crucial for the plant's respiratory processes. In woody plants, where the cork layer may block other forms of gas exchange, lenticels provide a necessary route for the plant's internal metabolic needs

FUNCTIONS OF PERIDERM

The periderm plays several vital roles in the life of a plant. As the plant continues to grow and expand in diameter, the periderm provides critical functions such as protection, water conservation, and gas exchange.

1. **Protection from Desiccation and Pathogens:** One of the primary functions of the periderm is to protect internal tissues from water loss (desiccation) and pathogens. The suberized cork cells of the phellem are impermeable to water and gases, which helps minimize evaporation and prevents the entry of harmful microorganisms. This barrier is particularly important in preventing water loss in plants that grow in arid environments or during periods of low moisture availability.
2. **Mechanical Protection:** The thick, dead cork cells of the phellem also provide mechanical protection to the plant. They act as a physical barrier that helps protect the underlying tissues from damage due to external stresses, such as abrasion, herbivory, or weather conditions like storms and frost.
3. **Facilitating Gas Exchange via Lenticels:** While the cork

openings for the exchange of gases, such as oxygen and carbon dioxide, between the plant and the environment. This is essential for the plant's respiratory needs and is especially important in woody plants where the bark can otherwise block gas exchange.

4. **Reducing Transpiration:** The periderm helps to reduce transpiration, or the loss of water vapor from the plant, by acting as a barrier to water loss. This is particularly important in dry conditions where minimizing water loss can be crucial for the plant's survival. The suberin in the cork cells of the phellem creates a waterproof layer that significantly limits water evaporation from the plant's surface.
5. **Serves as a Secondary Dermal System:** As the plant grows in girth, the periderm takes over the protective role previously carried out by the epidermis. It becomes the primary dermal tissue system responsible for safeguarding the plant's internal tissues from external threats. The periderm is therefore an essential part of the plant's secondary dermal system, ensuring the plant remains well-protected as it matures.

The periderm is a crucial secondary tissue that provides multiple protective functions for plants undergoing secondary growth. It forms from the cork cambium and includes components such as the cork (phellem), secondary cortex (phelloderm), and lenticels. These tissues work together to protect the plant from environmental stresses, reduce water loss, facilitate gas exchange, and serve as a mechanical barrier. The periderm is essential for the long-term health and survival of the plant, especially in woody species and those that experience significant secondary growth.

CONCLUSION

The diverse tissues of a plant body are intricately coordinated to ensure the plant's survival, growth, and adaptation to its environment. Meristematic tissues, located at the tips of roots and shoots, are responsible for driving plant development by producing new cells that contribute to primary growth. These tissues allow for the continuous formation of new plant structures, enabling plants to expand and respond to environmental conditions. As the plant matures, some of the cells from meristematic tissues differentiate into permanent tissues that perform specialized functions, such as conducting water and nutrients, storing energy, and providing structural support. These permanent tissues include xylem, phloem, parenchyma, collenchyma, and sclerenchyma, each of which plays a unique role in the overall functioning of the plant.

Mechanical tissues, such as sclerenchyma and collenchyma, are essential for maintaining the structural integrity of the plant, ensuring that it can withstand external forces such as wind or the weight of its own growth. These tissues provide rigidity and strength, supporting the plant's ability to stand upright, transport fluids, and protect vital tissues. The periderm, which develops during secondary growth, provides an important protective layer for woody plants, shielding them from physical damage, pathogens, and water loss. This layer includes the cork, cork cambium, and phelloderm, all of which contribute to the plant's resilience and adaptability over time.

A thorough understanding of plant tissue anatomy is crucial in various fields such as forestry, agriculture, horticulture, and biotechnology. In forestry, knowledge of tissue structures helps in selecting trees for specific environments, ensuring their longevity and productivity. In agriculture and horticulture, optimizing tissue functions can lead to more efficient crop production, improved disease resistance, and better yield quality. In biotechnology, tissue engineering and plant genetic modification rely on manipulating specific tissues to enhance desirable traits or develop new varieties with enhanced resistance to pests or environmental stressors insights into how plants grow, survive, and thrive, supporting advancements in environmental management, sustainable agriculture, and biotechnological innovations.

QUESTIONS:

- Explain the structure and functions of meristematic tissues. Discuss their role in plant growth and development.
- Describe the different types of meristems found in plants. How do apical, intercalary, and lateral meristems contribute to plant growth?
- What are the characteristics and functions of simple permanent tissues? Explain the role of parenchyma, collenchyma, and sclerenchyma in plant physiology.
- Discuss the structure and function of complex permanent tissues in plants. How do xylem and phloem contribute to the transport of water, minerals, and food in plants?
- Describe the various mechanical tissues in plants. How do collenchyma, sclerenchyma, and xylem fibres provide support and protection to plant structures?
- Explain the origin, structure, and function of periderm in plants. How does it contribute to the plant's secondary growth and protection?
- What are lenticels, and how do they facilitate gas exchange in plants? Discuss their significance in the periderm layer.
- Compare the roles of meristematic tissues and permanent tissues in plant growth. How do these tissues work together to ensure plant survival and adaptation?

CHAPTER 6

SECONDARY GROWTH AND ANATOMICAL VARIATIONS

Secondary growth is a critical process in the development of dicotyledonous plants and gymnosperms, contributing to an increase in the girth or diameter of roots and stems. This growth occurs after the initial elongation of the plant, and it is essential for the formation of woody tissues, which provide structural support and facilitate the transport of water, nutrients, and food throughout the plant. Secondary growth is typically initiated by the activity of lateral meristems, namely the vascular cambium and cork cambium, which lead to the production of secondary xylem and phloem, as well as the protective periderm. This growth is fundamental to the plant's ability to expand its vascular system, accommodate more metabolic activity, and respond to the stresses of the environment.

In normal secondary growth, the vascular cambium forms between the primary xylem and phloem, producing secondary xylem (wood) toward the inside and secondary phloem toward the outside. This continuous production of vascular tissues allows the plant to increase its girth and sustain its growing needs. The cork cambium, in turn, produces the periderm, which replaces the epidermis as the plant's outer protective layer, shielding the plant from environmental stresses such as desiccation, pathogens, and physical injury. Secondary growth is most prominent in dicotyledons and gymnosperms, where it results in the development of the characteristic woody stems and roots. This process is not observed meristems for their growth in length but lack the ability to increase girth through secondary growth.

Secondary growth does not always follow a typical pattern, and several plant species exhibit anomalous secondary growth, deviating from the conventional pattern seen in most dicots and gymnosperms. Such deviations may involve irregularities in the arrangement or development of vascular tissues, and they are often observed in monocotyledons (e.g., palms, bananas) that do not usually undergo secondary growth. In these plants, the vascular cambium may arise from different sources or show irregular patterns of activity. For example, some monocots form intrafascicular cambium between vascular bundles or exhibit concentric rings of vascular tissue. These anomalous growth patterns enable the plant to adapt its structure to environmental conditions that may not be conducive to typical growth processes, such as restricted space, mechanical stress, or the need for enhanced rigidity.

The process of secondary growth in plants is also highly influenced by environmental conditions, leading to specialized adaptations in various habitats such as aquatic, dry, saline, and epiphytic environments. In aquatic habitats, plants often have modified secondary growth that allows them to maintain structural integrity in the absence of strong support from soil. For instance, some aquatic plants may develop large, flexible stems with enhanced vascular tissue to maintain buoyancy and facilitate water movement through the plant. In dry or xerophytic conditions, secondary growth may involve the formation of thicker bark or the development of storage tissues like parenchyma to store water, which helps the plant survive during periods of drought. Saline environments, which are characterized by high salt concentrations, may lead to specialized adaptations in secondary growth, such as the accumulation of salt in vacuoles or modifications in the vascular cambium that protect against the effects of salinity on water uptake. In epiphytic plants, which grow on other plants, secondary growth can be more focused on the production of aerial roots or modifications that enable them to collect nutrients and water from the air, rather than from the soil.

The secondary growth is essential for the development of woody tissues in dicotyledonous plants and gymnosperms, providing the structural support needed for the plant's growth and survival. While the normal patterns of secondary growth lead to an increase in girth through the production of secondary xylem and phloem, deviations and anomalous growth patterns allow plants to adapt to a wide range of ecological conditions. By modifying their secondary growth processes, plants can thrive in diverse habitats, from aquatic environments to arid and saline regions, showcasing the remarkable flexibility and adaptability of plant growth strategies.

6.1 Normal Secondary Growth

Normal Secondary Growth in Plants: A Comprehensive Overview

Secondary growth is the process by which plants increase in girth or thickness over time, primarily through the activity of lateral meristems, particularly the **vascular cambium** and **cork cambium** (phellogen). This growth occurs after the initial elongation of the plant and is most prominent in **dicotyledons** and **gymnosperms**, where it leads to the formation of woody tissues. Secondary growth plays a pivotal role in supporting the plant structurally, improving the transport of water and nutrients, and facilitating the plant's adaptation to environmental conditions. It is responsible for the development of wood, bark, and the overall increase in girth of plant stems and roots, allowing for long-term survival, especially in perennial plants.

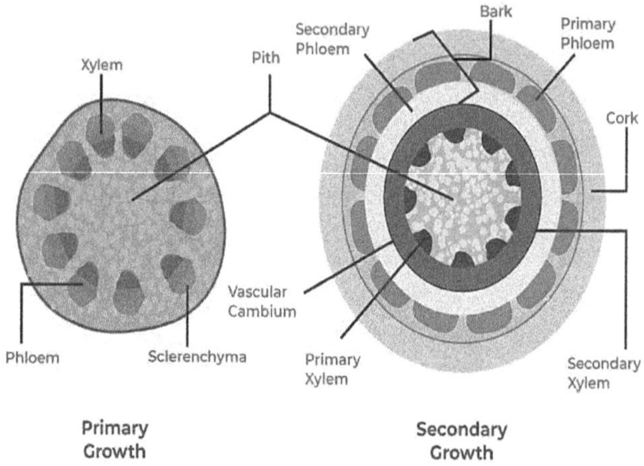

Figure: Normal Secondary Growth in a Dicot Stem

Vascular Cambium: The Heart of Secondary Growth

The vascular cambium is a lateral meristem that plays the central role in secondary growth by producing two distinct types of tissues: secondary xylem (wood) and secondary phloem. It forms a continuous cylindrical ring around the stem or root, located between the primary xylem and phloem. The vascular cambium is crucial for the thickening of stems and roots in plants that undergo secondary growth.

Origin of Vascular Cambium

The vascular cambium arises from two distinct sources:

- **Intra-fascicular cambium:** This cambium develops from the cells within the vascular bundles of the stem or root. It is located between the xylem and phloem in the vascular bundles of the primary plant body.

- **Inter-fascicular cambium:** This cambium arises from the parenchyma cells situated between the vascular bundles.

As the plant grows, the intra-fascicular and inter-fascicular cambium meet and fuse to form a continuous cambial ring that encircles the stem or root. This fusion is vital for the maintenance of the meristematic activity needed for secondary growth.

Activity of Vascular Cambium

The vascular cambium is the primary tissue responsible for producing the vascular tissues involved in secondary growth. Its activity results in the formation of secondary xylem and secondary phloem. The cambium divides, producing secondary xylem towards the inside of the plant and secondary phloem towards the outside. In general, more secondary xylem is produced than secondary phloem, contributing to the thickening of the stem and root. The cambium's activity is seasonal, with the growth rings forming in response to varying environmental conditions such as temperature and moisture. The cambium is most active during the growing season, leading to the formation of annual growth rings, which are often used in dendrochronology (tree-ring dating).

Cork Cambium (Phellogen) and Periderm Formation

As the plant grows in girth, the epidermis, which is initially responsible for protecting the plant, is replaced by a secondary protective covering called the periderm. The formation of the periderm is largely driven by the cork cambium (also known as phellogen), a secondary meristem that arises in the cortex of stems and roots.

6.2 Origin and Activity of Cork Cambium

The cork cambium is derived from cells of the cortex or sometimes from the vascular cambium itself. Its primary function is to produce the outer protective tissue of the plant body, the phellem (or cork), which consists of dead cells with suberized (wax-coated) walls that are impermeable to water and gases. On the inside, the cork cambium produces phelloderm, which is a layer of living parenchyma cells that provide additional support and storage.

Formation of Periderm

The periderm is the composite tissue that replaces the epidermis during secondary growth. It consists of the cork (phellem), the cork cambium (phellogen), and the phelloderm. The periderm provides a protective barrier against desiccation, pathogens, and mechanical damage. Over time, as the plant continues to grow, the cork cambium divides to produce new layers of cork, eventually leading to the formation of lenticels, which are small openings in the bark that facilitate gas exchange, allowing the plant to maintain cellular respiration despite the impermeable outer layer of cork.

Growth Rings and Wood Types: Understanding the Structure of Woody Tissues

Secondary growth results in the formation of wood, which consists of two main parts: heartwood and sapwood. The annual growth rings that form within wood are indicative of the plant's growth cycle, and they vary in appearance based on the environmental conditions during the growing season.

Annual Rings and Wood Types

Annual rings are formed by the alternating production of early wood (also known as spring wood) and late wood (or autumn wood). Early wood is produced during the early part of the growing season when water is abundant, and it is typically characterized by larger, thinner-walled xylem cells. Late wood is formed later in the growing season, typically under conditions of water scarcity or reduced growth, and is composed of smaller, thicker-walled xylem cells.

Heartwood: The central region of the tree trunk, consisting of non-functional, dark-colored xylem. Heartwood is formed as the plant ages and the older xylem cells become filled with resin, oils, and other substances that make them non-conductive. Although it no longer plays a role in water conduction, heartwood provides structural support to the tree.

- **Sapwood**: The outer portion of the xylem, which is still functional in transporting water and minerals from the roots to the leaves. Sapwood is lighter in color and typically surrounds the heartwood.

The alternating layers of early and late wood in each growth ring allow for the determination of a tree's age and the conditions in which it grew during specific years.

Medullary Rays and Tyloses: Structural Adaptations for Lateral Conduction

The vascular tissues, **medullary rays** and **tyloses** are crucial components of secondary growth that contribute to the plant's functionality.

- **Medullary Rays**: These are radial strips of parenchyma cells that extend from the center of the stem (the pith) outward to the periphery. They are important for lateral conduction of water and nutrients, as they connect the xylem and phloem within the stem. Medullary rays also play a role in storing

- **Tyloses:** Tyloses are balloon-like projections that form from the parenchyma cells of the xylem. These projections extend into the vessel lumens of xylem cells, blocking the passage of water and preventing its movement. Tyloses are often found in older wood and contribute to the formation of heartwood by reducing the conductivity of the xylem.

Normal secondary growth is a vital process in the life cycle of dicotyledonous plants and gymnosperms, leading to the thickening of stems and roots. The activity of the vascular cambium and cork cambium ensures that plants can produce woody tissues like secondary xylem and secondary phloem, as well as the protective periderm. The formation of growth rings, heartwood, sapwood, and the presence of specialized structures such as medullary rays and tyloses allow for efficient water conduction, structural support, and adaptations to environmental conditions. Understanding these processes provides insight into plant development, longevity, and survival strategies, especially in perennial species that undergo continuous growth over many years.

6.3 Tissue Organization in Different Environments: Hydrophytes, Xerophytes, Halophytes, and Epiphytes

Secondary growth, the increase in thickness or girth of plant organs, is a hallmark feature of dicotyledonous plants and gymnosperms. In certain species, particularly in some dicots and monocots, secondary growth occurs in an anomalous manner. These unusual growth patterns may represent adaptive strategies to particular environmental conditions or evolutionary specializations that enhance the plant's survival, mechanical support, and flexibility. This chapter delves into the anomalous secondary growth patterns observed in **Tinospora**, **Bignonia**, **Boerhaavia**, and **Dracaena**, each of which demonstrates unique modifications in their vascular tissue organization.

A. Tinospora (Menispermaceae): Formation of Secondary Vascular Bundles in the Cortex

Tinospora, a member of the Menispermaceae family, exhibits anomalous secondary growth characterized by the formation of secondary vascular bundles in the cortex, a feature uncommon in most plants. This deviation from typical vascular organization is essential for its survival in its native environments.

Anomalous Growth Features in Tinospora

- **Secondary Vascular Bundles in the Cortex:** The cambium in Tinospora does not remain confined to the primary vascular bundles but extends into the cortex, giving rise to secondary vascular bundles. These bundles form concentric rings, contributing to the thickening of the stem.
- **Medullary Bundles in the Pith:** To secondary vascular bundles in the cortex, **medullary bundles** are present within the pith. These bundles add another layer of vascular tissue, enhancing the plant's capacity to conduct water and nutrients across the stem.

Adaptation and Ecological Significance

The formation of additional vascular bundles in the cortex and pith is an adaptive strategy that allows Tinospora to thrive as a **climbing plant**. The increased flexibility and structural support provided by the concentric vascular bundles help the plant to better support its climbing habit. The presence of medullary bundles within the pith contributes to the storage of nutrients and water, which is beneficial for survival in fluctuating environmental conditions.

B. Bignonia (Bignoniaceae): Uneven Activity of the Vascular Cambium

Bignonia, a member of the Bignoniaceae family, displays an anomalous secondary growth pattern resulting from **uneven activity** of the vascular cambium. This feature is particularly significant for plants that rely on the mechanical strength of their stems, such as climbers or woody vines.

Anomalous Growth Features in Bignonia

- **Crescent-Shaped Xylem**: The vascular cambium in Bignonia does not produce uniform layers of secondary xylem. Instead, the xylem develops in a **furrowed pattern**, forming crescent-shaped or ridged structures along the stem. This irregular growth results in a stem surface with distinct ridges and furrows.
- **Phloem Wedges**: Between these xylem ridges, **phloem wedges** are formed, further contributing to the unique structure of the stem. The distribution of xylem and phloem in this manner enhances the plant's ability to support itself while allowing for the efficient transport of water, nutrients, and photosynthates.

ADAPTATION AND ECOLOGICAL SIGNIFICANCE

This anomalous growth pattern is an adaptation that provides mechanical strength and flexibility, which is critical for the survival of **climbing plants**. The ridged stems offer increased resistance to mechanical stress, such as wind or physical damage, while the unique arrangement of phloem and xylem optimizes the plant's vascular functions. The uneven cambial activity also allows the plant to respond to environmental pressures by adjusting its vascular tissue distribution, providing flexibility without compromising the plant's structural integrity.

C. Boerhaavia (Nyctaginaceae): Multiple Rings of Vascular Bundles

Boerhaavia, a member of the Nyctaginaceae family, exhibits a form of anomalous secondary growth characterized by the presence of multiple rings of vascular bundles. This modification is another example of how plants can adapt their internal structure to enhance storage capacity and mechanical strength.

Anomalous Growth Features in Boerhaavia

- **Concentric Rings of Vascular Bundles**: In Boerhaavia, **multiple rings of vascular bundles** are formed as a result of activity from the **extra-stelar cambium**. This cambium is responsible for generating concentric rings of vascular bundles, which increases the overall vascular network within the stem.
- **Accessory Cambia**: In addition to the primary vascular cambium, **accessory cambia** arise at different points in the plant's life cycle, forming new vascular bundles. These accessory cambia contribute to the plant's ability to produce additional vascular tissues in response to growth needs.

Adaptation and Ecological Significance

The formation of multiple rings of vascular bundles provides Boerhaavia with **enhanced storage** and **structural strength**. This allows the plant to store larger amounts of water and nutrients, which is particularly advantageous in environments where resources are variable or scarce. The increased vascular tissue and the formation of additional cambial layers also provide greater mechanical support, allowing the plant to withstand physical stress and environmental challenges such as drought or wind.

D. Dracaena (Monocot): Secondary Growth in Monocots

Dracaena, a genus of monocots, presents an interesting case of for secondary growth. Most monocots, such as grasses, only grow in length and do not exhibit the thickening of stems seen in dicots. The dracaena, which includes tree-like species, demonstrates an exceptional ability to undergo secondary growth.

Anomalous Growth Features in Dracaena

- **Secondary Vascular Bundles:** Unlike most monocots, Dracaena develops secondary vascular bundles that arise from a secondary meristem called the secondary thickening meristem. This meristem is responsible for producing new vascular tissues, contributing to the plant's ability to increase in girth.
- **Concentric Arrangement:** The secondary vascular bundles are arranged in concentric rings, but unlike dicots, they are not arranged in a single continuous cambial ring. These bundles are scattered throughout the ground tissue, resulting in a unique pattern of vascular tissue distribution.

Adaptation and Ecological Significance

The ability of Dracaena to develop secondary vascular bundles supports the upright posture of this tree-like monocot, allowing it to grow in height and diameter. The thickened stems provide both mechanical support and an enhanced capacity for water and nutrient transport, which is vital for the plant's survival in tree-like forms. The development of secondary growth in Dracaena is an evolutionary adaptation that allows it to overcome the typical limitations of monocots, enabling these plants to thrive in competitive environments.

Anomalous secondary growth in Tinospora, Bignonia, Boerhaavia, and Dracaena showcases the remarkable diversity of plant adaptation to varying ecological conditions. These plants illustrate how secondary growth can deviate from the typical patterns observed in most dicots and gymnosperms, offering specialized mechanisms that enhance survival in challenging environments. Whether it is the climbing habit of Tinospora, the mechanical strength of Bignonia, the enhanced storage in Boerhaavia, or the tree-like growth of Dracaena, these anomalous growth patterns demonstrate the plasticity of plant development and highlight the importance of seconda.

Conclusion

Secondary growth plays a critical role in enhancing the structural support, longevity, and storage capacity of plants. This growth, which occurs through the activity of vascular and cork cambium, leads to the thickening of stems and roots, allowing plants to support larger structures and better withstand environmental pressures. In dicots and gymnosperms, secondary growth typically follows a predictable pattern where the vascular cambium produces secondary xylem (wood) inward and secondary phloem outward, while the cork cambium forms protective layers of bark. This growth pattern provides strength, durability, and the ability to store nutrients and water, which are essential for the long-term survival of many plants. Some plants exhibit anomalous growth patterns that deviate from the typical secondary growth process, often as an adaptation to specific ecological pressures. For instance, some plants in tropical or arid environments may exhibit irregular cambium activity or even lack the formation of wood altogether, opting for alternative mechanisms of support and resource allocation. These deviations are often an adaptive response to unique environmental challenges, enabling plants to thrive in niches where standard growth patterns might be inefficient.

The organization of plant tissues varies significantly across different environmental conditions, further emphasizing the plants, tissues are often modified for buoyancy and gas exchange, with specialized aerenchyma that helps maintain the plant's structure in water. In contrast, plants growing in arid or saline environments tend to have thickened cuticles, sunken stomata, and specialized tissues for water storage and salt regulation. These adaptations allow plants to conserve water, reduce transpiration, and survive in harsh conditions where other species may struggle. The ability of plants to modify their anatomical structures in response to environmental factors highlights their remarkable plasticity, allowing them to inhabit a wide range of ecosystems—from dense forests to dry deserts to saline marshes.

This chapter underscores the importance of anatomical diversity in the survival and functionality of plants across diverse ecosystems. By understanding how plants adapt their growth patterns and tissue organization to meet ecological demands, we gain valuable insights into their resilience and potential applications in agriculture, horticulture, and environmental conservation. Through these adaptations, plants can continue to thrive in ever-changing and challenging environments, ensuring their role in maintaining the balance of ecosystems worldwide.

QUESTIONS

- Define secondary growth and explain its importance in dicotyledonous plants and gymnosperms.
- Describe the origin and activity of vascular cambium. How does it contribute to secondary growth?
- What is cork cambium, and how does it contribute to the formation of periderm in plants?
- Explain the difference between heartwood and sapwood. How are annual rings formed in secondary growth?

- Discuss the anomalous secondary growth in Tinospora and its adaptive significance.
- Describe the secondary growth patterns in Dracaena and explain its adaptation in monocots.
- How do hydrophytes, xerophytes, halophytes, and epiphytes adapt their tissue organization to thrive in their respective environments?
- Compare the structural adaptations of xerophytes and halophytes to their habitats.

CHAPTER 7

ANALYTICAL INSTRUMENTS IN BIOLOGICAL RESEARCH

Advancements in biological research are fundamentally reliant on the development and application of sophisticated analytical instruments that provide precise quantitative and qualitative insights into the biochemical and physiological processes within living organisms. These instruments have revolutionized how scientists study molecular interactions, cellular activities, and physiological responses, enabling more accurate measurements and detailed analysis than ever before. From determining the concentration of specific molecules in biological samples to observing the dynamics of complex biochemical reactions, these tools are indispensable in modern biological research. This chapter delves into four essential instruments—pH meter, colorimeter, spectrophotometer, and ultracentrifuge—providing a comprehensive overview of their principles, components, calibration procedures, and diverse applications across various fields of biological sciences.

The pH meter, one of the most commonly used instruments in biological laboratories, measures the acidity or alkalinity of a solution by detecting the concentration of hydrogen ions (H^+) present in the sample. The pH scale, ranging from 0 to 14, indicates whether a substance is acidic (pH $<$ 7), neutral (pH = 7), or alkaline (pH $>$ 7). A pH meter typically consists of a reference electrode and a glass electrode, both of which are immersed in the sample to measure the potential difference between them, which is then translated into a pH value. Calibration of the pH meter is crucial to ensure accuracy, typically involving the use of standard buffer solutions at known pH values. In biological systems, maintaining the proper pH is essential for enzyme activity, cellular processes, and the stability of biochemical reactions, making the pH meter invaluable in studies ranging from enzyme kinetics to the monitoring of cellular environments.

The colorimeter is another fundamental tool, primarily used to measure the concentration of colored compounds in a solution based on their absorption of specific wavelengths of light. It works on the principle that substances absorb light at characteristic wavelengths, and the amount of light absorbed is directly proportional to the concentration of the substance. A colorimeter uses a light source, a filter to select a particular wavelength, and a detector to measure the intensity of the transmitted light. Calibration is performed using standards with known concentrations, allowing for the precise determination of unknown sample concentrations. In biological research, colorimeters are frequently employed in experiments such as enzyme assays, where the change in color reflects the activity of enzymes or the presence of substrates. They are also useful in quantifying metabolites, proteins, or other biomolecules in complex biological samples, facilitating research in biochemistry, clinical diagnostics, and environmental monitoring.

The spectrophotometer expands on the principles of the colorimeter by providing more detailed spectral analysis across a wider range of wavelengths, from ultraviolet (UV) to visible light and sometimes even into the infrared (IR) region. Spectrophotometry relies on the measurement of light absorption by a sample at specific wavelengths, providing data on the concentration of particular molecules or the structure of biomolecules. This instrument typically consists of a light source, a monochromator or filter system to select wavelengths, a sample holder, and a detector. Calibration is achieved through the use of known concentration standards to of biomolecules such as nucleic acids, proteins, or pigments. Spectrophotometers are indispensable in molecular biology, where they are used for nucleic acid quantification (e.g., DNA or RNA concentrations), protein assays, and studying enzyme activities. They also play a vital role in pharmacology, environmental science, and food analysis, where monitoring the interaction of light with samples provides insights into chemical composition and structure.

The ultracentrifuge represents one of the most powerful analytical tools in biological research, enabling the separation of macromolecules, organelles, and even cells based on their size, shape, and density through high-speed centrifugation. This instrument operates by spinning samples at extremely high speeds, generating centrifugal forces that cause components of the sample to separate into distinct layers or bands. The ultracentrifuge is equipped with a rotor that holds the sample tubes, and the speed and duration of centrifugation can be adjusted depending on the nature of the sample. Ultracentrifugation is often used to isolate subcellular organelles, separate proteins based on their molecular weight, or purify macromolecules such as DNA and RNA. In addition, it is essential in protein studies, particularly when separating protein complexes or determining molecular weight distributions. Calibration of the ultracentrifuge involves ensuring that the speed and temperature are accurately controlled, as these factors can significantly influence the separation efficiency and quality of results. The ultracentrifuge is a cornerstone in cellular biology, biochemistry, and molecular genetics, enabling the detailed analysis of cellular components and their interactions.

These instruments—pH meters, colorimeters, spectrophoto meters, and ultracentrifuges—form the backbone of modern biological research. They empower scientists to quantify and analyze a broad range of biological phenomena with unprecedented precision, thereby advancing our understanding of life at molecular, cellular, and systemic levels. Whether studying cellular metabolism, enzyme activity, molecular structure, or the function of complex biological systems, these tools are essential for the continuous progress of biological and biomedical research. Their applications extend beyond the laboratory, influencing fields like clinical diagnostics, biotechnology, agriculture, and environmental science, where precise measurements and data-driven insights are crucial for innovation and problem-solving.

7.1 pH Meter: Principle, Calibration, and Applications

The pH meter is an essential tool in biological and chemical research, providing a precise and reliable method for measuring the hydrogen ion concentration (H^+) in a solution, which in turn indicates the acidity or alkalinity of that solution. pH is a logarithmic scale defined as:

$$pH = -\log_{10} [H^+]$$

where $[H^+]$ represents the concentration of hydrogen ions in moles per liter. The pH scale typically ranges from 0 to 14, with values less than 7 indicating an acidic environment, values greater than 7 indicating an alkaline or basic environment, and a value of 7 representing neutrality.

The pH meter operates on an electrochemical principle, wherein it uses a combination of two electrodes to measure the potential difference between them, which is directly related to the concentration of hydrogen ions in the sample. The glass electrode is sensitive to H^+ ions, while the reference electrode provides a stable, known potential. The potential difference between the two electrodes is then measured and correlated to a pH value using the Nernst equation, which describes the relationship between the electrode potential and the hydrogen ion concentration. This allows

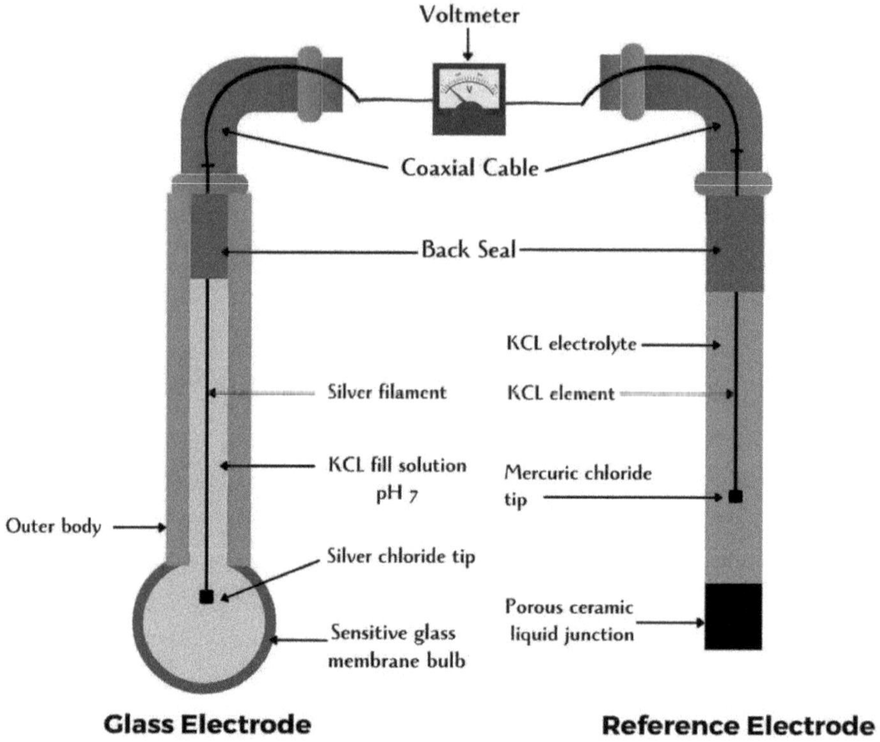

Figure: Diagram of a pH Meter Setup

COMPONENTS OF A pH METER

1. **Glass Electrode:** The glass electrode is the most critical component of the pH meter. It is specifically designed to be sensitive to hydrogen ions in the solution. The electrode consists of a glass membrane that allows the passage of H^+ ions, which causes a change in the electrical potential. This change in potential is measured and converted to a pH value. The glass electrode is typically made from a special glass that has a high ion-exchange capacity for hydrogen ions.
2. **Reference Electrode:** The reference electrode provides a stable, known potential that serves as a baseline for measuring the potential difference. Common reference electrodes

include the calomel electrode (Hg/Hg_2Cl_2) and the silver/silver chloride (Ag/AgCl) electrode. The stability of the reference electrode ensures that any changes in potential can be attributed to the sample's hydrogen ion concentration, and not due to fluctuations in the reference.

3. **Measuring Circuit**: The measuring circuit in the pH meter is responsible for amplifying the small potential difference generated between the glass and reference electrodes. The circuit then converts this potential difference into a readable pH value. It does so by using an internal calibration curve that correlates potential differences with known pH values. The circuit also compensates for temperature variations, ensuring that the pH readings are accurate across different temperatures.
4. **Digital Display**: The pH meter typically features a digital display that outputs the final pH value. Once the potential difference between the electrodes is measured and processed, the result is shown as a numerical value on the digital screen. Many modern pH meters also provide additional features, such as the ability to record data, display trends, and store previous readings for later analysis.
5. **Temperature Compensator**: pH is temperature-dependent, and fluctuations in temperature can alter the ionization of substances in solution, affecting the hydrogen ion concentration and, consequently, the pH. The temperature compensator automatically adjusts the pH value to account for variations in temperature. This ensures that the pH readings are accurate and reliable regardless of the temperature of the solution being measured. Some pH meters include an integrated temperature sensor that works in tandem with the pH electrode to continuously monitor and adjust the readings.

Calibration of the pH Meter

Calibration is a crucial step in ensuring the accuracy and reliability of pH measurements. A pH meter should be calibrated regularly—ideally before each use—to correct for any drifts in the electrode's sensitivity and to ensure that the readings are accurate.

Two-Point or Three-Point Calibration:

- The most common calibration method involves using standard buffer solutions with known pH values. For a two-point calibration, the pH meter is calibrated using two standard buffer solutions—typically one with a pH of 7.0 (neutral) and another with either a pH of 4.0 (acidic) or pH 10.0 (alkaline), depending on the expected pH range of the sample. This method is suitable for most general applications.
- **Three-point calibration** is recommended when a higher degree of precision is required or when the pH range of the sample spans a wider range. This method involves the use of three standard buffers, commonly pH 4.0, 7.0, and 10.0, providing a more accurate calibration across the full pH scale.

Calibration Procedure:

1. **Prepare Standard Buffers**: Always use fresh, properly prepared buffer solutions at the correct pH values. Buffer solutions should be purchased from reputable sources, and their expiration dates should be checked to ensure accuracy.
2. **Rinse the Electrode**: Before immersing the electrode into the buffer solutions, it should be rinsed with distilled or deionized water to remove any residues or contaminants that could affect the readings.

3. **Immerse the Electrode**: Place thc glass electrode in the first buffer solution and allow the meter to stabilize. The pH value will be displayed on the meter. If necessary, adjust the meter to match the pH value of the buffer. Repeat the process for the second (and third, if performing a three-point calibration) buffer solution.
4. **Store the Calibration Data**: After calibration, the pH meter will store the calibration data for use during measurements. It is important to regularly check and recalibrate the meter if the results appear inconsistent.

APPLICATIONS OF PH METERS

The pH meter is widely used in many areas of biological and chemical research, as pH is a critical factor in numerous biochemical and physiological processes. Some of the key applications of pH meters include:

1. **Monitoring pH in Cell Culture Media**: In cell biology and biotechnology, the pH of cell culture media is closely monitored to maintain an optimal environment for cell growth. Most mammalian cells grow best in slightly acidic to neutral conditions, and deviations from the ideal pH range can lead to cellular stress or affect cell metabolism. pH meters are used routinely to measure and adjust the pH of culture media, ensuring that cells have the best conditions for proliferation and differentiation.
2. **Soil and Water Analysis in Environmental Biology**: The pH of soil and water is a vital parameter in environmental biology, affecting plant growth, nutrient availability, and microbial activity. Soil pH influences the solubility of minerals and nutrients, impacting their uptake by plants. Similarly, the pH of water affects aquatic life, as many species have narrow

assess the health of soils and aquatic environments, guiding ecological management and conservation efforts.

3. **Biochemical Experiments Involving Enzyme Activity or Fermentation**: The pH of a solution significantly influences the activity of enzymes, many of which function optimally within a specific pH range. For example, enzymes in the stomach, like pepsin, work best in acidic environments, while enzymes in the small intestine require a more neutral pH. In biochemical experiments, pH meters are used to track pH changes in reaction mixtures, ensuring that enzymatic activity is occurring under optimal conditions. Similarly, in fermentation processes, such as in brewing or the production of biofuels, pH control is essential for the efficiency of microbial metabolism.
4. **Clinical Diagnostics (e.g., Blood and Urine pH)**: pH meters are also used in clinical diagnostics to measure the pH of bodily fluids, such as blood and urine. The pH of blood is tightly regulated, with deviations from the normal range (7.35–7.45) indicating underlying health issues like acidosis or alkalosis. Monitoring the pH of urine can provide valuable insights into kidney function, metabolic disorders, or urinary tract infections. In clinical settings, pH meters are used to conduct quick and accurate pH tests on patient samples, providing critical information for diagnosis and treatment.
5. **Food and Beverage Industry**: pH plays an important role in the quality control and production of food and beverages. For example, pH is a key factor in the production of cheese, yogurt, and fermented products, influencing texture, flavor, and safety. In the food industry, pH meters are used to monitor fermentation processes, assess the acidity of fruits and vegetables, and ensure the proper formulation of products such as sauces, jams, and beverages.

6. **Aquaculture.** In aquaculture, maintaining the right pH levels in water is crucial for the health of aquatic organisms, such as fish, shellfish, and algae. pH meters are used to monitor and regulate the pH of aquaculture systems, preventing stress and ensuring the optimal growth and reproduction of aquatic species.

The pH meter is an indispensable instrument in both research and industry, providing accurate, real-time measurements of the pH of various solutions. Its ability to quantify hydrogen ion concentration allows for precise control over environments critical to the success of biological, biochemical, and industrial processes. From maintaining optimal conditions for cell cultures and enzymes to ensuring the health of ecosystems and the quality of food products, pH meters play a central role in many fields. Understanding the principles behind pH measurement, proper calibration techniques, and applications of pH meters helps researchers, clinicians, and industry professionals to make informed decisions, optimize processes, and achieve reliable results.

7.2 Colorimeter: Components, Working Mechanism, and Uses

A colorimeter is an analytical instrument used to measure the absorbance or transmittance of light passing through a colored solution. This measurement is crucial in determining the concentration of a specific substance within the solution, particularly substances that exhibit a characteristic color.

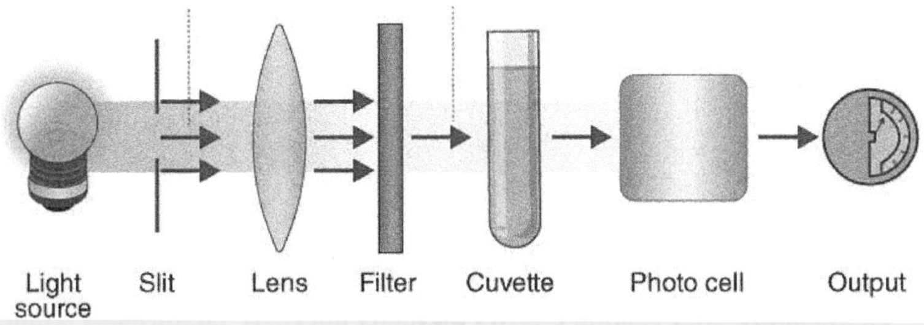

The fundamental principle behind colorimetry is Beer-Lambert's law, which states that the absorbance of light is directly proportional to the concentration of the colored substance and the path length of the solution. The relationship is expressed as:

$$A = \varepsilon cl$$

where:

- A is the absorbance of the solution (unitless),
- ε is the molar absorptivity (also known as the molar absorption coefficient, with units $L \cdot mol^{-1} \cdot cm^{-1}$),
- c is the concentration of the substance (in mol/L),
- l is the path length through which the light passes, usually measured in centimeters (cm).

The absorbance, in this case, is the fraction of light absorbed by the sample, while the transmittance (the ratio of transmitted light to incident light) is inversely related to absorbance. According to Beer-Lambert's law, by measuring the absorbance of a solution at a specific wavelength, the concentration of the colored substance can be determined. This is because each substance absorbs light at particular wavelengths based on its molecular structure.

Components of a Colorimeter

A typical colorimeter consists of several essential components that work together to measure the absorbance or transmittance of light. These components include:

1. **Light Source**: The light source is responsible for emitting light of a specific wavelength or a range of wavelengths. Most colorimeters use a tungsten filament lamp, which provides a broad spectrum of light. Some modern colorimeters may use LEDs for specific wavelengths, such as red, green, or

blue, to target specific analytes. The light source is essential for providing the initial light that passes through the sample solution.

2. **Filter System:** The filter system selectively transmits light of a specific wavelength that is most appropriate for the sample being analyzed. Colored glass filters or interference filters are commonly used in colorimeters to isolate the desired wavelength from the broader spectrum of light emitted by the light source. The choice of filter depends on the absorption characteristics of the substance being measured. For instance, if the sample absorbs blue light, a blue filter will be selected to allow only blue light to pass through the solution.
3. **Cuvette:** The cuvette is a small, transparent container that holds the sample solution. The cuvette is typically made of quartz or glass, as these materials are transparent to the visible spectrum and do not interfere with the measurement. The cuvette is usually standardized in terms of path length, often 1 cm, to ensure consistency in measurements. The solution is placed inside the cuvette, and light from the light source passes through it to be measured.
4. **Photocell/Detector:** The photocell or detector is a critical component in the colorimeter. It measures the amount of light that passes through the sample and is transmitted to the other side. The detector then converts this transmitted light into an electrical signal, which can be quantified. The amount of light that is absorbed by the sample corresponds to the difference between the light that passes through the sample and the light that enters the detector. The more the sample absorbs, the less light is detected.
5. **Display Unit:** The display unit shows the result of the absorbance or transmittance calculation. Modern colorimeters

some colorimeters, the display may show the transmittance value, which can then be converted into absorbance using the appropriate formula. In certain applications, the display might also provide real-time data or trends for continuous monitoring.

WORKING MECHANISM

The colorimeter works through the following sequence of events:

1. **Light Passage**: A specific wavelength of light is selected by the filter system and directed onto the sample solution in the cuvette. This wavelength is chosen based on the absorbance spectrum of the substance being analyzed, ensuring that it is absorbed efficiently by the target molecule.
2. **Absorption and Transmission**: As the light passes through the colored solution, a portion of the light is absorbed by the substance in the solution, while the remaining light passes through the sample. The absorption depends on the concentration of the substance and its ability to absorb light at the selected wavelength. The rest of the transmitted light passes through the sample and exits the cuvette.
3. **Detection**: The transmitted light is then measured by the photocell or detector on the other side of the cuvette. The detector captures the intensity of the transmitted light, which is inversely related to the amount of light absorbed by the sample.
4. **Calculation and Display**: The colorimeter calculates the absorbance (or transmittance) based on the measured intensity of the transmitted light. If absorbance is measured, it is calculated using the formula:

$$A = -\log_{10}\left(\frac{I_t}{I_0}\right)$$

where I_t is the transmitted light intensity, and I_0 is the incident light intensity. The absorbance value can then be related to the concentration of the analyte in the solution, using the Beer-Lambert law. The final result is displayed on the digital screen.

Applications of Colorimeters

Colorimeters are widely used in biological, chemical, and clinical laboratories for various quantitative and qualitative analyses. Some of the major applications include:

1. **Estimation of DNA, RNA, and Protein Concentrations**: One of the most common uses of colorimeters is in the quantification of biological macromolecules, such as DNA, RNA, and proteins. These macromolecules often form colored complexes with specific reagents that absorb light at particular wavelengths. For example, nucleic acids can be quantified by measuring their absorbance at 260 nm, while proteins are commonly measured using the Bradford or Biuret assays, which produce color changes related to protein concentration.
2. **Enzyme Activity Studies**: Colorimetric methods are widely used to study enzyme kinetics. In these studies, the enzyme catalyzes a reaction that produces a colored product or changes the color of a substrate. By measuring the change in absorbance over time, researchers can monitor enzyme activity, calculate reaction rates, and analyze the effects of inhibitors or activators on enzyme function.
3. **Water and Soil Quality Assessment**: Colorimeters play a crucial role in environmental biology, particularly in the assessment of water and soil quality. The concentration of various ions, such as nitrates, phosphates, and iron, can be

colored complexes with reagents that can be measured for their concentration. Monitoring the quality of water and soil is essential for maintaining healthy ecosystems and ensuring safe drinking water.

4. **Clinical Use in Blood Glucose, Bilirubin, and Hemoglobin Estimation**: In clinical settings, colorimeters are used for diagnostic purposes, such as determining blood glucose levels, bilirubin levels, and hemoglobin concentration. In the case of blood glucose, colorimetric assays based on the enzymatic conversion of glucose to a colored product are commonly used. Bilirubin, which is related to liver function, can be quantified by its characteristic absorption of light at specific wavelengths. Hemoglobin levels, essential for diagnosing anemia, can also be determined through colorimetric methods that rely on the light absorption properties of hemoglobin.
5. **Food and Beverage Industry**: Colorimeters are used in the food and beverage industry for quality control and product development. For example, the color of fruit juices, sauces, and beverages is an important quality parameter. Colorimetric methods can be used to assess color changes during processing, packaging, and storage, ensuring that products maintain their expected appearance and consumer appeal.
6. **Pharmaceutical Industry**: In pharmaceutical laboratories, colorimeters are employed for drug formulation and quality control. The concentration of certain active pharmaceutical ingredients (APIs) and excipients can be monitored using colorimetric assays. These tests ensure that pharmaceutical products meet the required specifications for potency and purity.

The colorimeter is an essential tool in laboratories across many fields, providing a straightforward and accurate method for determining the concentration of substances based on their color properties. By applying Beer-Lambert's law, colorimeters allow for the quantification of biological macromolecules, enzyme activities, environmental pollutants, and clinical markers. With its simplicity, speed, and versatility, the colorimeter remains a cornerstone in biological, environmental, and clinical analysis, playing a crucial role in research, diagnostics, and quality control across various industries.

7.3 Spectrophotometer: Types, Principles, and Applications

The spectrophotometer is a versatile and advanced analytical instrument that extends the principle of colorimetry, enabling precise measurements across a much broader range of wavelengths, from ultraviolet (UV) through visible light and into the infrared (IR) spectrum. It operates based on Beer-Lambert's law, which states that the absorption of light by a solution is proportional to both the concentration of the solute and the path length through which the light passes. This allows for accurate quantification of a substance based on its absorbance at a specific wavelength. Beer-Lambert's law is represented already in previous section.

This principle forms the foundation for the spectrophotometer's ability to quantify substances in solution by analyzing the intensity of light absorbed at specific wavelengths.

While colorimeters typically use a single wavelength of light, spectrophotometers offer much greater versatility by allowing for a broader spectrum of wavelengths, providing more detailed information about the absorption characteristics of a substance. This is especially useful in applications such as studying the structure and properties of molecules, detecting impurities, and performing complex biochemical assays.

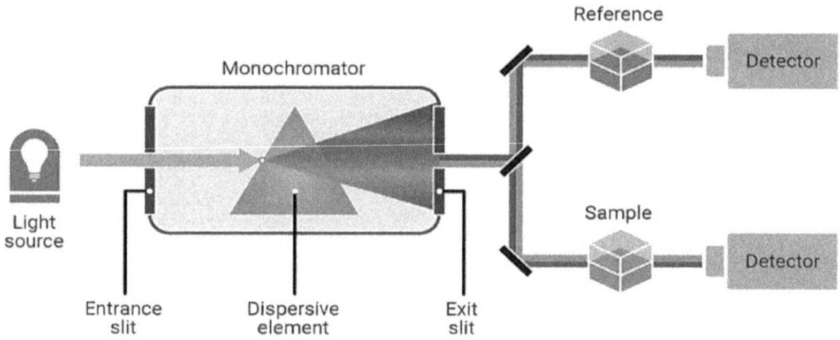

Figure: UV-Visible Spectrophotometer Diagram

TYPES OF SPECTROPHOTOMETERS

Spectrophotometers come in various configurations, each designed for specific applications that require precise light measurement across different spectral ranges. The main types of spectrophotometers include:

1. **UV-Visible Spectrophotometer**: This is the most commonly used spectrophotometer, which operates across the ultraviolet (UV) and visible light ranges, typically from 190 nm to 700 nm. It is widely used for determining the concentration of nucleic acids (DNA, RNA), proteins, and other biomolecules. The UV-Vis spectrophotometer is also used to study enzyme kinetics, perform quality control on chemical compounds, and assess the presence of specific molecular groups in samples. It is a critical tool in molecular biology, biochemistry, and environmental studies.
2. **Infrared (IR) Spectrophotometer**: This type of spectrophotometer operates in the infrared range (typically 700 nm to 1 mm) and is used to measure molecular vibrations. IR spectrophotometers provide insight into the structure

of organic compounds, detecting functional groups and molecular bonds. IR spectroscopy is particularly valuable in organic chemistry for structural analysis, as it can identify specific bonds and functional groups within molecules. It is used in pharmaceutical and materials science applications.

3. **Double Beam Spectrophotometer**: In a double beam spectrophotometer, the light from the source is split into two paths: one path goes through the sample, and the other serves as a reference. This configuration allows for real-time compensation of fluctuations in the light source or environmental factors. The reference beam helps maintain accurate measurements by ensuring that any changes in the light intensity or other external conditions do not affect the measurement of absorbance from the sample. Double beam spectrophotometers are commonly used in high-precision applications, such as pharmaceutical quality control and scientific research.
4. **Fluorescence Spectrophotometer**: A fluorescence spectrophotometer detects light emitted by a molecule after it absorbs incident light and then re-emits it at a longer wavelength. This is useful for studying molecules that naturally fluoresce or that are tagged with fluorescent probes. Fluorescence spectrophotometry is widely used in molecular biology, cell biology, and analytical chemistry for applications such as detecting low concentrations of biomolecules, investigating protein interactions, and performing high-sensitivity assays. It provides greater sensitivity than absorbance-based methods, making it valuable in detecting trace amounts of substances.

COMPONENTS OF A SPECTROPHOTOMETER

A spectrophotometer consists of several key components that work together to measure the absorbance or transmittance of light by a sample. These components are critical to the functioning of the instrument and ensure accurate and reliable measurements.

1. **Light Source**: The light source is responsible for producing the beam of light that is directed through the sample. The type of light source used depends on the wavelength range of interest:
   - o **Deuterium lamp**: Typically used for UV measurements (190–400 nm).
   - o **Tungsten lamp**: Used for the visible range (400–700 nm) of light.
   - o **Xenon or halogen lamps**: Can cover a broader range, including UV and visible spectra.
2. **Monochromator**: The monochromator is a critical component that isolates specific wavelengths from the broader light spectrum produced by the light source. This is typically achieved using diffraction gratings or prisms that separate the light into its constituent wavelengths. The monochromator allows the user to select the precise wavelength of light that corresponds to the maximum absorbance of the substance being studied.
3. **Sample Holder**: The sample holder, typically a cuvette, is where the sample solution is placed. The cuvette is positioned in the light path, and the light passes through the solution, where some is absorbed based on the chemical properties of the sample. Cuvettes are usually made of materials like quartz or glass, depending on the wavelength range used.

4. **Detector:** The detector captures the light that passes through the sample and converts the light intensity into an electrical signal. Common types of detectors include:
   - o **Photomultiplier tubes (PMTs):** Highly sensitive detectors that are typically used for low light intensities, especially in fluorescence spectrophotometry.
   - o **Diode array detectors:** These allow for simultaneous detection of multiple wavelengths, providing rapid scanning of a broad spectrum.
5. **Microprocessor and Display:** The microprocessor processes the data from the detector and calculates the absorbance or transmittance based on the light intensity detected. The processed results are then displayed on a digital screen, and in more advanced models, data can be stored for further analysis. Some spectrophotometers are connected to specialized software for enhanced data analysis, such as creating absorbance spectra or generating calibration curves for quantification.

Applications of Spectrophotometers

Spectrophotometers have a broad range of applications across multiple scientific disciplines due to their ability to measure light absorption at specific wavelengths. Some of the key applications of spectrophotometers include:

1. **Quantification of Nucleic Acids and Proteins:** UV-Vis spectrophotometers are widely used in molecular biology for quantifying nucleic acids (DNA and RNA) and proteins. The absorbance of nucleic acids at 260 nm and proteins at 280 nm is commonly measured to determine their concentration in a sample. The ratio of absorbance at 260 nm to 280 nm (A260/

A280) is used to assess the purity of DNA or RNA, with a ratio of approximately 1.8 indicating pure DNA.

2. **Determination of Enzyme Kinetics:** Spectrophotometers are used to study enzyme kinetics by measuring the rate of reaction in real time. Enzyme reactions often produce colored products, and the absorbance of these products can be measured at specific wavelengths to monitor the progress of the reaction. This data can be used to calculate parameters such as the reaction rate and enzyme efficiency.
3. **Detection of Impurities in Pharmaceutical Products:** In pharmaceutical quality control, spectrophotometers are used to detect impurities and degradation products in drug formulations. By measuring absorbance at specific wavelengths, it is possible to identify and quantify contaminants, ensuring the purity and safety of pharmaceutical products.
4. **Analysis of Chlorophyll, Pigments, and Secondary Metabolites in Plants:** Spectrophotometers are used in plant science to analyze the concentration of chlorophyll and other pigments in plant tissues. By measuring the absorbance of light at specific wavelengths, researchers can assess the photosynthetic efficiency of plants and analyze secondary metabolites such as flavonoids and alkaloids, which have various biological activities.
5. **Monitoring Microbial Growth:** In microbiology, spectrophotometers are frequently used to measure the optical density (OD) of microbial cultures. The OD at 600 nm (OD600) is often used to estimate the growth of bacteria or yeast in culture media, providing a quick and non-invasive method to monitor growth rates.
6. **Environmental Monitoring:** Spectrophotometers play a critical role in environmental monitoring, particularly in assessing water quality. They are used to measure the concentration of pollutants such as nitrates, phosphates,

heavy metals, and other contaminants in water samples. These measurements are crucial for monitoring ecosystem health and detecting pollution levels.

7. **Food and Beverage Industry:** Spectrophotometers are used in the food industry to monitor the color, quality, and concentration of ingredients in food and beverages. For example, the color intensity of fruit juices or the concentration of antioxidants in foods can be analyzed using spectrophotometry, ensuring product consistency and quality.

Spectrophotometers are indispensable tools in modern scientific research and industrial applications, offering precise and reliable measurements of light absorption across a wide range of wavelengths. By extending the principles of colorimetry, spectrophotometers provide detailed insights into molecular characteristics, concentrations, and behaviors. Whether for quantifying biomolecules, studying enzyme reactions, or analyzing environmental samples, the versatility and accuracy of spectrophotometers make them essential in fields ranging from biochemistry to environmental science.

7.4 Ultracentrifuge: Principle, Design, and Applications

Ultracentrifugation is a technique used to separate particles in a solution based on their size, shape, and density by subjecting them to extremely high centrifugal forces, often reaching up to 100,000 revolutions per minute (rpm). The principle of ultracentrifugation is grounded in the concept of sedimentation, where particles within a solution experience centrifugal forces that cause them to move towards the bottom of a container, depending on their mass and density. The force experienced by a particle in an ultracentrifuge is given by the following formula:

$$F = m \cdot r \cdot \omega^2$$

where:

- F is the centrifugal force,
- m is the mass of the particle,
- r is the radial distance from the center of rotation, and
- ω is the angular velocity (the rate of rotation).

At high speeds, the centrifugal force generated causes particles to sediment at different rates, allowing for their separation. This process can be described by two main principles:

1. **Sedimentation Velocity**: In this mode, particles are separated based on their rate of sedimentation under the influence of centrifugal force. Larger, denser particles move faster and sediment at the bottom of the tube quicker than smaller or less dense particles.
2. **Sedimentation Equilibrium**: This process occurs when a particle reaches a point where the centrifugal force pulling it downward is balanced by the diffusion force trying to keep it in suspension. This approach is often used to determine the density of macromolecules or particles in a mixture.

Ultracentrifugation is an extremely useful technique in molecular biology, biochemistry, and cell biology for separating and analyzing various biological macromolecules and organelles.

Design and Types of Ultracentrifuges

Ultracentrifuges are designed to generate very high speeds and are typically used for the separation of complex mixtures. The design varies based on the intended application, and ultracentrifuges come in two main types:

1. **Preparative Ultracentrifuge**: This type is used for the large-scale separation of biomolecules, organelles, and other cellular components. It is primarily used in preparative work,

where large volumes of samples need to be processed. The preparative ultracentrifuge is designed to handle multiple sample tubes or containers, and it is equipped with a high-speed rotor that spins the sample at extremely high velocities to separate components effectively.

2. **Analytical Ultracentrifuge:** Analytical ultracentrifuges are used for more detailed analysis of macromolecules, where their behavior can be studied in real-time. These instruments are primarily employed to examine properties such as molecular weight, size distribution, and conformational changes of macromolecules. The optical system in analytical ultracentrifuges allows the monitoring of sedimentation profiles, which provides valuable data on molecular interactions and the hydrodynamic properties of proteins, nucleic acids, or other biological macromolecules.

MAJOR COMPONENTS OF AN ULTRACENTRIFUGE

An ultracentrifuge consists of several essential components that enable its high-speed operation and ensure accurate separations. These components include:

1. **Rotor:** The rotor is a crucial part of the ultracentrifuge that holds the sample tubes. It is designed to rotate at extremely high speeds and can accommodate different types of sample containers, such as tubes or bottles. The rotor is typically made from durable materials like titanium or carbon fiber, which can withstand the immense forces generated during high-speed centrifugation.
2. **Vacuum System:** The vacuum system is used to reduce air resistance and friction, which can generate heat and hinder the performance of the centrifuge. By creating a vacuum, the

3. **Cooling System:** The cooling system is essential in maintaining a low temperature during ultracentrifugation. High-speed rotation generates a significant amount of heat, which could potentially denature or damage biological samples. To prevent this, ultracentrifuges are equipped with cooling systems that maintain a controlled temperature during the separation process, ensuring that samples remain stable.
4. **Drive System:** The drive system generates the high-speed rotation necessary for ultracentrifugation. It consists of motors and bearings that enable the rotor to reach extremely high speeds while maintaining stability and precision.
5. **Optical Systems (in Analytical Models):** In analytical ultracentrifuges, optical systems are used to monitor sedimentation in real time. These systems typically consist of a light source and detectors that measure the absorption or scattering of light as particles sediment. This data is critical for studying the dynamics of macromolecules in solution and understanding their molecular properties.

Applications of Ultracentrifugation

Ultracentrifugation is a powerful tool in various scientific fields, particularly in the isolation and study of macromolecules, cells, and organelles. Some of the major applications include:

1. **Isolation of Cellular Organelles:** Ultracentrifugation is commonly used to isolate specific cellular organelles, such as mitochondria, ribosomes, nuclei, and lysosomes, from complex cell homogenates. By adjusting the centrifugation speed and time, researchers can effectively separate organelles based on their size, density, and sedimentation properties. This technique is invaluable in cellular biology, where studying isolated organelles can provide insights into their structure and function.

2. **Separation of DNA, RNA, Proteins, and Viruses:** Ultracentrifugation is widely used for the separation and purification of nucleic acids (DNA and RNA), proteins, and even viruses. It can be used to separate these biomolecules from contaminants or to concentrate them from dilute solutions. This process is often coupled with density gradient centrifugation, which allows for even more precise separation based on the density of the components.
3. **Study of Protein-Protein or Protein-DNA Interactions:** Analytical ultracentrifugation is a powerful method for studying molecular interactions, such as protein-protein or protein-DNA interactions. By observing the sedimentation behavior of protein complexes, researchers can determine their size, shape, and interaction dynamics. This is particularly useful for understanding the mechanisms of cellular processes, such as DNA replication, transcription, and translation.
4. **Lipoprotein Analysis in Clinical Diagnostics:** Ultracentrifugation is also applied in clinical diagnostics to analyze lipoproteins in blood plasma. Lipoproteins, such as high-density lipoprotein (HDL) and low-density lipoprotein (LDL), are important biomarkers in cardiovascular disease. Ultracentrifugation can be used to isolate and quantify these lipoproteins, providing valuable information for diagnosing lipid metabolism disorders.
5. **Density Gradient Centrifugation for DNA Isolation:** One of the most well-known applications of ultracentrifugation is density gradient centrifugation, particularly for isolating DNA. For example, cesium chloride gradient ultracentrifugation is commonly used to separate DNA molecules based on their density. This method is especially useful for purifying plasmid

6. **Characterization of Nanoparticles:** Ultracentrifugation is increasingly used to characterize nanoparticles, including those used in drug delivery systems. By separating nanoparticles based on their size and density, researchers can assess their stability, purity, and uniformity. This is critical for ensuring the efficacy and safety of nanomedicines.

Ultracentrifugation is a cornerstone technique in modern molecular biology and biochemistry. Its ability to separate particles based on size, shape, and density has made it an indispensable tool in the study of cellular components, biomolecules, and molecular interactions. From isolating cellular organelles to analyzing protein complexes and studying macromolecular properties, ultracentrifugation continues to be essential for both basic research and clinical applications. The high precision and versatility of ultracentrifuges ensure their continued relevance in the advancing fields of molecular biology, pharmacology, and diagnostics.

CONCLUSION

Analytical instruments such as pH meters, colorimeters, spectrophotometers, and ultracentrifuges are essential tools in modern biological and biochemical research, providing precise measurements and enabling detailed analysis of complex biological systems. These instruments, although grounded in fundamental physical principles, offer a wide range of applications across various scientific disciplines, from molecular biology to environmental monitoring and clinical diagnostics. For instance, pH meters measure the acidity or alkalinity of a solution by assessing the concentration of hydrogen ions, which is critical in experiments involving enzyme activity, cellular processes, and chemical reactions. Colorimeters and spectrophotometers, which measure light absorption or transmission at specific wavelengths, are vital for quantifying the concentration of substances in a sample, such as proteins, nucleic acids, or pigments.

Spectrophotometry, in particular, allows researchers to analyze the molecular composition of samples by measuring how they interact with light, enabling studies in fields like protein quantification, DNA sequencing, and metabolic analysis.

Ultracentrifuges are used to separate components of biological mixtures based on their size, shape, and density, an essential technique in protein purification, DNA extraction, and cellular fractionation. The high-speed spinning of samples generates centrifugal forces that help isolate organelles, macromolecules, and other particles for further study. These instruments, though incredibly powerful, require a strong understanding of their principles, calibration procedures, and limitations to ensure accurate and reliable results. Calibration ensures the precision of measurements, while awareness of each instrument's limitations—such as sensitivity, resolution, and sample size constraints—prevents errors and ensures the validity of experimental outcomes.

A comprehensive understanding of how these instruments function, how to calibrate them, and their potential sources of error is crucial for generating reliable data in experimental biology. Whether in the study of biochemical reactions, environmental pollution monitoring, or disease diagnostics, the accurate use of analytical instruments forms the cornerstone of scientific discovery and technological advancement in both research and applied sciences.

QUESTIONS

- Explain the principle, components, and calibration procedure of a pH meter, and describe its applications in biological research.
- Discuss the working mechanism of a colorimeter and explain its applications in the estimation

- Describe the different types of spectrophotometers and their applications in biological and biochemical research.
- What is the principle of ultracentrifugation? Discuss the design and major components of an ultracentrifuge and its applications in isolating cellular organelles.
- Compare and contrast the working principles of a colorimeter and a spectrophotometer, highlighting their differences and similarities in biological applications.
- Explain the importance of calibration in analytical instruments such as pH meters, colorimeters, and spectrophotometers. How does calibration affect the accuracy of experimental results?
- Discuss the role of ultracentrifugation in the separation and analysis of biomolecules. Provide examples of its applications in protein and nucleic acid research.
- How does the Beer-Lambert law apply to both colorimetry and spectrophotometry? Discuss its significance in quantitative analysis in biological research.

CHAPTER 8

ADVANCED MICROSCOPY AND IMAGING TECHNIQUES

Microscopy is an indispensable tool in biological research, enabling the study of cellular structures and physiological processes that are invisible to the naked eye. Over time, advancements in microscopy techniques have revolutionized our ability to visualize biological systems at an increasingly detailed level. Light microscopy, including methods like fluorescence and phase contrast microscopy, allows for real-time observation of live cells, enhancing our understanding of cellular functions and protein dynamics. Fluorescence microscopy, in particular, uses specific dyes to target biomolecules, providing insights into protein localization and gene expression. Phase contrast microscopy, enhances the contrast of transparent samples, allowing for the observation of cellular structures without staining, making it ideal for living cell studies.

To light microscopy, electron microscopy (SEM, TEM, STEM) has provided unparalleled resolution, enabling visualization of cellular components at the nanoscale. SEM allows for detailed imaging of cell surfaces, while TEM provides insights into internal cellular structures like organelles. Scanning transmission electron microscopy (STEM) merges the benefits of both SEM and TEM, offering a comprehensive look at both surface and internal structures. The rise of confocal microscopy has further enhanced three-dimensional imaging, enabling clear views of thick samples by eliminating out-of-focus light, and digital imaging microscopy techniques have vastly expanded our understanding of biology, offering unprecedented insights into molecular interactions, cellular dynamics, and tissue organization, with future innovations promising even greater imaging capabilities.

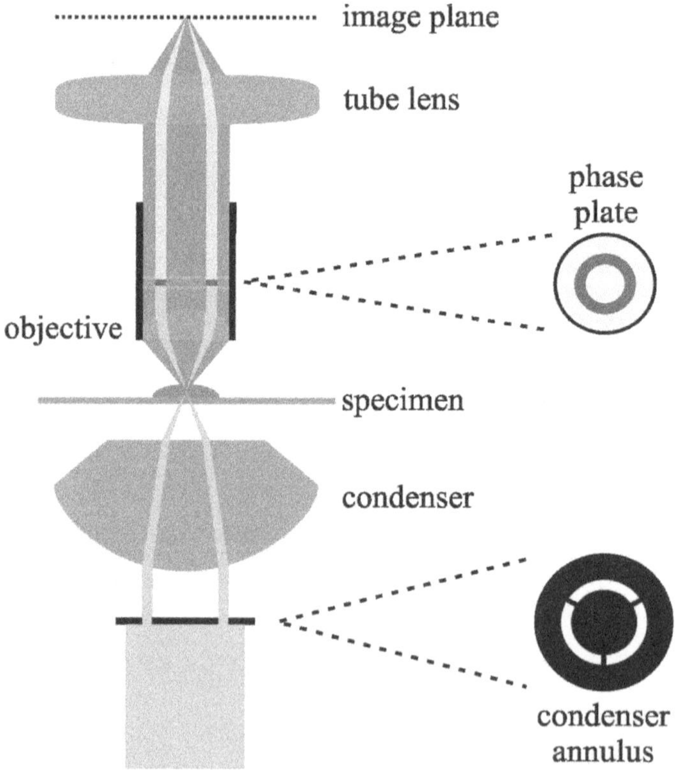

Figure: Phase Contrast Microscopy Workflow

8.1 Light and Electron Microscopy (SEM, TEM, STEM)

Microscopy is a cornerstone of biological research, providing the essential tools to observe the hidden world of cells and subcellular structures. Light microscopy and electron microscopy (SEM, TEM, STEM) are the two primary methods for studying specimens in detail. While light microscopy remains widely accessible and versatile, electron microscopy offers extraordinary resolution, allowing scientists to visualize structures at the molecular and atomic levels.

This chapter delves into the principles, methods, and applications of light and electron microscopy, exploring their capabilities, limitations, and role in advancing biological and material science.

Light Microscopy

Light microscopy is one of the oldest and most widely used techniques for studying biological specimens. It is an essential tool for visualizing larger cellular structures, tissues, and microorganisms. By magnifying specimens with visible light, light microscopy provides a straightforward and versatile approach to study biological samples.

Principle of Light Microscopy

The principle of light microscopy is based on the interaction of light with the specimen. Visible light passes through the specimen or is reflected from it, and the transmitted or reflected light interacts with various components of the specimen. The resulting patterns of light and dark areas, which arise due to differences in refractive indices or staining, are captured by lenses and projected onto the viewer's eye or a camera. The lenses focus the light and magnify the image of the specimen, typically within the range of 40x to 1000x magnification, although higher magnifications can be achieved with advanced techniques like oil immersion.

Types of Light Microscopes

1. **Brightfield Microscopy**: This is the most common type of light microscopy, where light passes directly through the sample. It is best suited for stained specimens that absorb light. In brightfield microscopy, the specimen appears dark against a bright background. This type of microscopy is

morphology and structures, such as cell shape, size, and basic tissue architecture. However, it is limited by contrast when observing transparent or unstained samples.

2. **Darkfield Microscopy**: In darkfield microscopy, light is directed at the sample at an angle, and only the light scattered by the specimen enters the objective lens. This enhances the contrast, making the specimen appear bright against a dark background. This technique is particularly useful for observing live cells and microorganisms without the need for staining, providing high contrast images of transparent or unstained specimens. It is commonly used for studying the movement and behavior of microorganisms and live cell cultures.
3. **Fluorescence Microscopy**: Fluorescence microscopy utilizes ultraviolet (UV) light to excite specific fluorescent molecules or dyes within the specimen. The specimen then emits light at a longer wavelength, which is captured by the microscope. This method allows for the observation of specific components within cells, such as proteins, organelles, or nucleic acids, that have been tagged with fluorescent markers. Fluorescence microscopy is widely used in molecular and cellular biology to study protein localization, gene expression, and cellular dynamics. By using different fluorophores, scientists can observe multiple targets simultaneously in a single sample, providing powerful insights into complex biological processes.

APPLICATIONS OF LIGHT MICROSCOPY

Light microscopy plays a crucial role in various fields of research, from microbiology to histology. It is instrumental in the examination of cellular morphology, tissue organization, and the behavior of microorganisms. Some applications include:

- Visualizing cell division and cellular structures like the nucleus, cytoplasm, and cell membrane.
- Studying tissue samples to identify pathological changes such as cancerous cells.
- Observing the growth and morphology of microorganisms in clinical microbiology.

Despite its broad applicability, light microscopy has its limitations. Its resolution is constrained by the wavelength of visible light, meaning it is incapable of observing structures smaller than approximately 200 nm. Thus, fine structures like subcellular organelles and macromolecules remain beyond the reach of conventional light microscopy.

Electron Microscopy (EM)

Electron microscopy (EM) is a powerful imaging technique that surpasses light microscopy in terms of resolution. Unlike light microscopy, which uses visible light, electron microscopy uses electron beams to illuminate the specimen. Electrons have much shorter wavelengths than visible light, which allows for much higher resolution and the ability to resolve fine details at the molecular and atomic levels. Electron microscopes can achieve magnifications of up to 10 million times, enabling scientists to observe structures such as viruses, macromolecules, and subcellular components.

Transmission Electron Microscopy (TEM)

Transmission electron microscopy (TEM) is one of the most commonly used types of electron microscopy. TEM works by passing a beam of electrons through a thin specimen. The electrons interact with the specimen, and the transmitted electrons are captured to form provides extremely high resolution, making it possible to observe intracellular structures, including organelles, macromolecular complexes, and even individual molecules.

Sample Preparation for TEM: The preparation of samples for TEM is a complex process. Specimens must be fixed to preserve their structure, dehydrated, and embedded in resin to make them easier to slice into ultra-thin sections. These thin sections are required because electrons can only penetrate thin materials. After sectioning, the sample is placed in a vacuum chamber and subjected to electron bombardment, producing an image that can be magnified and analyzed.

Resolution: TEM is capable of achieving resolution up to 0.1 nm, allowing it to visualize fine details such as the structure of membranes, ribosomes, viruses, and protein complexes at the molecular level. This resolution surpasses that of light microscopy by orders of magnitude, making it the go-to technique for observing the ultrastructure of cells and viruses.

Applications of TEM: TEM is particularly useful for:

- Observing subcellular structures, such as the endoplasmic reticulum, mitochondria, and Golgi apparatus.
- Studying the detailed structure of viruses and bacteria.
- Investigating the molecular organization of materials at the atomic scale.

Scanning Electron Microscopy (SEM)

Scanning electron microscopy (SEM) differs from TEM in that it scans the surface of a specimen rather than passing electrons through it. In SEM, a focused beam of electrons is directed at the surface of the specimen, and the scattered electrons are captured to create a high-resolution image. SEM allows for the examination of three-dimensional surfaces, providing detailed information about the morphology and surface topography of samples.

Sample Preparation for SEM: Specimens are typically coated with a thin layer of a conductive material, such as gold or carbon, to prevent charging and ensure the efficient flow of electrons. Unlike TEM, SEM samples do not need to be sliced into thin sections, making it easier to study the surface features of bulkier specimens.

Resolution: SEM can achieve resolution in the range of 1-10 nm, enabling detailed imaging of surface structures, including cell membranes, surface morphology of tissues, and the arrangement of materials at the nanoscale.

Applications of SEM: SEM is particularly useful for:

- Studying the surface topography of biological samples, such as plant cells, animal tissues, and microorganisms.
- Analyzing materials science samples to examine the surface features of metals, ceramics, and polymers.
- Imaging the morphology and surface structures of microorganisms and other small organisms.

Scanning Transmission Electron Microscopy (STEM)

Scanning transmission electron microscopy (STEM) is a hybrid technique that combines the principles of both TEM and SEM. STEM uses a finely focused electron beam that scans across the specimen, with transmitted electrons detected to form an image. This technique provides the high resolution of TEM with the ability to analyze surface features like SEM.

Resolution: STEM is capable of achieving atomic-scale resolution, often below 1 nm, making it one of the most powerful imaging techniques available for the study of biological and material samples at the atomic level.

Applications of STEM: STEM is used for:

4. Atomic-level imaging of biological samples, such as thin sections of tissues.
5. Studying the fine structure of materials, including semiconductor materials and nanomaterials.
6. Analyzing surface structures in combination with 3D tomography.

ADVANTAGES AND LIMITATIONS OF ELECTRON MICROSCOPY

Advantages of Electron Microscopy:

- **High Resolution**: Electron microscopes provide exceptional resolution, allowing for the observation of structures at the molecular and atomic levels.
- **Detailed Imaging**: TEM, SEM, and STEM enable the visualization of fine cellular and subcellular structures, providing crucial insights into the ultrastructure of cells, tissues, and materials.
- **3D Imaging**: SEM and STEM allow for the generation of three-dimensional images, which are valuable for studying surface structures and complex materials.

Limitations of Electron Microscopy:

- **Complex Sample Preparation**: Electron microscopy requires extensive sample preparation, including fixation, dehydration, and sectioning, which can be time-consuming and may alter the structure of the specimen.

- **Inability to Observe Living Samples:** Electron microscopy operates in a vacuum, which makes it impossible to observe living organisms or cells in their natural state.
- **High Cost and Expertise:** Electron microscopes are expensive, and their operation requires specialized training and expertise.
- **Limited Field of View:** While electron microscopes provide incredible resolution, they typically offer a smaller field of view compared to light microscopes.

Both light and electron microscopy are indispensable tools for biological research, each with its unique strengths and applications. Light microscopy provides a versatile and accessible means of observing cells, tissues, and microorganisms, while electron microscopy offers unparalleled resolution for studying fine cellular details and subcellular structures. Together, these techniques have advanced our understanding of the complexity of biological systems and materials science, enabling groundbreaking discoveries in fields ranging from molecular biology to nanotechnology. As technology continues to advance, these imaging techniques are expected to evolve further, offering even more detailed insights into the intricate world of biological and material science.

8.2 Phase Contrast and Confocal Microscopy

Microscopy techniques have evolved significantly over the years, with various methods designed to enhance the ability to visualize biological structures with higher precision and contrast. Among the most influential techniques are phase contrast microscopy and confocal microscopy, each with its own strengths and applications.

specimens, especially those that are transparent and difficult to visualize with traditional light microscopy. This section explores the principles, features, and applications of these two advanced imaging techniques.

PHASE CONTRAST MICROSCOPY

Phase contrast microscopy is a specialized type of light microscopy developed to enhance contrast in transparent specimens without the need for staining. This makes it particularly valuable for observing living, unstained biological samples, such as cells and microorganisms. Unlike conventional brightfield microscopy, which relies on light absorption and transmission, phase contrast microscopy exploits differences in the refractive index of different parts of a specimen.

PRINCIPLE OF PHASE CONTRAST MICROSCOPY

The basic principle of phase contrast microscopy involves the manipulation of phase shifts in light as it passes through various components of a specimen. When light passes through a transparent object, such as a cell, different structures within the cell, such as the nucleus, cytoplasm, and organelles, refract light to different extents due to their varying refractive indices. These differences in refraction cause phase shifts in the light waves. Phase contrast microscopy converts these phase differences into variations in amplitude (brightness) through a specialized optical system. This process enhances contrast, making otherwise invisible or faint cellular components more distinct, even without the use of stains or dyes.

Sample Preparation and Resolution

One of the primary advantages of phase contrast microscopy is that it requires no sample preparation involving staining or fixation, which is especially beneficial for live cell imaging. The technique works well for observing living cells in their natural state, making it invaluable for studying cellular processes such as mitosis, motility, and dynamic changes in cell shape. The resolution of phase contrast microscopy is similar to that of conventional light microscopy, typically up to 0.2 μm. While this is sufficient for observing cellular components such as the nucleus and large organelles, finer structures like subcellular components may not be fully resolved.

Applications of Phase Contrast Microscopy

Phase contrast microscopy is widely used in many biological and medical research applications, particularly when it is essential to observe live cells in an unstained, natural environment. Some notable applications include:

- **Live cell imaging**: Monitoring the movement, growth, and behavior of living cells over time.
- **Cellular processes**: Observing cellular processes like mitosis (cell division), changes in cell shape during motility, and other dynamic processes like phagocytosis or intracellular transport.
- **Microbial studies**: Studying the morphology and motility of microorganisms without the need for staining, which could interfere with their natural behavior.

While phase contrast microscopy provides high contrast for transparent samples, it does come with some limitations, including optical artifacts such as halos around edges that may obscure fine other techniques like electron microscopy, which can visualize finer cellular structures.

CONFOCAL MICROSCOPY

Confocal microscopy is a more advanced imaging technique that offers significantly improved resolution over conventional light microscopy. This technique uses laser light to scan specimens at various depths, enabling the capture of high-resolution, three-dimensional (3D) images. Confocal microscopy has become a cornerstone in biological research, particularly for applications that require detailed 3D imaging of thick tissue samples or studying cellular dynamics in vivo.

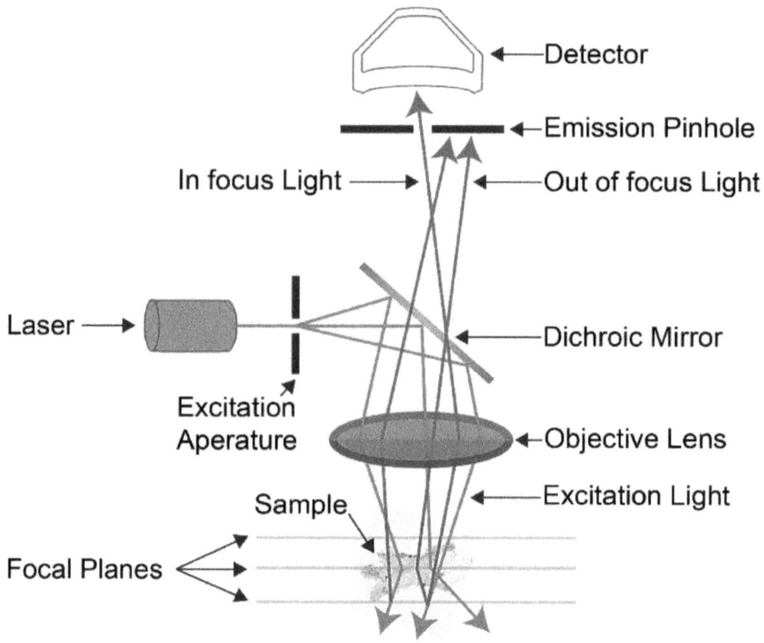

Figure: *Confocal Microscopy Imaging Process*

Principle of Confocal Microscopy

The core principle behind confocal microscopy is its ability to focus a laser beam onto a single point within the specimen and capture emitted light only from that focal point. This is achieved using a special optical arrangement that includes a pinhole aperture. The pinhole blocks out-of-focus light from other parts of the specimen, ensuring that only light emitted from the plane of focus is collected. As the laser scans the specimen point by point, layer by layer, a high-resolution image is obtained. By compiling these individual images from different focal planes, researchers can reconstruct detailed 3D images of the specimen.

One of the key advantages of confocal microscopy is that it allows for optical sectioning. Unlike traditional microscopy, where light from out-of-focus regions contributes to the image, confocal microscopy only collects light from the in-focus regions. This significantly improves image clarity, particularly when studying thick or complex samples like tissues. As a result, confocal microscopy is widely used for three-dimensional imaging of cellular and tissue architecture.

Sample Preparation and Resolution

For confocal microscopy, specimens must typically be labeled with fluorescent dyes or fluorescent proteins to highlight specific structures or components within the sample. These fluorescent labels are excited by the laser light and emit light at longer wavelengths, which is captured by the microscope. The resolution of confocal microscopy is significantly better than conventional light microscopy, typically in the range of 0.1 μm, allowing for more detailed imaging of cellular structures, organelles, and macromolecules.

Because of its ability to acquire high-resolution images from

Researchers can visualize the organization of cells and tissues in 3D, which is crucial for understanding developmental processes, cellular interactions, and disease mechanisms.

APPLICATIONS OF CONFOCAL MICROSCOPY

Confocal microscopy has broad applications across multiple fields of biological and biomedical research. Some of the most common uses include:

- **3D Imaging of Tissues**: Confocal microscopy enables the visualization of entire tissues in three dimensions, allowing researchers to study tissue architecture and cellular arrangements in ways that traditional microscopy cannot.
- **Fluorescent Protein Localization**: By using genetically encoded fluorescent proteins (e.g., GFP), confocal microscopy enables the study of protein localization in living cells. This is particularly useful for understanding cellular signaling, protein trafficking, and organelle dynamics.
- **Developmental Biology**: The ability to visualize developing organisms at high resolution makes confocal microscopy invaluable in developmental biology. Researchers can observe processes like embryogenesis, organ formation, and cell differentiation in real-time.
- **Neuroscience**: In neuroscience, confocal microscopy is often used to study the structure and connectivity of neurons in the brain. This allows for detailed observations of dendritic branching, synaptic connections, and neuronal activity in animal models.

Advantages and Limitations

Confocal microscopy offers several key advantages over traditional light microscopy:

- **High resolution**: The technique provides significantly better resolution, allowing for the observation of subcellular structures and the generation of high-quality 3D images.
- **Optical sectioning**: Confocal microscopy enables the imaging of thick samples without the need for physical sectioning, maintaining sample integrity.
- **Fluorescence imaging**: The ability to use multiple fluorescent dyes enables researchers to observe different cellular components simultaneously, providing a powerful tool for studying complex biological processes.

However, there are some limitations associated with confocal microscopy:

- **Cost**: Confocal microscopes are typically much more expensive than conventional light microscopes, making them less accessible to some laboratories.
- **Photobleaching**: Fluorescent dyes can degrade over time when exposed to light, limiting the duration of imaging experiments. This phenomenon, known as photobleaching, can affect the accuracy and reliability of results.
- **Depth penetration**: Although confocal microscopy provides superior resolution for surface imaging, its ability to penetrate thick samples is still limited. This can be particularly challenging when imaging tissues or samples that are several micrometers in thickness.

Both phase contrast microscopy and confocal microscopy have

resolution and contrast. Phase contrast microscopy allows for the study of living cells without staining, making it ideal for observing cellular processes in real time. The confocal microscopy offers a higher level of resolution and the ability to generate three-dimensional images of thick samples, making it an invaluable tool in developmental biology, tissue imaging, and fluorescence-based studies. Despite their unique advantages, both techniques come with certain limitations, such as optical artifacts in phase contrast microscopy and photobleaching in confocal microscopy. Nevertheless, these techniques have become indispensable for advancing our understanding of the intricate and dynamic processes occurring within living organisms.

8.3 Photomicrography and Digital Imaging Techniques

The field of microscopy has seen revolutionary advancements with the introduction of photomicrography and digital imaging techniques, which have significantly improved the way biological specimens are visualized, documented, and analyzed. These advancements have provided researchers with more powerful tools to capture and process images, facilitating deeper insights into the structure and behavior of microscopic organisms and cells. Photomicrography, a technique that has been in use for decades, is complemented by digital imaging technologies that enable real-time imaging, enhanced analysis, and quantification, further pushing the boundaries of biological research. This section explores the principles, applications, and advantages of both photomicrography and digital imaging techniques.

PHOTOMICROGRAPHY

Photomicrography is the practice of capturing high-resolution photographs through a microscope, and it has long been a vital tool in biological research. It involves attaching a camera or digital sensor to the microscope and using the microscope's magnifying capabilities to photograph specimens at various levels of magnification. The images captured through photomicrography are invaluable for documenting experimental results, preserving data for long-term storage, and providing visual evidence for academic publications.

PRINCIPLE OF PHOTOMICROGRAPHY

In photomicrography, the camera or digital sensor records the image produced by the microscope's objective lenses. The optical system of the microscope focuses light from the specimen to form an image, which is then captured by the camera. Modern photomicrography typically employs high-quality digital cameras or CCD (charge-coupled device) sensors that are capable of capturing sharp, detailed images. These images can be further enhanced or processed using image-editing software to improve features such as contrast, brightness, and resolution, leading to high-quality visuals that facilitate in-depth analysis.

While sample preparation depends on the type of microscopy being used (e.g., brightfield, fluorescence, or phase contrast), the primary goal of photomicrography is to record the specimen's appearance at various magnifications, thus enabling detailed observation of biological structures and processes. It is an indispensable tool for biological researchers, providing permanent records of research findings and a means for publication in academic journals.

APPLICATIONS OF PHOTOMICROGRAPHY

Photomicrography is commonly used in many areas of biological and medical research. Some of its key applications include:

- **Documenting experimental results**: Researchers use photomicrography to capture critical images that form part of their experimental records, ensuring that visual data is

- **Publishing images**: High-quality images captured through photomicrography are often used in research publications, presentations, and scientific papers to visually communicate findings.
- **Long-term preservation**: Photomicrography helps in archiving images for long-term storage, allowing researchers to revisit and reanalyze data over time.
- **Educational purposes**: Microscopic images captured through photomicrography serve as educational tools in teaching biology, providing visual examples of cellular structures, microbial morphology, and tissue architecture.

Photomicrography remains a vital technique, particularly when high-quality, high-magnification images are needed for documentation, publication, or detailed analysis.

Digital Imaging Techniques

The integration of digital imaging into microscopy has brought profound changes to the way researchers capture and process images of biological specimens. Digital imaging involves the use of electronic sensors, such as digital cameras and CCD sensors, to convert the light captured by the microscope into an electronic signal, which is then processed and displayed on a computer. This technology allows for real-time imaging, enhanced contrast, and digital processing, making it an essential tool for modern biological research.

Principle of Digital Imaging Techniques

In digital imaging, light from the microscope is detected by a digital camera or CCD sensor, which then converts this light into an electronic signal. This signal is processed by specialized software that enhances and displays the image on a computer monitor. Digital imaging offers several advantages over traditional photographic methods, such as immediate image viewing, digital storage, and the ability to apply various image-processing techniques to enhance specific features of the specimen.

One of the key features of digital imaging is its ability to enhance and modify images in real-time. For instance, researchers can adjust contrast, brightness, and resolution to improve the visibility of certain structures or make specific features stand out. Image filters can be applied to isolate particular aspects of the sample, such as fluorescent signals or specific wavelengths of light, providing enhanced clarity and contrast.

Applications of Digital Imaging Techniques

Digital imaging has had a significant impact on many areas of research, particularly in biological sciences. Its applications span across real-time imaging, quantitative analysis, and high-throughput screening, among others. Notable applications include:

- **Real-time imaging**: In live-cell imaging, digital microscopy allows researchers to capture images of dynamic biological processes, such as cell division, intracellular transport, and protein interactions, as they happen in real-time.
- **Time-lapse photography**: Digital imaging enables time-lapse photography, which is invaluable for studying slow or long-term processes like the growth of plants or the development of organisms over several hours or days.
- **High-throughput screening**: In drug discovery, digital imaging techniques are used to screen large numbers of samples rapidly. High-resolution imaging allows researchers to examine the effects of potential drugs on cells, tissues, or

- **Quantitative analysis:** Digital imaging enables precise measurements of features such as cell count, fluorescence intensity, and the localization of specific proteins. By analyzing these features quantitatively, researchers can gain insights into cellular processes like gene expression, signaling, and protein trafficking.
- **Fluorescence microscopy**: Digital imaging enhances the sensitivity and accuracy of fluorescence microscopy by allowing researchers to capture detailed images of fluorescently labeled molecules in living cells, thereby tracking specific molecular interactions in real-time.

Advantages of Digital Imaging

Digital imaging offers several advantages over traditional microscopy and photographic methods:

- **Quantification**: One of the most significant benefits of digital imaging is its ability to quantify various biological phenomena, such as fluorescence intensity, cell proliferation, and protein localization. This is invaluable for researchers who require precise, reproducible measurements to support their hypotheses.
- **High sensitivity**: Digital imaging systems are highly sensitive, capable of capturing even low-intensity light. This is particularly important when working with faint signals or in low-light conditions, which are common in fluorescence or confocal microscopy.
- **Data storage**: Unlike traditional photographic images, digital images can be stored easily in digital formats, allowing for efficient archiving, sharing, and retrieval of large datasets. This enables researchers to preserve and access images without the need for physical storage space.

- **Enhanced contrast**: Through digital processing, researchers can reduce noise and enhance specific features of the specimen, improving the overall quality of the images. This is particularly helpful when working with samples that have low contrast or when fine details need to be highlighted.
- **Advanced analysis tools**: Digital imaging software provides powerful tools for analyzing images, such as measuring distances between structures, quantifying pixel intensities, and tracking the movement of particles or cells.

Limitations of Digital Imaging

Despite its many advantages, digital imaging does have some limitations. High-resolution imaging, such as that required for capturing very fine cellular structures or ultrastructural features, may require specialized, expensive equipment. While digital images offer significant flexibility in post-processing, excessive manipulation of images may lead to potential artifacts or distortions. The capturing high-quality digital images from thick samples may still be challenging, particularly when working with complex tissues or multi-layered structures.

Photomicrography and digital imaging techniques have profoundly transformed the way biological specimens are visualized and analyzed. While photomicrography remains an essential tool for documenting and preserving experimental results, digital imaging has revolutionized microscopy by enabling real-time visualization, quantitative analysis, and the ability to enhance images digitally. The combination of both techniques has enabled researchers to observe biological processes with greater precision, while also providing powerful tools for data storage and sharing. With continuous advancements in digital imaging technologies, the future of microscopy looks promising, offering even more sophisticated methods to explore the microscopic world in unprecedented detail.

CONCLUSION

Advanced microscopy techniques have revolutionized biological research, offering researchers unparalleled tools for examining cellular and molecular structures in both living and non-living organisms. Light microscopes, including fluorescence and bright-field microscopes, enable the study of cellular morphology and the behavior of live cells in relatively low magnification. For ultrastructural analysis, electron microscopes (such as scanning electron microscopes, or SEM, and transmission electron microscopes, or TEM) provide much higher magnification and resolution, allowing scientists to observe the fine details of cellular components like membranes, organelles, and macromolecular complexes at the nanoscale. These powerful imaging methods have been integral in understanding cellular processes, including protein interactions, cellular organelle function, and the morphology of microorganisms.

For dynamic live-cell imaging, techniques like phase contrast microscopy and confocal microscopy have become indispensable. Phase contrast microscopy enhances the contrast of transparent living cells without the need for staining, enabling real-time observations of cell dynamics, including mitosis and cellular migration. Confocal microscopy, uses laser light to scan samples and generate high-resolution images of thick specimens, providing optical sections that can be digitally reconstructed into 3D models. This method is particularly valuable in studying the dynamics of cellular structures, protein localization, and interactions within living organisms.

The advent of digital imaging and photomicrography has expanded the capabilities of traditional microscopy, facilitating high-resolution imaging, quantitative analysis, and more detailed visualization. Digital cameras and software for image processing enable researchers to capture, store, and analyze microscopic data with increased precision and efficiency. These advancements also allow for large-scale image analyses, contributing to fields such as cell biology, microbiology, and biomedical research.

Each microscopy technique comes with its own set of advantages and limitations, making it crucial for researchers to understand their principles. The choice of technique must align with the specific goals of an experiment, such as the level of detail required, the type of specimen being studied, and whether live-cell imaging is necessary. A solid grasp of these methods ensures that scientists can make informed decisions, enabling them to optimize their experimental design and achieve the most accurate, reliable results.

QUESTIONS

- Discuss the principles, types, and applications of light microscopy. How does it compare with electron microscopy in terms of resolution and magnification?
- Explain the working principle of Transmission Electron Microscopy (TEM). What are the advantages and limitations of TEM in biological research?
- Describe the principles of Scanning Electron Microscopy (SEM) and its applications. How does SEM differ from TEM in terms of sample preparation and imaging?
- What is Scanning Transmission Electron Microscopy (STEM), and how does it combine the principles of TEM and SEM? Discuss its applications in atomic-level imaging.
- Explain the principle of phase contrast microscopy and its advantages for observing living cells. How does it differ

from conventional light microscopy in terms of contrast and resolution?

- What is confocal microscopy, and how does it enhance three-dimensional imaging of specimens? Discuss its applications and limitations in biological research.
- Discuss the role of photomicrography in microscopy. How does it contribute to the documentation and publication of experimental results?
- What are the advantages of digital imaging techniques in microscopy? Explain how digital imaging has revolutionized the field of biological research.

CHAPTER 9

SEPARATION AND IMMUNOLOGICAL TECHNIQUES

Separation techniques and immunological assays are indispensable tools in biological research, providing critical insights into the composition and behavior of complex biological samples. These methods enable scientists to purify biomolecules like proteins, nucleic acids, lipids, and metabolites, and also facilitate the identification, quantification, and functional analysis of specific molecules. Electrophoresis and chromatography are among the most widely used separation techniques, each with its own principle and application in separating biomolecules based on properties like size, charge, affinity, and hydrophobicity. Electrophoresis, for instance, takes advantage of an electric field to separate molecules such as DNA, RNA, and proteins, allowing researchers to study their molecular weight, charge, and purity. Gel electrophoresis (both agarose and polyacrylamide) is commonly employed for DNA and protein analysis, while capillary electrophoresis is utilized for high-resolution separation of small molecules. Similarly, chromatography, which includes techniques like gas chromatography (GC), liquid chromatography (HPLC), and affinity chromatography, provides a robust method for separating biomolecules based on their physical and chemical properties. Affinity chromatography, for example, is used for the purification of proteins based on their specific binding interactions with ligands, making it ideal for isolating antibodies, enzymes, and receptor proteins.

To separation techniques, immunological assays are pivotal for the detection and quantification of target molecules, such as antigens or antibodies, within a sample. These assays harness the specificity of the immune system to bind antibodies or antigens, and their applications are widespread in diagnostics, vaccine development, and disease monitoring. The Radioimmunoassay (RIA) is a highly sensitive technique that uses radiolabeled antigens or antibodies to detect and quantify the presence of specific molecules in a sample. Despite its sensitivity, RIA has been largely replaced by more advanced, safer methods due to concerns about radioactivity. The Enzyme-Linked Immunosorbent Assay (ELISA) offers a non-radioactive and highly sensitive alternative. ELISA uses an enzyme-linked antibody to detect the presence of a target antigen, producing a colorimetric, fluorescent, or chemiluminescent signal that correlates with the concentration of the target molecule. ELISA is widely used for detecting infectious diseases, measuring hormone levels, and assessing immune responses. These separation and immunological techniques not only enable the purification and identification of biomolecules but also allow for quantitative and qualitative analysis, providing invaluable data in molecular biology, clinical diagnostics, and biochemistry research. The continuous refinement of these methods, with advancements in automation and sensitivity, ensures that they remain foundational to both basic and applied biosciences.

9.1 Electrophoresis and Chromatography

In modern biological research, the ability to separate and analyze complex mixtures of biomolecules is crucial for understanding cellular function, disease mechanisms, and biochemical pathways. Electrophoresis and chromatography are two of the most essential techniques used for these purposes. These methods allow for the isolation, identification, and quantification of proteins, nucleic acids, and other biological molecules, which are often present in complex, heterogeneous mixtures. This section delves into the principles, applications, and variations of both electrophoresis and chromatography, highlighting their importance in scientific research and clinical diagnostics.

Electrophoresis

Electrophoresis is a technique that utilizes an electric field to separate charged biomolecules, such as proteins, nucleic acids, and other charged compounds, based on their size, charge, and other properties. When an electric current is applied to a medium, molecules migrate towards the electrode with the opposite charge. The rate at which molecules move through the medium depends on factors such as the size, shape, and charge density of the molecules as well as the composition of the medium itself. Electrophoresis is commonly performed using gels made of agarose or polyacrylamide, which provide a matrix for the separation of molecules.

Principle of Electrophoresis

In electrophoresis, charged molecules, when subjected to an electric field, move toward the electrode of opposite charge. The rate at which these molecules migrate is inversely proportional to their size and directly proportional to their charge. Smaller molecules or those with higher charge densities will travel faster through the gel matrix, while larger molecules or those with lower charge densities will move more slowly. The pH and ionic strength of the buffer used in electrophoresis can significantly influence the rate of migration.

Types of Electrophoresis

1. Agarose Gel Electrophoresis:

- **Principle:** Agarose gel electrophoresis is commonly used to is made of agarose, a polysaccharide that forms a porous structure. The size of the pores in the agarose gel determines how easily molecules can move through it.

- **Applications:** This technique is widely used in genetic studies, PCR product verification, restriction fragment length polymorphism (RFLP) analysis, and genetic fingerprinting.

2. Polymerase Gel Electrophoresis (PAGE):

- **Principle:** PAGE, particularly **SDS-PAGE** (Sodium Dodecyl Sulfate-Polyacrylamide Gel Electrophoresis), is used for the separation of proteins based on their size. SDS is a detergent that denatures proteins and gives them a negative charge, allowing them to migrate through the polyacrylamide gel based solely on size.
- **Applications:** SDS-PAGE is routinely used in protein identification, molecular weight determination, and the analysis of protein purity. It is a standard technique in proteomics, enabling the separation and visualization of complex protein mixtures.

3. Isoelectric Focusing (IEF):

- **Principle:** IEF separates proteins based on their isoelectric point (pI), the pH at which the protein has no net charge. In this technique, proteins migrate through a pH gradient until they reach the point where their charge is neutral, and their migration stops.
- **Applications:** IEF is primarily used for the separation of proteins with different pIs, enabling the identification of protein isoforms and the analysis of post-translational modifications.

4. Two-Dimensional Gel Electrophoresis (2D-GE):

- **Principle:** 2D-GE combines IEF and SDS-PAGE to separate proteins by both their charge and size. The first dimension separates proteins based on their pI, while the second dimension separates them based on molecular weight.
- **Applications:** 2D-GE is a powerful tool for analyzing complex protein mixtures, studying protein modifications, and identifying proteins in cell lysates or other biological samples.

Applications of Electrophoresis

Electrophoresis has a wide range of applications in molecular biology, biochemistry, and clinical diagnostics. Some of the most common applications include:

- **Protein and Nucleic Acid Purification:** Electrophoresis allows for the isolation of specific nucleic acids and proteins, which can be further analyzed or used in subsequent experiments.
- **Genetic Studies:** Electrophoresis is a critical tool for DNA fingerprinting, genetic mutation analysis, and the study of genetic diversity.
- **Forensic Analysis:** Electrophoresis is used in forensic science for analyzing DNA samples, helping to solve crimes and identify individuals.
- **Clinical Diagnostics:** Electrophoresis is used to detect genetic mutations, identify protein biomarkers, and diagnose viral infections.

Chromatography

Chromatography is a versatile separation technique that relies on two phases: a stationary phase and a mobile phase. This technique exploits the differing affinities of molecules for the two phases, allowing for the separation of complex mixtures into individual components. Chromatography is widely used in the purification and analysis of biomolecules, including proteins, nucleic acids, lipids, and small molecules.

PRINCIPLE OF CHROMATOGRAPHY

In chromatography, a mixture is introduced onto a stationary phase (such as a solid or liquid) and is carried through it by a mobile phase (a liquid or gas). The components of the mixture interact with the stationary phase to different extents, causing them to travel at different rates. These varying rates of movement result in the separation of the components. Depending on the type of chromatography, the interaction between the components and the stationary phase can be based on size, charge, polarity, or affinity.

TYPES OF CHROMATOGRAPHY

1. Thin-Layer Chromatography (TLC):

- **Principle**: TLC is a simple form of chromatography in which a thin layer of adsorbent (usually silica gel) is spread on a flat surface, and the sample is applied as a spot. The mobile phase (typically a solvent) moves through the stationary phase by capillary action, causing the components of the mixture to separate.
- **Applications**: TLC is commonly used for the qualitative analysis of small molecules such as lipids, amino acids, and other organic compounds. It is a low-cost, rapid technique for monitoring the progress of reactions and for the identification of compounds.

2. High-Performance Liquid Chromatography (HPLC):

- **Principle:** HPLC is a more sophisticated form of column chromatography in which the mobile phase (a liquid) is pumped under high pressure through a column packed with a solid adsorbent. This technique provides high resolution and sensitivity for separating complex mixtures.
- **Applications:** HPLC is extensively used in the pharmaceutical, biochemistry, and clinical laboratories for the purification of proteins, peptides, and nucleic acids, as well as for quantifying small molecules like drugs, hormones, and metabolites.

3. Gas Chromatography (GC):

- **Principle:** GC is similar to HPLC, but instead of a liquid, a gas is used as the mobile phase. The mixture is injected into a column where it is separated based on the volatility of the components.
- **Applications:** GC is used to detect volatile organic compounds in environmental samples, as well as in the analysis of metabolic products and drug testing.

4. Affinity Chromatography:

- **Principle:** Affinity chromatography separates biomolecules based on their specific interactions with ligands immobilized on the stationary phase. For example, antibodies may be used to capture antigens, or a substrate may be used to isolate an enzyme.
- **Applications:** This technique is widely used for the purification of proteins, enzyme assays, antibody isolation, and nucleic acid separation. It is highly specific and can yield highly purified biomolecules.

5. Size Exclusion Chromatography (SEC):

- **Principle:** SEC separates molecules based on their size. Larger molecules elute first, as they are excluded from entering the pores of the stationary phase, while smaller molecules take longer to elute as they can enter the pores and are slowed down.
- **Applications:** SEC is used for the size determination of proteins, molecular weight estimation, and for the removal of small contaminating molecules from protein solutions.

APPLICATIONS OF CHROMATOGRAPHY

Chromatography is indispensable in many areas of research and industry. Some of the key applications include:

- **Protein Purification and Characterization:** Chromatography is widely used to purify proteins and other biomolecules to study their structure, function, and interactions.
- **Quantification of Metabolites:** Chromatographic techniques, particularly HPLC and GC, are essential for quantifying metabolites in biological samples, such as blood, urine, and tissue extracts.
- **Analyzing Complex Mixtures:** Chromatography is used to analyze complex biological mixtures, such as blood and urine, for the identification of biomarkers, disease indicators, and drug metabolites.
- **Drug Testing and Quality Control:** Chromatography is used in the pharmaceutical industry for drug testing, quality control, and formulation analysis.

Both electrophoresis and chromatography are indispensable techniques in modern biological and biochemical research. Electrophoresis offers a reliable and efficient method for separating nucleic acids and proteins based on size, charge, and other molecular properties, while chromatography provides a powerful tool for isolating and purifying biomolecules from complex mixtures. These techniques are widely used in diagnostics, drug development, and molecular biology, continuing to advance with technological innovations that improve sensitivity, resolution, and throughput. The combination of these methods has enabled the detailed analysis of cellular components, aiding in the understanding of biological processes at the molecular level.

9.2 Organelle and Cell Separation

The separation of cellular components is a fundamental aspect of cell biology and molecular research. Techniques that isolate specific organelles, cells, or sub-cellular structures are critical for studying their functions, structures, and roles within the cell. Methods such as centrifugation, density gradient separation, and magnetic bead-based techniques are widely used to isolate high-purity samples of specific organelles or cells for further analysis. These techniques rely on differences in the size, shape, density, or specific interactions of cellular components, enabling the isolation and detailed examination of structures that are otherwise difficult to study in bulk mixtures.

CENTRIFUGATION

Centrifugation is a core technique in cellular and organelle separation. It utilizes centrifugal force to separate components of a mixture based on differences in their size, shape, and density. When a sample is subjected to rapid spinning in a centrifuge, the components are forced to move outward, forming layers or "fractions" within the tube, with the denser components pelleting at the bottom, while less dense components remain suspended in the supernatant. The

TYPES OF CENTRIFUGATION

1. Differential Centrifugation:

- **Principle:** Differential centrifugation is a method where samples are centrifuged at progressively higher speeds to separate components based on their size and density. Initially, the heavier components, such as the nucleus, are pelleted at lower speeds, while lighter components, such as mitochondria and ribosomes, remain in the supernatant and are collected for further centrifugation.
- **Applications:** Differential centrifugation is commonly used for the isolation of cellular organelles such as the nucleus, mitochondria, lysosomes, and peroxisomes. It is a versatile method used for extracting components from cells, such as during sub-cellular fractionation experiments where each organelle is further analyzed.

2. Density Gradient Centrifugation:

- **Principle:** This method involves layering the sample over a density gradient medium, such as sucrose or cesium chloride, which is then subjected to centrifugation. The components of the sample will migrate to positions within the gradient that match their density, with denser components forming distinct bands at the bottom of the gradient.
- **Applications:** Density gradient centrifugation is particularly useful for separating sub-cellular organelles, viral particles, and macromolecules like nucleic acids and proteins. It is widely used for the isolation of organelles like endoplasmic reticulum, Golgi apparatus, vesicles, and mitochondria, as well as for purifying virus particles or ribosomes.

3. Ultracentrifugation:

- **Principle:** Ultracentrifugation involves the use of extremely high centrifugal forces, often exceeding 100,000 rpm. These high speeds enable the separation of smaller and less dense particles, allowing for the purification of even the finest sub-cellular components.
- **Applications:** Ultracentrifugation is particularly valuable in the high-precision isolation of macromolecules like proteins, lipids, and nucleic acids. It is widely used in proteomics and other research fields that require detailed analysis of biomolecules, including large-scale protein purification and the study of complex biological samples.

Applications of Centrifugation in Organelle and Cell Separation

Centrifugation is essential for a wide range of research applications. Its ability to isolate different cellular fractions has made it an invaluable tool in:

- **Cell fractionation:** The isolation of different organelles for functional studies. This can include mitochondria for studying energy metabolism, nuclei for gene expression, or lysosomes for understanding cellular waste processing.
- **Purification of macromolecules:** High-speed centrifugation is used for the purification of proteins, nucleic acids, and other biomolecules, which can be further characterized using techniques like Western blotting, enzyme assays, and spectrometry.
- **Diagnostic applications:** Centrifugation is used in clinical laboratories to isolate and purify components such as

platelets, and exosomes from blood samples for diagnostic purposes.

- **Drug development:** In pharmaceutical research, centrifugation is applied to purify pharmaceutical agents or to isolate cellular components involved in drug response.

Magnetic Bead-based Separation

Magnetic bead-based separation is a powerful technique that allows for the isolation of specific cells, proteins, or nucleic acids based on their affinity to magnetic beads. These beads are coated with ligands (such as antibodies, streptavidin, or other molecular tags) that specifically bind to the target molecules. Once the beads are bound to the target, a magnetic field is applied to separate the bead-bound target from the rest of the sample. This technique is particularly useful when high specificity and purity are required for the isolation of specific cell types or biomolecules.

Principle of Magnetic Bead-based Separation

Magnetic beads are functionalized with various ligands that have a high affinity for the target molecule. When the sample containing the target molecule (e.g., cells, proteins, or nucleic acids) is mixed with the magnetic beads, the target molecules bind to the ligands on the beads. After incubation, a magnetic field is applied, which pulls the bead-bound molecules to a specific location, while the rest of the sample can be washed away. This process ensures that only the specific target is isolated.

Applications of Magnetic Bead-based Separation

1. Isolating Specific Cell Types:

- Magnetic bead-based separation is extensively used in immunology and cell biology to isolate specific cell types, such as stem cells, T cells, or B cells, from complex mixtures. By using antibodies or ligands that specifically recognize surface markers on the target cells, this technique allows for the isolation of high-purity populations of cells.
- **Applications:** Isolation of immune cells for studies on immune responses, stem cell research, and cell therapy.

2. Protein Purification:

- Magnetic beads are also used for isolating specific proteins from a mixture. By attaching an affinity tag (such as His-tag or GST-tag) to the protein of interest, the protein can be captured by beads coated with an anti-tag antibody. The bound protein can then be eluted and analyzed.
- **Applications:** Purification of tagged proteins for structural studies, enzyme assays, and proteomics.

3. Analysis of Specific Biomarkers:

- Magnetic beads can be used to capture biomarkers from biological samples, facilitating the analysis of specific proteins, nucleic acids, or other molecules. This method is particularly useful for detecting low-abundance biomarkers in clinical diagnostics, where high sensitivity is required.
- **Applications: Biomarker detection, pathogen identification,** and **early disease diagnosis.**

Advantages of Magnetic Bead-based Separation

- **High Specificity**: Magnetic bead-based methods can achieve high specificity due to the tailored ligands used to capture target molecules.
- **Simplicity and Speed**: The process is relatively straightforward and can be performed quickly, making it suitable for high-throughput applications.
- **Scalability**: Magnetic bead-based techniques can be scaled up for large-scale purification or isolated analysis of complex mixtures, making them ideal for both research and industrial applications.

Both centrifugation and magnetic bead-based separation are indispensable tools in cell biology, molecular biology, and diagnostics. Centrifugation provides a highly efficient means to separate cellular components based on their size, shape, and density, with applications ranging from organelle isolation to high-precision protein purification. Magnetic bead-based separation, on the other hand, offers unparalleled specificity and sensitivity, making it an essential technique for isolating specific cells, proteins, and biomarkers in both research and clinical settings. These methods, often used in combination, have revolutionized our ability to study the molecular and cellular components of life, offering new insights into disease mechanisms, drug discovery, and therapeutic applications.

9.3 Radioimmunoassay (RIA) and ELISA

Immunoassays are a group of analytical techniques used to detect and quantify substances based on their ability to bind to specific antibodies. These assays are widely used in clinical diagnostics, biochemical research, and environmental testing due to their specificity and sensitivity. Two of the most important and widely applied immunoassays are Radioimmunoassay (RIA) and Enzyme-Linked Immunosorbent Assay (ELISA). Both of these methods have distinct principles, applications, and advantages, but they share a common focus on detecting and quantifying target molecules through specific antibody-antigen interactions.

Radioimmunoassay (RIA)

Radioimmunoassay (RIA) is a highly sensitive analytical technique used to measure the concentration of specific antigens or antibodies by utilizing radioactively labeled substances. RIA was one of the earliest immunoassays developed and revolutionized the measurement of small molecules in biological samples, such as hormones, drugs, and certain metabolites. While RIA is now largely replaced by non-radioactive methods, it remains an important historical method for the detection of low-abundance biomarkers.

Principle of RIA

In RIA, the principle involves the competition between a radioactively labeled antigen (called a tracer) and an unlabeled antigen in the sample for binding to a specific antibody. The amount of radioactivity measured after the competition reflects the concentration of the target antigen or antibody in the sample. The process involves several key steps:

1. The antibody is introduced into a sample containing both the unlabeled antigen (target) and a known quantity of the radioactively labeled antigen (tracer).
2. The tracer and the target antigen compete for binding sites on the antibody.
3. After incubation, the excess unbound antigen is separated,

4. The amount of radioactivity is inversely proportional to the concentration of the target molecule in the sample—higher concentrations of antigen will displace more of the labeled tracer, leading to lower radioactivity.

APPLICATIONS OF RIA

- **Hormone Detection:** RIA is commonly used for measuring concentrations of hormones, including thyroid hormones, insulin, and corticosteroids.
- **Drug Monitoring:** RIA is used in clinical settings to monitor levels of therapeutic drugs, such as anti-seizure medications, corticosteroids, and analgesics.
- **Detection of Small Molecules:** It is used for the detection of substances like vitamins, amino acids, and steroids in biological samples.
- **Research Applications:** RIA is employed in studies involving immune system responses, tumor markers, and neurotransmitter levels in neuroscience research.

ADVANTAGES AND LIMITATIONS OF RIA

1. Advantages:

- **High Sensitivity:** RIA is capable of detecting very low concentrations of substances (picomolar to nanomolar levels), making it ideal for applications requiring high sensitivity.
- **Specificity:** RIA can be highly specific, allowing for accurate measurements of particular molecules in complex samples.

2. Limitations:

- **Radioactive Hazard:** The use of radioactively labeled substances in RIA requires careful handling, special safety protocols, and disposal procedures, which may pose risks to laboratory personnel.

- **Disposal and Environmental Concerns:** Radioactive waste disposal and regulatory compliance can be costly and cumbersome, limiting the widespread use of RIA.
- **Replacement by Non-radioactive Methods:** Due to the advancement of more accessible and safer techniques (such as ELISA), RIA has been largely replaced in many areas by non-radioactive assays.

ENZYME-LINKED IMMUNOSORBENT ASSAY (ELISA)

Enzyme-Linked Immunosorbent Assay (ELISA) is a non-radioactive immunoassay technique that is widely used to detect and quantify target molecules in a sample. ELISA uses an enzyme-labeled antigen or antibody to generate a detectable signal, making it safer and easier to perform compared to RIA. Since its development, ELISA has become the most commonly employed method for various types of immunoassays in research and clinical diagnostics.

Principle of ELISA

In ELISA, the detection of the target molecule is based on the ability of an enzyme-labeled antigen or antibody to catalyze a color change or generate a detectable signal upon substrate addition. The process involves the following steps:

1. **Coating:** An antigen or antibody is immobilized onto the surface of a microplate (usually a 96-well plate).
2. **Sample Incubation:** The sample containing the target molecule is added to the plate. The target antigen (or antibody) in the sample binds to the immobilized antigen (or antibody) on the surface

3. **Detection:** After washing away unbound components, a substrate for the enzyme is added. The enzyme catalyzes a reaction that results in a color change or fluorescence, which can be measured quantitatively.
4. **Signal Measurement:** The color change or fluorescence intensity correlates with the concentration of the target molecule in the sample.

TYPES OF ELISA

1. Direct ELISA:

- **Principle:** In direct ELISA, the antibody or antigen is directly conjugated to the enzyme. This enzyme-labeled antibody or antigen binds to the target antigen or antibody in the sample. The signal is generated by the enzyme's action on the substrate.
- **Applications:** Used for detecting simple antigens or antibodies, such as during viral infections or allergen detection.

2. Indirect ELISA:

- **Principle:** In indirect ELISA, a primary antibody binds to the target antigen, and a secondary antibody, which is enzyme-labeled and specific to the primary antibody, binds to the primary antibody. This allows amplification of the signal.
- **Applications:** Used to detect antibodies in serum or for diagnostic testing of diseases such as **HIV** or **Hepatitis**.

3. Sandwich ELISA:

- **Principle:** A capture antibody is used to bind to the target antigen, followed by the addition of a detection antibody, which is enzyme-labeled. This "sandwich" technique provides a high level of specificity and is often used for detecting larger antigens.

- **Applications**: Commonly used for detecting large antigens such as **cytokines, growth factors**, and **biomarkers** in clinical samples.

4. Competitive ELISA:

- **Principle**: In competitive ELISA, the target antigen in the sample competes with a labeled antigen for binding to the antibody. The signal generated is inversely proportional to the concentration of the target antigen in the sample.
- **Applications**: Used for detecting small molecules like **hormones, drugs**, or **toxins.**

APPLICATIONS OF ELISA

- **Infectious Disease Testing**: ELISA is widely used in clinical diagnostics for the detection of **infections** such as **HIV, Hepatitis B and C**, and **malaria.**
- **Cancer Biomarker Detection**: ELISA is used to detect **tumor markers** in blood or tissue samples, helping in the diagnosis and monitoring of various cancers.
- **Cardiac Disease**: Detection of biomarkers associated with **heart disease**, such as **troponin** and **B-type natriuretic peptide (BNP)**, is commonly performed using ELISA.
- **Food Safety**: ELISA is also used in the food industry to detect contaminants such as **allergens, toxins**, and **pathogens.**

ADVANTAGES AND LIMITATIONS OF ELISA

1. **Advantages:**
   - o **Non-radioactive**: ELISA does not involve the use of radioisotopes, eliminating the need for stringent safety

- o **High Throughput**: ELISA can be easily automated for large-scale testing, making it suitable for high-throughput screening and clinical diagnostics.
- o **Versatility**: ELISA can be adapted to various formats, including direct, indirect, sandwich, and competitive ELISA, making it suitable for a wide range of applications.

1. **Limitations**:
   - o **Standardization Issues**: ELISA assays require careful standardization to ensure reproducibility and accurate results. Variations in reagents, antibodies, and protocols can affect sensitivity and specificity.
   - o **Matrix Effects**: The presence of interfering substances in the sample (e.g., lipids, proteins, or salts) can influence the assay's sensitivity, especially in complex samples like serum or plasma.

Both Radioimmunoassay (RIA) and Enzyme-Linked Immunosorbent Assay (ELISA) are powerful immunoassays that have found widespread applications in clinical diagnostics, research, and biotechnology. While RIA is highly sensitive and specific, its use of radioactivity limits its application due to safety concerns. ELISA, on the other hand, has become the gold standard in immunoassay techniques due to its non-radioactive nature, ease of automation, and versatility in detecting a wide range of analytes. Together, these techniques have greatly advanced our ability to monitor biomolecules with high precision and contribute to advancements in healthcare and scientific research.

CONCLUSION

Separation techniques like electrophoresis and chromatography, along with immunological assays such as radioimmunoassay (RIA) and enzyme-linked immunosorbent assay (ELISA), are cornerstone methods in modern biological research. These techniques enable the purification, detection, and quantification of biomolecules with high sensitivity and specificity, making them essential for a wide range of applications in molecular biology, biochemistry, and medical diagnostics. Electrophoresis, particularly gel electrophoresis, utilizes an electric field to separate biomolecules, such as proteins or nucleic acids, based on their size, charge, and conformation. This method is invaluable for studying gene expression, protein analysis, and DNA sequencing, allowing researchers to identify and characterize individual components within complex biological mixtures.

Chromatography, including liquid chromatography (LC) and gas chromatography (GC), offers another powerful tool for separating biomolecules based on their chemical properties, such as polarity, charge, or molecular weight. High-performance liquid chromatography (HPLC), a specific form of liquid chromatography, is particularly useful for isolating pure compounds from complex biological samples, such as proteins, lipids, and metabolites. These separation techniques not only allow for the isolation of individual molecules but also enable detailed analysis of their structure, function, and interactions, providing valuable insights into cellular processes and metabolic pathways.

Immunological assays like RIA and ELISA play a critical role in detecting and quantifying biomolecules, particularly in clinical and diagnostic settings. RIA utilizes radioactive isotopes to measure the concentration of specific antigens or antibodies in a sample, providing highly sensitive and precise quantification. ELISA, on the other hand, employs enzyme-linked antibodies to detect and quantify biomolecules with the added advantage of being less hazardous than RIA. ELISA is widely used in diagnostics for detecting infections, measuring hormone levels, and monitoring immune responses.

development. By isolating specific biomolecules, researchers can study their roles in health and disease, identify biomarkers for early detection, and develop targeted treatments. The ability to purify, detect, and quantify biomolecules with high sensitivity and specificity has greatly advanced fields such as cancer research, immunology, and drug development, making these methods indispensable tools in both basic and applied biological sciences.

QUESTIONS

- What is electrophoresis, and how is it used for protein and nucleic acid analysis?
- Describe the principles and applications of different chromatography techniques like TLC, HPLC, and GC.
- Explain the types of centrifugation techniques and their applications in cell and organelle separation.
- What is Radioimmunoassay (RIA), and how is it used to detect specific antigens or antibodies?
- How does ELISA work, and what are the different types used in clinical diagnostics?
- What is magnetic bead-based separation, and how is it used in isolating specific cells or proteins?
- What is Two-Dimensional Gel Electrophoresis (2DGE), and how is it useful in protein analysis?
- How do electrophoresis and chromatography differ in separating biological samples for research and diagnostics?

CHAPTER 10

FUNDAMENTALS OF BIOSTATISTICS

Biostatistics plays a crucial role in the analysis and interpretation of biological, environmental, and health-related data. It is the foundation upon which scientific studies in these fields are built, enabling researchers to draw meaningful conclusions from their data and make evidence-based decisions. One of the primary goals of biostatistics is to design studies that minimize bias and maximize the accuracy and reliability of results. This involves choosing appropriate sampling methods, such as random sampling, stratified sampling, or cluster sampling, to ensure that the sample is representative of the population being studied. Understanding central tendency measures like the mean, median, and mode is also essential for summarizing data and identifying patterns or trends. These measures provide insights into the "average" behavior or characteristic of a population, which is critical for interpreting large datasets in fields like epidemiology, clinical research, and environmental science.

Hypothesis testing is another cornerstone of biostatistics, allowing researchers to make inferences about a population based on sample data. This involves formulating null and alternative hypotheses and using statistical tests, such as the t-test, chi-square test, or analysis of variance (ANOVA), to determine whether observed differences or relationships are statistically significant. In this process, the p-value plays a key role in assessing the likelihood that the observed results occurred by chance. Biostatisticians also rely on different statistical models, such as regression analysis and survival analysis.

instance, regression models can be used to examine the relationship between an independent variable and a dependent variable, while survival analysis is employed in medical research to estimate the time until an event, such as death or disease recurrence, occurs. The interpretation of these models requires a strong understanding of statistical concepts to ensure that conclusions drawn are valid and meaningful, particularly in high-stakes areas such as public health policy and clinical decision-making.

10.1 Sampling, Scaling, and Data Collection

In biostatistics, the accuracy and reliability of the results depend largely on the methods used to gather and analyze data. Proper sampling, scaling, and data collection are crucial steps in the research process, as they ensure that conclusions drawn from studies are meaningful, representative, and statistically valid. This section will explore these methods in detail, discussing the various sampling techniques, types of scales, and approaches to data collection that are used in biological, environmental, and health sciences.

SAMPLING

Sampling is the process of selecting a subset of individuals or observations from a larger population to estimate the characteristics or parameters of that population. Given that it is often impractical or impossible to study an entire population, sampling allows researchers to draw inferences about a population by analyzing a smaller, manageable sample. The goal of sampling is to ensure that the sample is representative of the population, minimizing biases and maximizing the reliability of the results. In biostatistics, this is particularly important, as the outcomes of clinical trials, epidemiological studies, and public health interventions often depend on the quality of the sample.

TYPES OF SAMPLING METHODS

1. **Random Sampling:** Random sampling is the simplest and most commonly used method of sampling. In this approach, every individual in the population has an equal chance of being selected, ensuring that the sample is unbiased. Random sampling is essential in eliminating selection bias and improving the generalizability of study results.
   - o *Example*: In a clinical study testing a new drug, researchers might randomly select 100 patients from a hospital to participate, ensuring that the sample reflects the diversity of patients in the hospital population.
   - o *Advantages*: Eliminates selection bias, is simple to execute, and generally provides a good representation of the population.
   - o *Limitations*: Can be resource-intensive and difficult to implement in very large populations or when specific subgroups must be represented.
2. **Systematic Sampling:** Systematic sampling involves selecting every nth individual from a population. For example, every 10th individual from a list of patients or participants could be chosen. While this method can be more convenient than random sampling, it assumes that the population is organized in a way that does not introduce periodicity that could bias the sample.
   - o *Example*: Researchers might select every 10th person from a registry of diabetes patients to participate in a study on the effectiveness of a new treatment.
   - o *Advantages*: Simpler to implement than random sampling, especially when working with lists or databases.

- o *Limitations*: If there is an underlying pattern or periodicity in the population (e.g., patients listed by the time of arrival), the sample could be biased.

3. **Stratified Sampling:** Stratified sampling divides the population into distinct subgroups, or strata, based on specific characteristics (such as age, gender, or disease severity). Then, random samples are taken from each stratum. This approach ensures that all relevant subgroups are represented in the sample, making it especially useful when certain groups are small but crucial for the study.
   - o *Example*: A public health survey might stratify the population into different age groups and then randomly select participants from each age group to ensure that both young and elderly individuals are adequately represented.
   - o *Advantages*: Ensures that all subgroups are represented, reducing the potential for bias and improving the precision of the estimates.
   - o *Limitations*: More complex to implement and requires knowledge of the population's structure.

4. **Cluster Sampling:** In cluster sampling, the population is divided into clusters, which are often based on geographical or administrative boundaries (e.g., schools, hospitals, or neighborhoods). A random selection of clusters is made, and all individuals within the selected clusters are surveyed. This approach is particularly useful when the population is widespread or difficult to access in its entirety.
   - o *Example*: A study on the health outcomes of children in a city might select several schools randomly and then survey all the children within those schools.
   - o *Advantages*: Cost-effective and practical, especially when studying large or geographically dispersed populations.

- *Limitations*: Can lead to less precision than other methods, especially if the clusters are not homogeneous.

5. **Convenience Sampling:** Convenience sampling involves selecting individuals who are easiest to access or recruit. This method is often used in preliminary research, pilot studies, or when resources are limited. While it is convenient, convenience sampling is typically prone to biases and is not always representative of the broader population.
   - *Example*: A researcher might survey attendees at a local community center or clinic because they are easily accessible.
   - *Advantages*: Quick and cost-effective.
   - *Limitations*: High risk of bias and limited generalizability.

SCALING

Scaling refers to the process of transforming raw data into measurable units that facilitate meaningful analysis. In biostatistics, scaling is crucial for ensuring that data can be compared, interpreted, and analyzed in a way that provides insights. The choice of scale is determined by the nature of the data being collected and the analysis to be conducted.

Types of Scales

1. **Nominal Scale:** Data on the nominal scale consist of categories without any intrinsic order. This scale is used to label variables without implying any quantitative relationship.

- *Example*: Blood types (A, B, AB, O), gender (male, female), or the presence or absence of a disease.
- *Use*: Nominal scales are used for categorical data where each

2. **Ordinal Scale:** Data on the ordinal scale can be ordered or ranked, but the intervals between the values are not uniform. This scale is often used when the exact difference between categories is not important but the rank or order is.
   - *Example*: Likert scale in surveys (e.g., strongly agree, agree, neutral, disagree, strongly disagree), stages of disease progression.
   - *Use*: Ordinal scales are useful when the data can be ordered but cannot be quantified with exact intervals.
3. **Interval Scale:** Interval data have both order and equal intervals between values but lack a true zero point. This means that while you can determine the difference between two values, you cannot make meaningful ratios.
   - *Example*: Temperature measured in Celsius or Fahrenheit.
   - *Use*: Interval scales are often used in scientific measurements where the difference between values is important, but a true zero is not relevant.
4. **Ratio Scale:** The ratio scale has all the properties of the interval scale, but with a true zero point, allowing for meaningful comparisons of ratios. This scale is the most advanced and flexible for quantitative analysis.
   - *Example*: Height, weight, time, income.
   - *Use*: Ratio scales are used in situations where exact measurements and the ability to calculate meaningful ratios are important.

DATA COLLECTION

Data collection is the process of gathering information that will be used for analysis in research studies. Effective data collection methods are crucial for ensuring the accuracy, validity, and reliability of the results. In biostatistics, data collection can be categorized into two primary types: experimental data collection and observational data collection.

Types of Data Collection

1. **Experimental Data Collection:** Experimental data collection involves the manipulation of variables to test specific hypotheses in a controlled setting. Researchers actively intervene in the study to test cause-and-effect relationships. This method allows for more control over confounding variables and provides more reliable conclusions regarding causality.

- *Example*: A clinical trial testing the efficacy of a new drug on lowering blood pressure. In this case, the researcher manipulates the independent variable (drug type) and observes its effect on the dependent variable (blood pressure).
- *Advantages*: Can establish causality, controlled environment minimizes confounding variables.
- *Limitations*: May not reflect real-world conditions, can be resource-intensive.

2. **Observational Data Collection:** Observational data collection involves gathering information without intervening or manipulating the study environment. This method is used when experiments are impractical or unethical, such as in epidemiological studies where the goal is to observe patterns and associations in natural settings.

- *Example*: A study examining the relationship between air pollution levels and respiratory diseases in different urban areas.
- *Advantages*: More realistic and applicable to real-world

- *Limitations*: Cannot establish causality, more prone to confounding factors and biases.

The processes of sampling, scaling, and data collection are the foundational building blocks of biostatistics. Each step is essential for ensuring that the data collected is representative, accurate, and interpretable, leading to valid scientific conclusions. Proper understanding and implementation of these methods ensure that studies in biological, environmental, and health sciences can provide meaningful insights and guide effective decision-making.

10.2 Central Tendency and Dispersion

In biostatistics, the concepts of central tendency and dispersion are fundamental for understanding and summarizing data. Central tendency measures provide an overview of the "center" or "typical" value of a dataset, while dispersion measures describe the spread or variability of data points. Together, these measures offer valuable insights into the characteristics of a dataset, helping researchers and analysts interpret data, compare groups, and make informed decisions. This section delves into the key concepts and calculations of central tendency and dispersion.

Central Tendency

Central tendency refers to statistical measures that summarize the central point of a data set. These measures provide insight into the general behavior or trend of the data and help us understand where the data points tend to cluster. The three most common measures of central tendency are the **mean**, **median**, and **mode**, each serving a unique purpose depending on the type of data and distribution.

1. **Mean (Arithmetic Average):**
   The mean is the sum of all values in the dataset divided by the number of values. It is the most commonly used measure

of central tendency because it takes into account every data point in the dataset, offering a balanced central value.

- Formula:

$$\text{Mean} = \frac{\sum_{i=1}^{n} x_i}{n}$$

Where x_i represents each value in the dataset, and is the total number of values.

- Example: In a clinical study examining the age of patients, if the ages are 45,50,55, and 60, the mean age is:

$$\text{Mean} = \frac{45 + 50 + 55 + 60}{4} = 52.5$$

So, the average age of the patients is 52.5 years.

The mean is particularly useful when the data is symmetrically distributed, but it can be heavily influenced by outliers (extremely high or low values).

2. **Median:**

The median is the middle value of a dataset when the data points are arranged in ascending or descending order. It is particularly useful when the data is skewed or contains outliers, as it is not influenced by extreme values. If the dataset has an odd number of values, the median is the middle value. If there is an even number of values, the median is the average of the two middle values.

- Example: Consider the dataset 3,6,9,12. Arranging the values in order, the median is 9, the middle value of the dataset. If the dataset were 1,3,6,9,12, the median would be the average of 6 and 9 , resulting in:

$$\text{Median} = \frac{6 + 9}{2} = 7.5$$

The median provides a better measure of central tendency when the data includes outliers, as it is not affected by extreme values.

3. Mode:

The mode is the value that appears most frequently in the dataset. It is the only measure of central tendency that can be used with nominal data (categorical data without a meaningful order) and is helpful for understanding the most common value in a dataset.

- Example: In a dataset of exam scores: 56, 58, 59, 59, 60, 61, the mode is 59, as it appears twice while the other values appear only once.

A dataset can have more than one mode (bimodal, trimodal) if multiple values appear with the same highest frequency, or no mode if all values appear with the same frequency.

DISPERSION

Dispersion refers to the extent to which the data points in a dataset spread out or vary. While central tendency provides an idea of the center of the data, measures of dispersion offer insight into the variability or consistency of the data. These measures are essential for understanding the degree of uncertainty or reliability of data, particularly in clinical trials, epidemiological studies, and other research areas where variability is important. The three primary measures of dispersion are **range, variance**, and **standard deviation.**

1. Range:

The range is the simplest measure of dispersion and is calculated by subtracting the minimum value from the maximum value in the dataset. The range provides a basic idea of the spread of data but does not account for how the data points are distributed within that range.

- Formula:

$$\text{Range} = \text{Max value} - \text{Min value}$$

- Example: For a dataset of ages: 23,30,35,40,45, the range would be:

$$\text{Range} = 45\text{-}23 = 22$$

The range indicates that the data points span 22 years. While this provides a basic sense of spread, the range can be influenced by extreme values and does not offer detailed information about how the data is distributed.

2. **Variance:**

Variance measures how much individual data points differ from the mean. It is calculated as the average of the squared differences between each data p[...]ula for variance is:

$$\text{Variance} = \frac{\sum_{i=1}^{n} (x_i - \mu)^2}{n}$$

Where x_i represents each value in the dataset, and µ is the mean of the dataset.

- Example: For the dataset 3,6,9,12, with a mean of 7.5, the variance would be:

$$\text{Variance} = \frac{(3-7.5)^2 + (6-7.5)^2 + (9-7.5)^2 + (12-7.5)^2}{4}$$

$$= \frac{(20.25) + (2.25) + (2.25) + (20.25)}{4} = \frac{45}{4} = 11.25$$

Variance provides a numerical value that quantifies the degree of spread in the data. Because variance involves squaring the differences, the unit of variance is the square of the unit of the original data, which may be difficult to interpret directly.

3. **Standard Deviation:**

Standard deviation is the square root of the variance and provides a measure of how much individual data points deviate from the mean, in the same unit as the original data. It is one of the most commonly used measures of dispersion because it is easier

- Formula:

$$\text{Standard Deviation} = \sqrt{\text{Variance}}$$

- Example: Continuing from the previous example where the variance was 11.25, the standard deviation would be:

$$\text{Standard Deviation} = \sqrt{11.25} \approx 3.35$$

In clinical trials, for instance, standard deviation can help determine how much variation there is in patient responses to a treatment. A small standard deviation indicates that most patients' responses are similar to the mean, while a large standard deviation suggests significant variability in the responses.

Central tendency and dispersion are essential tools in biostatistics for summarizing and understanding data. While central tendency measures like the mean, median, and mode give us a sense of the typical value in a dataset, measures of dispersion such as range, variance, and standard deviation provide insights into the variability and reliability of the data. Together, these concepts allow researchers to interpret complex data, detect patterns, assess the effectiveness of interventions, and make informed decisions in fields like public health, clinical research, and epidemiology.

10.3 Hypothesis Testing and Statistical Significance

Hypothesis testing is a core concept in biostatistics and scientific research, enabling investigators to draw conclusions about populations based on sample data. It is a structured method for making decisions about whether a particular assumption (hypothesis) regarding a parameter or relationship within a dataset is likely to be true. In medical, environmental, and biological sciences, hypothesis testing is used to evaluate the effectiveness of treatments, determine associations between variables, and identify potential risk factors for diseases. This section delves into the fundamentals of hypothesis testing, the interpretation of p-values, and the concept of statistical significance.

Hypothesis Testing

At the heart of statistical inference is the idea of hypothesis testing. A hypothesis is a statement or assumption about a population parameter that can be tested using sample data. The process of hypothesis testing allows researchers to make objective decisions about these assumptions.

There are two types of hypotheses in statistical testing:

1. **Null Hypothesis (H_0)**: The null hypothesis represents a statement of no effect, no difference, or no association. It is the default or baseline assumption that the observed results are due to chance or random variation.
    - o *Example*: H_0: There is no difference in mean blood pressure between patients treated with Drug A and those treated with a placebo.
2. **Alternative Hypothesis (H_1 or Ha)**: The alternative hypothesis is what the researcher aims to prove. It suggests that there is a statistically significant effect, difference, or relationship.
    - o *Example*: H_1: Patients treated with Drug A have significantly lower mean blood pressure than those receiving the placebo.

Steps in Hypothesis Testing

The process of hypothesis testing follows a systematic sequence of steps:

1. **Formulate Hypotheses:** Clearly state the null and alternative hypotheses. The formulation must be precise and reflect the research question.
2. **Select the Significance Level (α):** The significance level (alpha) is the threshold probability used to determine whether to reject the null hypothesis. It reflects the acceptable risk of a Type I error (rejecting a true null hypothesis). Commonly, α is set at **0.05**, meaning a 5% risk of concluding an effect exists when it does not.
3. **Choose the Appropriate Statistical Test:** The choice of test depends on the type of data and the research question. Some commonly used statistical tests include:
   - o **t-test:** Compares the means of two groups.
   - o **ANOVA (Analysis of Variance):** Compares means among three or more groups.
   - o **Chi-square test:** Tests for association between categorical variables.
   - o **Z-test:** Compares proportions or means for large sample sizes.
   - o **Mann-Whitney U test or Wilcoxon test:** Non-parametric alternatives for comparing medians when data do not follow normal distribution.
4. **Calculate the Test Statistic:** A test statistic is a standardized value derived from sample data. It indicates how far the sample statistic is from the null hypothesis in standard error units.
5. **Compare with Critical Value or Use the p-value:** The test statistic is compared to a critical value from statistical tables (based on α and degrees of freedom), or alternatively, the **p-value** is used to make a decision.
6. **Make a Decision:**

- If the p-value $\leq \alpha$, **reject the null hypothesis** (evidence supports the alternative hypothesis).
- If the p-value $> \alpha$, **fail to reject the null hypothesis** (insufficient evidence to support the alternative).

P-VALUE AND STATISTICAL SIGNIFICANCE

The **p-value** (probability value) plays a critical role in hypothesis testing. It represents the probability of obtaining a result equal to or more extreme than what was actually observed, assuming that the null hypothesis is true.

- A low p-value (typically < 0.05) suggests that the observed data is unlikely under the null hypothesis, providing evidence to reject H_0.
- A high p-value (≥ 0.05) suggests the data is consistent with the null hypothesis, and we fail to reject H_0.

For example, suppose a researcher tests whether a new drug lowers blood pressure. If the p-value is 0.03, there is a 3% probability that the observed difference is due to chance alone, which is below the 5% threshold ($\alpha = 0.05$), and the result is considered statistically significant.

TYPES OF ERRORS IN HYPOTHESIS TESTING

In interpreting hypothesis tests, it is essential to understand the types of errors that can occur:

- **Type I Error (False Positive)**: Rejecting the null hypothesis when it is actually true. The probability of this error is the significance level (α).

- **Type II Error (False Negative)**: Failing to reject the null hypothesis when it is false. The probability of this error is denoted by β, and the power of a test is 1 - β.

A robust study design aims to minimize both errors, particularly by selecting an appropriate sample size and using suitable statistical methods.

Hypothesis testing is a cornerstone of empirical research in biostatistics, guiding scientists in making evidence-based conclusions about populations based on sample data. By structuring investigations around the null and alternative hypotheses and interpreting p-values within the context of a pre-defined significance level, researchers can assess whether observed differences are meaningful or likely due to chance. Properly conducted hypothesis tests enhance the reliability of scientific findings and support critical decisions in healthcare, public policy, and biological research.

10.4 Correlation, Regression, and ANOVA

In biostatistics, correlation, regression, and analysis of variance (ANOVA) are essential techniques used to explore relationships among variables, model data, and draw meaningful conclusions from experimental or observational studies. These statistical methods are commonly applied in health sciences, environmental studies, clinical trials, and epidemiological research to understand how variables interact, predict outcomes, and determine the significance of observed differences.

CORRELATION

Correlation is a statistical measure that describes the extent to which two variables are linearly related. It provides insight into whether increases or decreases in one variable correspond to increases or decreases in another.

- The **correlation coefficient (r)** quantifies the relationship:
  - o **r = +1:** Perfect **positive** correlation (as one variable increases, so does the other).
  - o **r = -1:** Perfect **negative** correlation (as one variable increases, the other decreases).
  - o **r = 0:** No linear correlation.

The closer the value of **r** to +1 or -1, the stronger the linear relationship. Correlation does not imply causation; it only indicates the degree of association.

- **Example:** A study might find a correlation of **r = 0.85** between smoking and lung cancer incidence, suggesting a strong positive association. Other confounding factors must be considered to establish causality.

There are different types of correlation methods:

- **Pearson's correlation coefficient:** Measures the linear correlation between two continuous variables.
- **Spearman's rank correlation:** A non-parametric test used when data are ordinal or not normally distributed.

REGRESSION

Regression analysis goes a step further than correlation by modeling the relationship between a dependent (outcome) variable and one or more independent (predictor) variables. It allows researchers to make predictions, evaluate the strength of predictors, and control for confounding variables.

1. **Linear Regression**
   Linear regression models a straight-line relationship between a dependent variable (Y) and an independent variable (X):

- β_0 is the intercept (the value of Y when X=0).
- β_1 is the slope (the change in Y for a one-unit change in X).
- ε is the error term (the difference between observed and predicted values).
- Example: Predicting BMI based on a person's height and weight. The model helps understand how these physical attributes relate to BMI and predict BMI for new individuals.

2. **Multiple Regression**

   Multiple regression involves two or more independent variables to predict the dependent variable:

$$Y = \beta_0 + \beta_1 X_1 + \beta_2 X_2 + \cdots + \beta_n X_n + \epsilon$$

This technique is useful when outcomes are influenced by several factors simultaneously.

- Example: Predicting patient survival using variables such as age, treatment type, blood pressure, and smoking history.

Multiple regression provides adjusted coefficients, allowing for the control of confounding variables and a better understanding of each predictor's independent effect.

ANOVA (Analysis of Variance)

ANOVA is a statistical method used to compare the means of three or more groups to determine if there are significant differences between them. Unlike the t-test (used for comparing two groups), ANOVA is designed for multi-group comparisons.

1. **One-Way ANOVA**

One-Way ANOVA tests the effect of **one independent variable (factor)** with multiple levels on a single continuous dependent variable.

- Example: Testing the effectiveness of three different blood pressure drugs. The null hypothesis (H_0) states that all group means are equal, while the alternative (H_1) states that at least one group mean differs.

$$F = \frac{\text{Between-group variance}}{\text{Within-group variance}}$$

A significant **F-statistic** suggests that at least one drug performs differently from the others.

2. **Two-Way ANOVA**

Two-Way ANOVA assesses the effects of two independent variables and their interaction on a dependent variable.

- **Example**: Studying the effect of gender (male/female) and diet type (vegetarian, non-vegetarian, vegan) on cholesterol levels. This test can identify:
  - The individual effect of **gender**.
  - The individual effect of **diet**.
  - The **interaction effect** (whether the effect of diet differs by gender).

Two-Way ANOVA helps researchers understand complex interactions in multifactorial studies, which are common in biomedical and environmental research.

APPLICATIONS AND IMPORTANCE

- In **epidemiology**, correlation and regression help identify potential risk factors for diseases.
- In **clinical trials**, ANOVA is used to compare treatment efficacy across multiple groups.

- In **public health**, regression models can predict outcomes like infection rates based on various predictors (e.g., vaccination status, demographic data).
- In **environmental health**, correlation analysis may identify links between pollutant exposure and respiratory outcomes.

Correlation, regression, and ANOVA are foundational tools in biostatistics that support data-driven decision-making and scientific discovery. While correlation identifies associations, regression allows for prediction and adjustment for multiple variables, and ANOVA enables comparisons across multiple groups. A thorough understanding of these techniques is essential for analyzing complex biological and medical data, improving healthcare outcomes, and advancing research in life sciences.

10.5 Probability Distributions: Binomial, Poisson, and Normal

Probability distributions are fundamental tools in biostatistics used to model and predict outcomes of random events. They provide the mathematical framework to describe the likelihood of different outcomes and are crucial in experimental design, statistical inference, and decision-making in biological and health sciences. This section focuses on three essential probability distributions: the binomial, Poisson, and normal distributions, each suited for different types of data and scenarios.

Binomial Distribution

The binomial distribution is used when an experiment consists of a fixed number of independent trials, each with only two possible outcomes: success or failure. It answers the question: "What is the probability of obtaining exactly k successes in n trials if each trial has the same probability of success p?"

MATHEMATICAL FORMULA:

$$P(X = k) = \binom{n}{k} p^k (1 - p)^{n-k}$$

Where:

- n total number of trials
- k number of successes
- p probability of success in a single trial
- $\binom{n}{k}$ combination of n items taken k at a time

Example: If a fair coin is flipped 10 times (n=10,p=0.5), the binomial distribution can be used to calculate the probability of getting exactly 6 heads.

Applications in Biostatistics:

- Estimating the probability of a patient responding to treatment.
- Modeling survival or failure in clinical trials (e.g., success rate of a vaccine).
- Analyzing genetic traits (e.g., inheritance patterns in Mendelian genetics).

Key Properties:

- Discrete distribution.
- Mean = np, Variance = $np\,(1 - p)$.
- The shape becomes more symmetric as ***n*** increases.

Poisson Distribution: The Poisson distribution is suitable for modeling the number of occurrences of an event in a fixed interval of time or space, where these events occur with a known constant

MATHEMATICAL FORMULA:

$$P(X = k) = \frac{\lambda^k e^{-\lambda}}{k!}$$

Where:

- λ the expected number of occurrences in a given interval
- *k* the number of occurrences
- e ≈ 2.718 (Euler's number)

Example: Suppose a call center receives an average of 5 calls per hour (λ = 5). The Poisson distribution can determine the probability of receiving exactly 7 calls in the next hour.

Applications in Biostatistics:

- Modeling the number of disease cases reported in a region per month.
- Estimating mutations in DNA sequences.
- Assessing the frequency of hospital admissions or emergency visits.

Key Properties:

- Discrete distribution.
- Mean = Variance = λ.
- Skewed to the right, especially when λ is small; becomes more symmetric as λ increases.

NORMAL DISTRIBUTION

The normal distribution, also known as the Gaussian distribution, is the most widely used continuous probability distribution in statistics. It describes data that cluster around a central mean (μ) and is characterized by its bell-shaped curve.

Mathematical Formula:

$$P(X = x) = \frac{1}{\sigma\sqrt{2\pi}} e^{-\frac{(x-\mu)^2}{2\sigma^2}}$$

Where:

- μ = mean of the distribution
- σ = standard deviation
- x = value of the random variable

Example: Human body temperatures typically follow a normal distribution with a mean of approximately 98.6° F and a small standard deviation. Similarly, IQ scores are designed to have a mean of 100 and a standard deviation of 15.

APPLICATIONS IN BIOSTATISTICS:

- Modeling physiological parameters (e.g., blood pressure, heart rate).
- Calculating confidence intervals and performing hypothesis testing.
- Standardizing scores (z-scores) for comparison across different metrics.

Key Properties:

- Continuous distribution.
- Symmetric around the mean: μ = median = mode.
- The total area under the curve is 1.
- Empirical Rule (68-95-99.7 Rule):
    - ~68% of values lie within ±1σ of the mean.

STANDARD NORMAL DISTRIBUTION:

- A special case where $\mu=0$ and $\sigma=1$.
- Any normal distribution can be converted into a standard normal distribution using the -score formula:

$$z = \frac{x - \mu}{\sigma}$$

This conversion facilitates comparison between different datasets and simplifies probability calculations using z-tables.

Understanding probability distributions is crucial in biostatistics as they form the backbone of statistical modeling and inference. Each distribution serves specific types of data and research questions:

- **Binomial** for discrete, binary outcome data with fixed trials.
- **Poisson** for modeling rare or time-based events.
- **Normal** for continuous, naturally occurring biological measurements.

Mastery of these distributions allows researchers to predict outcomes, assess risk, test hypotheses, and make evidence-based decisions across clinical, environmental, and public health domains.

CONCLUSION

Biostatistics serves as a foundational pillar in biological and health sciences by offering essential tools for the design, analysis, and interpretation of data. Its application spans a broad range of disciplines, from public health and epidemiology to molecular biology and clinical research. Sampling techniques, for instance, enable researchers to draw representative subsets from larger populations, ensuring that conclusions are statistically sound and generalizable. Descriptive statistics help summarize and visualize data trends, while inferential statistics allow scientists to make predictions or test hypotheses about biological phenomena. Hypothesis testing, through methods such as t-tests, ANOVA, and chi-square tests, provides a framework for determining whether observed patterns are statistically significant or merely due to chance.

The correlation and regression analyses help identify and quantify relationships between variables, revealing potential causal links or associations critical for understanding complex biological interactions. Probability distributions, including normal, binomial, and Poisson distributions, form the mathematical backbone of many statistical models, allowing for the accurate modeling of biological variability and uncertainty. These tools are particularly crucial in clinical trials, where rigorous statistical analysis is needed to evaluate the efficacy and safety of new drugs or treatments.

In genetics and genomics, biostatistics plays a pivotal role in analyzing large-scale data, such as gene expression profiles or genome-wide association studies, helping uncover genetic contributions to disease. In ecology and environmental science, statistical models are used to track population dynamics, assess biodiversity, and evaluate the impact of environmental changes. Ultimately, biostatistics empowers researchers to draw meaningful conclusions from complex data, reduce biases, and make evidence-based decisions that improve scientific understanding and health outcomes. Mastery of biostatistical principles not only enhances the reliability of research findings but also facilitates the translation of data into actionable knowledge in both research and applied biological sciences.

QUESTIONS:

- What is sampling in biostatistics, and why is it important?
- Explain the difference between random sampling and

- What are the four types of scales used in biostatistics? Give one example for each.
- Define central tendency. What are the three main measures of central tendency?
- What is the difference between variance and standard deviation?
- Explain the concept of hypothesis testing and its importance in biostatistics.
- What is correlation in biostatistics? How is it measured?
- What is the purpose of ANOVA in biostatistical analysis?

CHAPTER 11

STATISTICAL TOOLS AND SOFTWARE APPLICATIONS

In modern biostatistics, the integration of computational tools and software has revolutionized the way researchers handle data, perform analyses, and communicate findings. Among these tools, Microsoft Excel stands out as one of the most accessible and widely used platforms for data analysis in both academic and professional settings. Its intuitive interface, combined with powerful features for handling large datasets, makes it particularly valuable for biostatisticians, especially at the preliminary stages of data management and analysis. Excel allows for efficient data entry, storage, and organization using rows and columns, which are essential for clear data visualization. Its built-in functions support basic statistical calculations such as mean, median, mode, standard deviation, variance, and range, providing immediate insight into datasets without the need for complex programming.

One of the most significant features of Excel is its robust graphing and charting capabilities, which allow users to visually interpret data through bar charts, histograms, line graphs, scatter plots, and box plots. Visual representation of data helps identify patterns, outliers, and trends, making it easier to convey complex statistical concepts to diverse audiences. Excel supports the use of pivot tables, which are instrumental in summarizing large datasets, identifying relationships among variables, and performing subgroup analyses—an essential aspect of biostatistical reporting. Excel's Analysis advanced statistical operations, including t-tests, ANOVA, regression analysis, and correlation matrices, without requiring users to write code. Researchers can also automate repetitive tasks using macros and Visual Basic for Applications (VBA), thereby reducing the risk of human error and improving efficiency in longitudinal or large-scale studies.

In biostatistical research where accuracy and reproducibility are paramount, Excel serves as a powerful introductory tool that bridges the gap between raw data and more complex statistical software like R or SPSS. Its widespread availability ensures that even institutions with limited access to high-end analytical tools can engage in meaningful data analysis. However, it is essential for users to understand both the capabilities and limitations of Excel—especially regarding statistical rigor and reproducibility—so it is often used in conjunction with other software in more advanced studies. Nonetheless, as a practical and versatile tool, Microsoft Excel continues to be indispensable in the workflow of biostatisticians, streamlining tasks ranging from basic data entry to sophisticated analyses, and empowering users to derive meaningful insights with precision and clarity..

11.1 Using Excel for Biostatistical Analysis

Microsoft Excel has become an indispensable tool for professionals and students engaged in biostatistics due to its widespread availability, user-friendly interface, and powerful analytical capabilities. Whether conducting clinical trials, public health surveys, epidemiological research, or laboratory experiments, Excel provides the essential functionality needed to input, organize, visualize, and statistically analyze data. Although not a replacement for specialized statistical software such as SPSS, R, or SAS in complex research, Excel is an excellent platform for initial analyses, exploratory data visualization, and the generation of descriptive and inferential statistics in an accessible environment.

Data Entry and Organization

A cornerstone of effective biostatistical analysis is accurate and systematic data entry. Excel's spreadsheet format allows users to neatly organize data into rows and columns, mimicking a traditional data table. Typically, each row corresponds to a unique observation, subject, or event (e.g., a patient record), while each column represents a variable or field (e.g., age, gender, cholesterol level, treatment group).

Key Principles of Data Organization:

- **Headers:** Each column should have a clear, descriptive header (e.g., "Age," "BP_Systolic," "Treatment_Group") to maintain clarity.
- **Consistency:** Ensure consistent data types within each column. For example, avoid mixing numerical and textual values in a column labeled "Weight."
- **Avoid Merged Cells and Blanks:** Avoid merging cells or leaving unnecessary blank cells, as these can disrupt formula operations and data filtering.
- **Data Validation:** Use Excel's built-in "Data Validation" tool to restrict entries to acceptable formats or ranges, reducing data entry errors.

An organized dataset ensures seamless application of formulas and statistical tools, enabling faster, more accurate analysis.

Excel Functions for Biostatistical Analysis

Excel supports a wide array of built-in functions that facilitate various types of statistical analysis, from basic descriptive statistics to more

1. Descriptive Statistics

Descriptive statistics summarize and describe the central tendency, dispersion, and overall pattern of data. Common Excel functions include:

- **=AVERAGE(range)** – Calculates the mean (arithmetic average).
- **=MEDIAN(range)** – Returns the median, or middle value.
- **=MODE.SNGL(range)** – Identifies the mode, or most frequent value.
- **=STDEV.S(range)** – Calculates the sample standard deviation, measuring data spread.
- **=VAR.S(range)** – Computes the sample variance.
- **=MAX(range) and =MIN(range)** – Determine the maximum and minimum values.
- **=COUNT(range)** – Counts the number of numeric entries in a range.

Example: To calculate the average systolic blood pressure in column B from rows 2 to 101:

=AVERAGE(B2:B101)

These functions are fundamental when summarizing patient demographics, clinical measurements, or laboratory values in biomedical studies.

2. Probability Distributions

Excel includes specific functions to calculate probabilities and cumulative distributions for various theoretical models frequently used in biostatistics:

=NORM.DIST(x, mean, standard_dev, cumulative) – Calculates the normal distribution (cumulative or probability density).

=BINOM.DIST(number_s, trials, probability_s, cumulative) – Returns the probability from a binomial distribution.

=POISSON.DIST(x, mean, cumulative) – Computes probabilities based on the Poisson distribution.

These functions are particularly useful in modeling events such as disease incidence, mutation frequencies, or adverse event reporting.

Example: To compute the probability of exactly 3 adverse events occurring when the expected rate is 2:

=POISSON.DIST(3, 2, FALSE)

3. Correlation and Regression

Excel allows for the assessment of relationships between two or more variables using correlation and regression tools.

- **=CORREL(array1, array2)** – Calculates the Pearson correlation coefficient (r), indicating the strength and direction of a linear relationship between two variables.
- **=LINEST(known_y's, known_x's, const, stats)** – Performs linear regression analysis, providing slope, intercept, and optional statistics such as R^2 and standard errors.

Example: To analyze the correlation between hours of physical activity and cholesterol levels:

=CORREL(C2:C100, D2:D100)

Regression analysis can also be extended using the Analysis ToolPak, allowing users to compute residuals, ANOVA statistics, and regression coefficients in tabular form.

4. Hypothesis Testing

Statistical hypothesis testing is central to biostatistical research. Excel provides several functions to conduct common tests:

- **=T.TEST(array1, array2, tails, type)** – Compares the means of two datasets using Student's t-test.
    - o Type = 1 for paired, 2 for two-sample equal variance, 3 for unequal variance.
- **=CHISQ.TEST(actual_range, expected_range)** – Performs the chi-square test for categorical data.
- **=F.TEST(array1, array2)** – Tests whether two datasets have equal variances.

Example: To perform a two-tailed t-test on the systolic BP of two patient groups:

=T.TEST(A2:A51, B2:B51, 2, 2)

These tools enable rapid inferential analysis directly within Excel, supporting conclusions about treatment efficacy, population differences, or variable associations.

Advanced Statistical Tools: The Analysis ToolPak

While basic formulas are sufficient for many statistical tasks, Excel's Analysis ToolPak significantly expands its capabilities, making it a more comprehensive statistical platform.

To Enable the Analysis ToolPak:

1. Go to File > Options > Add-ins.
2. In the "Manage" box, select "Excel Add-ins" and click "Go."
3. Check "Analysis ToolPak" and click "OK."

Once activated, the ToolPak provides access to powerful tools such as:

- **Descriptive Statistics** – Generates a summary report with mean, median, mode, variance, standard deviation, range, and more.
- **Histogram** – Creates frequency distributions and graphical histograms.
- **ANOVA** – Performs one-way, two-factor with replication, and two-factor without replication ANOVA tests.
- **Regression** – Provides detailed linear regression outputs including coefficients, R^2, standard errors, and residuals.
- **t-Test and z-Test** – Performs hypothesis tests on sample means and proportions.

Example Workflow: To conduct a one-way ANOVA on blood pressure data from three treatment groups:

1. Navigate to Data > Data Analysis > ANOVA: Single Factor.
2. Select the data range and identify whether the data is grouped by columns.
3. Set the alpha level (e.g., 0.05) and click "OK."

The resulting output includes the **F-statistic**, **p-value**, and between-group vs within-group variances, supporting conclusions about statistical significance.

Graphing and Visualization in Biostatistics

Visual representation of data is essential in biostatistics for identifying patterns, summarizing distributions, and communicating results. Excel offers a wide range of charting tools:

- **Bar Charts and Column Charts** – Useful for comparing

- **Histograms** – Show the frequency distribution of numerical data.
- **Line Charts** – Ideal for trends over time or repeated measures.
- **Scatter Plots** – Display relationships between continuous variables, useful for correlation and regression.
- **Box Plots** – Available via Excel templates or custom formatting, used to show medians, quartiles, and outliers.

Excel allows customization of chart elements, including labels, titles, legends, gridlines, and data points, enhancing clarity and publication quality.

AUTOMATION WITH MACROS AND VBA

For researchers handling repetitive tasks such as formatting, data cleaning, or batch analysis, Excel's macro recorder and Visual Basic for Applications (VBA) scripting capabilities provide automation solutions. Macros can record a series of steps and replay them on new datasets, while VBA can be programmed to conduct complex loops, conditional analyses, or create user-defined functions.

Example Use Cases:

- Automatically formatting and summarizing weekly laboratory data.
- Creating buttons for executing regression models.
- Building interactive dashboards for real-time data updates.

Microsoft Excel offers a comprehensive environment for biostatistical analysis, from fundamental descriptive statistics to advanced hypothesis testing, correlation, and regression. Its user-friendly interface, combined with the versatility of functions, graphing tools, and the Analysis ToolPak, makes it ideal for students and researchers seeking quick and accurate statistical insights. While

Excel may not replace specialized statistical software for highly complex or large-scale data modeling, its accessibility and efficiency make it a practical and powerful tool in the biostatistician's toolkit. Mastery of Excel enables researchers to handle data confidently, streamline workflows, and derive meaningful conclusions that inform scientific inquiry and health decisions.

11.2 Graphing and Descriptive Statistics

In biostatistical research, visualizing data is as crucial as analyzing it numerically. Graphs provide intuitive, immediate insights into data patterns, trends, and anomalies that may not be apparent through tables or raw numbers alone. Microsoft Excel, widely used in academic and professional settings, offers a suite of charting tools that simplify data visualization and support statistical interpretation. This section explores the different types of graphs available in Excel and demonstrates how descriptive statistics can be used to summarize and communicate the essential features of a dataset.

GRAPHING IN BIOSTATISTICAL ANALYSIS

Graphs serve a dual purpose in statistics—they assist in preliminary data exploration and play a central role in presenting results to various audiences, from scientific peers to the general public. In biostatistics, common graph types include histograms, bar charts, scatter plots, box plots, and line graphs, each serving a specific analytical function.

1. Histograms

Histograms display the frequency distribution of a continuous variable by grouping data into bins or intervals. They are useful for identifying the shape of the distribution (normal, skewed, bimodal, etc.), spotting outliers, and evaluating the spread of the data.

- **Use Case in Biostatistics**

- **How to Create:**
  - o Select the data range.
  - o Go to the **Insert** tab.
  - o Click on **Insert Statistic Chart → Histogram.**
- **Customization Tips:** Adjust bin width to refine the granularity of distribution. Use axis labels and titles for clarity.

2. Bar Charts

Bar charts are typically used for categorical data to compare the magnitude of variables across different groups or conditions.

- **Use Case in Biostatistics:** Comparing the number of male and female participants, different treatment outcomes, or disease prevalence across regions.
- **How to Create:**
  - o Select the data range.
  - o Go to **Insert → Bar Chart**.
- **Horizontal vs. Vertical Bars:** Use horizontal bars when category names are long; vertical bars are ideal for short labels.

3. Scatter Plots

Scatter plots show the relationship between two continuous variables. Each point represents a pair of values, and the overall pattern can reveal trends, clusters, and potential outliers.

- **Use Case in Biostatistics:** Exploring relationships between age and cholesterol, dosage and response, or height and weight.
- **How to Create:**
  - o Highlight the two columns of related data.

- Click **Insert → Scatter Plot.**
- Select the basic scatter plot option.

- **Advanced Tip:** Add a **trendline** and display the **R^2 value** and **regression equation** to explore linear relationships.

4. Box Plots (Box-and-Whisker Plots)

Box plots summarize the central tendency and variability of data using medians, quartiles, and outliers. They provide a quick visual of skewness and help identify potential outliers.

- **Use Case in Biostatistics:** Comparing hemoglobin levels across treatment groups, visualizing interquartile ranges of reaction times, or evaluating variability in enzyme activity.
- **How to Create:**
  - Select your dataset.
  - Click **Insert → Statistical Chart → Box and Whisker** (available in Excel 2016 and later).
- **Customization Tip:** Label each box with group names to improve interpretability.

5. Line Graphs

Line graphs are ideal for showing changes in a variable over time or across ordered categories. They are especially helpful in longitudinal studies or time-series data.

- **Use Case in Biostatistics:** Tracking weight loss over weeks, plotting disease incidence over years, or monitoring glucose levels post-intervention.
- **How to Create:**
  - Select time-series data (e.g., date and measurement).
  - Go to **Insert → Line or Area Chart → Line Chart**

Line charts allow researchers to easily track trends and cyclical patterns, particularly in intervention studies and public health surveillance.

DESCRIPTIVE STATISTICS USING EXCEL

Descriptive statistics provide a quantitative summary of the main features of a dataset. These statistics include measures of central tendency (mean, median, mode), variability (range, standard deviation, variance), and distribution shape (skewness, kurtosis). Excel enables both manual calculation using formulas and automated summary through the **Data Analysis ToolPak**.

USING BUILT-IN FUNCTIONS

Common statistical measures can be calculated using Excel's formula functions:

- **Mean:** =AVERAGE(range)
- **Median:** =MEDIAN(range)
- **Mode:** =MODE.SNGL(range)
- **Standard Deviation:** =STDEV.S(range) (for sample) or =STDEV.P(range) (for population)
- **Variance:** =VAR.S(range)
- **Range:** =MAX(range) - MIN(range)
- **Skewness:** =SKEW(range)
- **Kurtosis:** =KURT(range)

Example: To compute the standard deviation of cholesterol levels in column C (rows 2–101):

=STDEV.S(C2:C101)

These formulas help researchers understand the spread and symmetry of data distributions.

Using the Analysis ToolPak for Descriptive Statistics

Excel's Analysis ToolPak can generate a comprehensive statistical summary with minimal effort. It compiles a report with various descriptive statistics in a single output table.

Steps to Generate Descriptive Statistics:

1. Enable the ToolPak:

- Go to File → Options → Add-ins.
- In the Manage box, select "Excel Add-ins" and click "Go."
- Check the "Analysis ToolPak" box and click "OK."

2. Run Descriptive Statistics:

- Click on the **Data** tab → **Data Analysis** (right side).
- Select **Descriptive Statistics** from the list and click "OK."
- Specify the input range (including labels if applicable).
- Check the box labeled "Summary statistics."
- Choose output location (same sheet or new sheet).
- Click **OK.**

Included Output Statistics:

- Mean, Median, Mode
- Standard Deviation, Variance
- Kurtosis, Skewness
- Range, Minimum, Maximum
- Count and Standard E

This functionality is ideal for researchers who need a quick statistical overview for presentations, reports, or publications.

Integrating Graphs and Descriptive Statistics

To enhance interpretation, it's beneficial to integrate graphs and numerical summaries. For example:

- Pair a **histogram** with mean and standard deviation values to understand both the shape and spread of data.
- Combine a **scatter plot** with the **correlation coefficient** and a **regression equation** to support claims of linear relationships.
- Use **box plots** alongside quartile and IQR statistics to visualize group differences in a clinical study.

Excel also allows for conditional formatting (e.g., color-coding high or low values), dynamic charts with drop-down filters, and interactive dashboards that combine multiple visual elements—all of which improve data storytelling and decision-making.

Graphing and descriptive statistics are foundational to biostatistical analysis. Microsoft Excel provides a comprehensive suite of tools for creating visualizations that enhance data interpretation and support statistical reasoning. From simple bar charts to detailed box plots, Excel enables researchers to visualize patterns, detect anomalies, and communicate findings effectively. Coupled with its powerful summary statistics tools, Excel empowers users to gain deeper insights into their data, paving the way for robust, evidence-based conclusions in the field of biological and health sciences. By mastering these Excel functionalities, biostatisticians and students alike can transform raw data into compelling, informative narratives that drive scientific progress.

11.3 Add-ins and Automation for Research Data

In modern research environments, particularly in biostatistics, managing large datasets and conducting complex statistical analyses can be time-consuming and error-prone if done manually. Microsoft Excel, while inherently robust, can be significantly enhanced through the use of add-ins and automation tools. These extensions expand the program's capabilities beyond its default features, making it a dynamic and customizable platform for researchers. This section explores the integration of add-ins such as the Analysis ToolPak, third-party tools, and the power of VBA automation, providing researchers with efficient workflows, reproducibility, and greater analytical depth.

Installing and Using the Analysis ToolPak

One of the most widely used add-ins for statistical analysis in Excel is the Analysis ToolPak. This add-in includes a collection of tools specifically designed to facilitate advanced statistical operations without requiring complex programming or external software. Once activated, it integrates seamlessly into the Excel interface, allowing users to perform sophisticated analyses with just a few clicks.

Key Features of the Analysis ToolPak:

- **ANOVA (Analysis of Variance):** Useful for comparing means across multiple groups to determine whether any statistically significant differences exist.
- **Regression Analysis:** Allows researchers to examine the relationship between one dependent variable and one or more independent variables.
- **t-Tests and z-Tests:** Used for hypothesis testing, particularly

- **Descriptive Statistics:** Quickly generates a summary including mean, median, standard deviation, and range.
- **Moving Average and Exponential Smoothing:** Time-series analysis tools used in longitudinal health studies or environmental monitoring.

STEPS TO INSTALL THE TOOLPAK:

1. Click on File → Options.
2. In the Options dialog box, select Add-ins.
3. At the bottom, in the "Manage" box, select Excel Add-ins and click Go.
4. In the Add-Ins window, check the box labeled **Analysis ToolPak**, then click OK.

Once activated, the Data Analysis button will appear on the Data tab under the Analysis group. From there, users can select the statistical test or analysis they wish to perform, choose their data range, and receive results instantly in the form of new worksheet outputs.

PRACTICAL APPLICATION:

For example, in a clinical study evaluating blood pressure changes before and after administering a new drug, a paired t-test can be performed using the ToolPak:

- Go to **Data → Data Analysis → t-Test: Paired Two Sample for Means.**
- Select the pre- and post-treatment data ranges.
- Choose an output range or new worksheet.
- Click **OK** to view the results including mean difference, t-statistic, and p-value.

This feature saves time and cnsures consistent analytical output, especially in research involving repetitive testing across subjects or groups.

AUTOMATION WITH EXCEL VBA

While add-ins like the Analysis ToolPak streamline many standard procedures, some tasks in research require custom solutions or need to be repeated across multiple datasets. In such scenarios, Visual Basic for Applications (VBA) becomes invaluable. VBA is a built-in programming language in Excel that enables users to automate repetitive tasks, create custom functions, and design interactive tools tailored to specific research workflows.

BENEFITS OF VBA IN RESEARCH DATA MANAGEMENT:

- **Automation of Data Cleaning:** Automate the removal of duplicates, handling of missing values, and normalization of datasets.
- **Report Generation:** Automatically generate charts, summary statistics, and formatted reports.
- **Batch Analysis:** Perform statistical tests on multiple variables or datasets without manual intervention.
- **Data Importing:** Pull data from external databases or APIs into Excel for seamless analysis.

WRITING A SIMPLE VBA MACRO:

To begin using VBA:

1. Press Alt + F11 to open the **VBA Editor**.

3. Write or paste your VBA code.
4. Press F5 to run the macro, or assign it to a button for quick access.

Example – Performing a t-Test via VBA:

```
Sub AutoTTest()

'This macro performs a t-test on data in columns A and B

Application.Run "ATPVBAEN.XLAM!TTest", Range("A2:A11"),

Range("B2:B11"), 2, 3, False, False

End Sub
```

This macro executes a two-sample t-test assuming unequal variances on data in columns A and B. When reused across multiple datasets, it eliminates manual effort and ensures uniform execution.

External Add-ins for Advanced Biostatistical Needs

While the Analysis ToolPak and VBA cover many general research tasks, certain statistical analyses in biostatistics—such as survival analysis, non-parametric tests, or complex regression models—require more specialized tools. Several third-party add-ins extend Excel's capabilities to cater to these advanced requirements.

1. XLSTAT

XLSTAT is one of the most comprehensive statistical add-ins available for Excel. It supports a wide range of analytical techniques:

- Multivariate analysis (e.g., PCA, cluster analysis)
- Survival analysis (Kaplan-Meier, Cox regression)
- Time series forecasting
- Clinical trials analysis

- Logistic and probit models
- Monte Carlo simulations

Advantages:

- User-friendly interface integrated with Excel
- Interactive visualizations and customizable output
- Regularly updated with new statistical methods

Use Case Example: A biostatistician studying cancer survival rates may use XLSTAT's Kaplan-Meier function to compare survival curves between treatment groups.

2. Analyse-it

`**Analyse-it** is another powerful Excel add-in tailored for medical statistics and diagnostic test evaluation. It offers:

- Confidence intervals and power analysis
- ROC curves and diagnostic test evaluation
- Method comparison (Bland-Altman, Passing-Bablok)
- Control charts and capability analysis

Use Case Example: A clinical researcher comparing diagnostic methods for diabetes might use Analyse-it to evaluate the sensitivity and specificity of new blood glucose testing devices.

3. Real Statistics Resource Pack

This free add-in enhances Excel with numerous additional statistical functions not available in the standard ToolPak. It includes:

- Advanced regression analysis
- Non-parametric tests (Mann-Whitney, Kruskal-Wallis)

- Chi-square tests with post-hoc analysis

Use Case Example: A public health researcher analyzing survey data with non-normal distributions might apply the Kruskal-Wallis test using this add-in for more accurate results.

Integrating Add-ins and VBA for Comprehensive Workflow Automation

For researchers aiming to build scalable and reproducible data analysis workflows, combining add-ins with VBA automation can yield powerful solutions. For instance:

- Use **Real Statistics Pack** for a test not available in the ToolPak.
- Automate execution via **VBA macros** for multiple datasets.
- Generate final reports with embedded charts using a VBA script.

This integration reduces human error, improves consistency, and saves time—particularly critical in longitudinal studies, epidemiological modeling, and high-throughput screening in biomedical research.

Microsoft Excel's flexibility as a statistical tool is greatly enhanced by its support for add-ins and automation through VBA. For researchers engaged in biostatistics, these tools offer the ability to go beyond basic spreadsheet functions and delve into powerful, efficient, and customized analysis workflows. Whether through the built-in Analysis ToolPak, advanced tools like XLSTAT or Analyse-it, or the use of VBA macros, Excel becomes a full-featured research platform. Mastering these capabilities empowers researchers to handle complex datasets, perform robust statistical analysis, and ensure reproducibility across projects—making Excel not just a spreadsheet tool, but a strategic asset in scientific inquiry.

CONCLUSION

Excel, owing to its widespread accessibility and versatile features, has become a vital tool for conducting biostatistical analysis in the life sciences. It offers a user-friendly interface that allows researchers to input, organize, and manipulate data efficiently, making it especially valuable for those without extensive programming experience. Excel enables users to compute basic descriptive statistics such as mean, median, mode, standard deviation, and variance, which are fundamental for understanding the distribution and variability within datasets. Its powerful charting tools support the creation of histograms, scatter plots, line graphs, and bar charts, aiding in the visual representation and interpretation of data trends.

For more advanced statistical operations, the Analysis ToolPak add-in significantly extends Excel's capabilities. This feature allows users to perform regression analysis, t-tests, ANOVA, correlation, and other inferential statistics, making it a practical alternative for preliminary data analysis or educational purposes. Excel supports the use of pivot tables for multidimensional data summaries, which are especially helpful in clinical studies and epidemiological research where large datasets are common.

Beyond built-in functions, Excel can be customized through Visual Basic for Applications (VBA), enabling automation of repetitive tasks such as data cleaning, formatting, or batch statistical computations. This automation not only enhances productivity but also minimizes human error, which is critical in maintaining the integrity of scientific data. Excel's compatibility with various data formats and its ability to integrate with other statistical software and databases further amplify its utility in research workflows.

Despite certain limitations in handling very large or highly complex datasets compared to specialized statistical software like R toolkit. Its flexibility, ease of use, and capacity for both basic and intermediate-level statistical analysis make it a valuable asset in biological research, healthcare analytics, environmental monitoring, and other life science applications where rapid, accurate data analysis is essential.

QUESTIONS:

- Explain how Microsoft Excel is used for biostatistical analysis and data organization.
- What are the key Excel functions used for biostatistical analysis? Provide examples for descriptive statistics, probability distributions, and regression.
- Discuss the process of creating common graphs in Excel, such as histograms, bar charts, and scatter plots.
- Describe the role of the Data Analysis ToolPak in generating descriptive statistics and conducting statistical tests in Excel.
- How can the Analysis ToolPak add-in be installed in Excel, and what are its applications in biostatistical analysis?
- What is the significance of using VBA (Visual Basic for Applications) in automating tasks within Excel for research purposes?
- Explain the use of external add-ins like XLSTAT and Analyse-it for advanced biostatistical analysis in Excel.
- What are the advantages of using Excel for biostatistical analysis in comparison to other specialized statistical software tools?

GLOSSARY OF KEY TERMS

A

- Accuracy: The closeness of a measured value to a standard or known value.
- Allele: A variant form of a gene found at a specific locus on a chromosome.
- Aneuploidy: A condition in which a cell has an abnormal number of chromosomes.
- Antigen: A substance that induces an immune response, especially the production of antibodies.
- Apomixis: A form of asexual reproduction that occurs via seeds without fertilization.
- Autotroph: An organism capable of producing its own food through photosynthesis or chemosynthesis.

B

- Biodiversity: The variety and variability of life forms within a given ecosystem, region, or on the entire Earth.
- Bioinformatics: The application of computer technology to manage and analyze biological data.
- Bioluminescence: The production and emission of light by living organisms.
- Biostatistics: A branch of statistics that deals with data relating to

C

- Carcinogen: A substance capable of causing cancer in living tissue.
- Catalyst: A substance that increases the rate of a chemical reaction without itself undergoing any permanent chemical change.
- Cell Cycle: The sequence of events in the life of a cell from its origin to its division into two daughter cells.
- Central Tendency: Statistical measures that identify a single score as representative of an entire distribution (mean, median, mode).
- Chromatography: A technique used to separate the components of a mixture based on differences in their movement through a medium.
- Chromosome: A thread-like structure of nucleic acids and protein that carries genetic information.
- Clone: An organism or cell produced asexually from one ancestor, to which it is genetically identical.
- Codon: A sequence of three nucleotides that together form a unit of genetic code in a DNA or RNA molecule.
- Confocal Microscopy: An optical imaging technique used for increasing optical resolution and contrast.
- Crossing Over: The exchange of genes between homologous chromosomes during meiosis.
- Cytokinesis: The division of the cytoplasm into two daughter cells.
- Cytoplasm: The material within a cell, excluding the nucleus, where many metabolic processes occur.

D

- Denaturation: The alteration of a protein's or DNA's natural structure by external factors like heat or pH.
- Descriptive Statistics: Methods for summarizing the key characteristics of a data set.
- Dispersion: Measures that describe the spread of data (range, variance, standard deviation).
- DNA Fingerprinting: A technique used to identify individuals based on their unique DNA patterns.

E

- Ecology: The study of interactions between organisms and their environment.
- Ecosystem: A biological community of interacting organisms and their physical environment.
- Electrophoresis: A method used to separate DNA, RNA, or proteins based on their size and charge.
- Endocytosis: A cellular process in which substances are brought into the cell.
- Endosymbiotic Theory: The theory that explains the origin of eukaryotic cells from prokaryotic organisms.
- Exocytosis: The process by which contents of a cell vesicle are released to the exterior.

F

- Fertilization: The union of male and female gametes to form a zygote.

G

- Gene Expression: The process by which the instructions in DNA are converted into a functional product, such as a protein.
- Gene Pool: The total genetic diversity found within a population or species.
- Genetic Drift: Random changes in gene frequencies in a population.
- Genotype: The genetic makeup of an individual organism.
- Germination: The process by which a seed develops into a new plant.

H

- Habitat: The natural environment where an organism lives.
- Haploid: A cell that contains a single set of chromosomes.
- Heredity: The transmission of genetic characteristics from parents to offspring.
- Histograms: A type of bar graph used to represent the frequency distribution of numerical data.
- Homeostasis: The maintenance of stable internal conditions in an organism.
- Hormone: A signaling molecule produced in the body that regulates physiology and behavior.
- Hypothesis Testing: A statistical method that uses sample data to evaluate a hypothesis about a population parameter.

I

- Immunology: The study of the immune system and immune responses.
- Inflorescence: The arrangement of flowers on a plant.
- Intron: A segment of DNA or RNA that does not code for proteins and interrupts the sequence of genes.

K

- Karyotype: A photograph or diagram of the chromosomes of a cell, arranged in pairs.

L

- Locus: The specific location of a gene or DNA sequence on a chromosome.
- Lysosome: A membrane-bound cell organelle that contains digestive enzymes.

M

- Meiosis: A type of cell division that reduces the number of chromosomes by half and produces four gamete cells.
- Micropyle: A small opening in the surface of a seed that allows the entry of water and gases during germination.
- Mitosis: A type of cell division resulting in two daughter cells each having the same number and kind of chromosomes as the parent nucleus.
- Mutation: A change in the DNA sequence that may lead to variations in traits or diseases.

N

- Neoplasm: An abnormal growth of tissue, which may be benign or malignant (cancer).
- Nucleotide: The basic structural unit of nucleic acids such as DNA and RNA.

O

- Oncogene: A gene that has the potential to cause cancer.
- Operon: A unit of genetic regulation found in bacteria and prokaryotes, consisting of genes with related functions.

P

- Pathogen: An organism that causes disease in its host.
- Phenotype: The observable characteristics of an organism resulting from the interaction of its genotype with the environment.
- Photomicrography: The process of taking photographs through a microscope.
- Plasmid: A small DNA molecule within a cell that is physically separated from chromosomal DNA.
- Poisson Distribution: A statistical distribution showing the probability of a given number of events occurring in a fixed interval of time or space.
- Polymerase Chain Reaction (PCR): A technique used to amplify small segments of DNA.
- Probability Distribution: A function that describes the likelihood of obtaining the possible values that a random variable can take.
- Protista: A kingdom of mostly single-celled eukaryotic organisms that are not fungi, plants, or animals.

R

- Recessive Trait: A trait that is expressed only when two copies of the gene are present.
- Regression Analysis: A statistical technique for modeling and analyzing the relationships between variables.
- Restriction Enzymes: Enzymes that cut DNA at specific sequences.

S

- Sampling: The process of selecting a representative group from the population under study.
- Standard Deviation: A measure of the amount of variation or dispersion of a set of values.
- Symbiosis: Interaction between two different organisms living in close physical association.

T

- T-Test: A statistical test used to compare the means of two groups.
- Taxonomy: The science of classifying organisms into ordered systems.
- Transcription: The process of copying a gene's DNA sequence into RNA.
- Translation: The process by which a protein is synthesized from the mRNA template.

V

- VBA (Visual Basic for Applications): A programming language developed by Microsoft that is used for writing macros to automate tasks in Microsoft Office applications.

LIST OF ABBREVIATIONS

- ANOVA – Analysis of Variance
- ATP – Adenosine Triphosphate
- AIDS – Acquired Immunodeficiency Syndrome
- BOD – Biochemical Oxygen Demand
- cDNA – Complementary DNA
- CDC – Centers for Disease Control and Prevention
- CFU – Colony Forming Unit
- CNS – Central Nervous System
- COD – Chemical Oxygen Demand
- COVID-19 – Coronavirus Disease 2019
- DNA – Deoxyribonucleic Acid
- DTP – Diphtheria, Tetanus, and Pertussis
- ECG – Electrocardiogram
- ELISA – Enzyme-Linked Immunosorbent Assay
- EMS – Emergency Medical Services
- FAO – Food and Agriculture Organization
- FISH – Fluorescence In Situ Hybridization
- FSH – Follicle Stimulating Hormone
- GC – Gas Chromatography
- GDP – Gross Domestic Product

- GH – Growth Hormone
- GHG – Greenhouse Gas
- GIS – Geographic Information System
- GNP – Gross National Product
- HIV – Human Immunodeficiency Virus
- HPLC – High-Performance Liquid Chromatography
- IAA – Indole Acetic Acid
- ICMR – Indian Council of Medical Research
- ICU – Intensive Care Unit
- IPR – Intellectual Property Rights
- IQ – Intelligence Quotient
- IR – Infrared
- IVF – In Vitro Fertilization
- LC50 – Lethal Concentration 50%
- LD50 – Lethal Dose 50%
- LH – Luteinizing Hormone
- LOD – Limit of Detection
- LQ – Lower Quartile
- MHC – Major Histocompatibility Complex
- mRNA – Messenger RNA
- NACO – National AIDS Control Organization
- NCBI – National Center for Biotechnology Information
- NDVI – Normalized Difference Vegetation Index
- NGO – Non-Governmental Organization
- NMR – Nuclear Magnetic Resonance

- NPV – Net Present Value
- PCR – Polymerase Chain Reaction
- PHC – Primary Health Center
- PM – Particulate Matter
- pH – Potential of Hydrogen
- QTL – Quantitative Trait Locus
- R&D – Research and Development
- RFLP – Restriction Fragment Length Polymorphism
- RNA – Ribonucleic Acid
- RQ – Respiratory Quotient
- SDS – Sodium Dodecyl Sulfate
- SEM – Scanning Electron Microscopy
- SPM – Suspended Particulate Matter
- STP – Standard Temperature and Pressure
- TB – Tuberculosis
- TCA – Trichloroacetic Acid
- TLC – Thin Layer Chromatography
- TP – Total Phosphorus
- TSS – Total Suspended Solids
- TDS – Total Dissolved Solids
- UV – Ultraviolet
- UTR – Untranslated Region
- VFA – Volatile Fatty Acids
- VLDL – Very Low-Density Lipoprotein

- WBC – White Blood Cell
- WHO – World Health Organization
- XRD – X-Ray Diffraction
- ZOI – Zone of Inhibition
- ZP – Zona Pellucida

REFERENCES AND BIBLIOGRAPHY

- Nelson, D. L., Cox, M. M. (2022). Lehninger Principles of Biochemistry (8th ed.). W.H. Freeman and Company.
- Alberts, B., Johnson, A., Lewis, J., et al. (2022). Molecular Biology of the Cell (7th ed.). Garland Science.
- Campbell, N. A., Urry, L. A., Cain, M. L., et al. (2023). Biology (13th ed.). Pearson Education.
- Peck, R., Olsen, C., Devore, J. (2023). Introduction to Statistics and Data Analysis (6th ed.). Cengage Learning.
- Glick, B. R., Pasternak, J. J., Patten, C. L. (2023). Molecular Biotechnology: Principles and Applications of Recombinant DNA (6th ed.). ASM Press.
- Salkind, N. J. (2022). Statistics for People Who (Think They) Hate Statistics (7th ed.). Sage Publications.
- Ribas-Maynou, J., Parra, A., Martínez-Díaz, P., et al. (2025). Protective role of extracellular vesicles against oxidative DNA damage. Biological Research, 58(14). BioMed Central
- Gizer, M., Önen, S., Erol, Ö. D., et al. (2025). Endocannabinoid system upregulates the enrichment and differentiation of human iPSC-derived spermatogonial stem cells via CB2R agonism. Biological Research, 58(13). BioMed Central
- Wang, J., Liu, M., Zhao, J., et al. (2025). Oxidative stress and dysregulated long noncoding RNAs in the pathogenesis of Parkinson's disease. Biological Research, 58(7). BioMed Central

- Ji, Q., Lv, Y., Hu, B., et al. (2024). Study on the therapeutic potential of induced neural stem cells for Alzheimer's disease in mice. Biological Research, 57(89). BioMed Central
- Powell, M. P., Verma, N., Sorensen, E., et al. (2023). Epidural stimulation of the cervical spinal cord for post-stroke upper-limb paresis. Nature Medicine, 29(3), 689–699. Mailman School of Public Health
- Mitrani, L. R., Tumasian, R. A. III, Vilches, S., et al. (2023). Racial differences in atrial fibrillation management between White and Black patients in transthyretin cardiac amyloid. American Journal of Cardiology, 187, 164–170. Mailman School of Public Health
- Rudolph, K. E., Williams, N. T., Miles, C. H., et al. (2023). All models are wrong, but which are useful? Comparing parametric and nonparametric estimation of causal effects in finite samples. Journal of Causal Inference, 11(1). Mailman School of Public Health
- Matheson, G. J., Ge, L., Zhang, M., et al. (2023). Parametric and non-parametric Poisson regression for modelling of the arterial input function in positron emission tomography. EJNMMI Physics, 10(1), 72. Mailman School of Public Health
- Shieh, D., Matheson, G. J., & Ogden, R. T. (2023). Nonlinear mixed-effects modeling approach for simplified reference tissue model. IEEE Transactions on Biomedical Engineering. Mailman School of Public Health
- Vest, N., Wenzel, K., Choo, T. H., et al. (2023). Trajectories of depression among patients in treatment for opioid use disorder: A growth mixture model secondary analysis of the XBOT trial. American Journal of Addiction, 32(3), 291–300. Mailman School of Public Health

www.ingramcontent.com/pod-product-compliance
Lightning Source LLC
LaVergne TN
LVHW052034080726
842905LV00051B/1200
* 9 7 9 8 8 9 9 8 4 1 5 6 9 *